A Taste of Croatia

Savoring the food, people and traditions of Croatia's Adriatic coast

by Karen Evenden

New Oak Press
Ojai, CA
www.atasteofcroatia.com

A Taste of Croatia

Published by New Oak Press
PO Box 940
Ojai CA 93024

First Edition

ISBN 9780980012002

Library of Congress Control Number: 2007938333

Cover and book design by Olga Singer

Printed in the United States on recycled, acid-free paper

Sixth Printing January 2014

Visit us on the web
www.atasteofcroatia.com

To Bill, the love of my life and my very best friend.
Thank you for taking me on this and so many wonderful life adventures.
My life has meaning because of you.

Contents
CONTENTS

Foreword

In the spirit of full disclosure, I feel it's only fair to let you know that Karen Evenden is one of my favorite people on earth. Karen's gracious sensibility when it comes to food, farming and community are easy to adore, as are her gentle nature and adventurous spirit. But even for those who are able to navigate the adventures of life easily, writing a cookbook can be quite a challenge.

In *A Taste of Croatia*, Karen has gone beyond the bounds of what makes a great cookbook. Instead, she has captured the spirit of a culture, a country and a cuisine—tying it all together with a collection of recipes that will make you want to run, not walk, to your kitchen and start cooking.

These days, we often hear about the benefits of eating fresh, seasonal, local foods that are grown and produced using sustainable methods, but it can be difficult to know exactly how to incorporate that into our busy lives without it being too complicated, time consuming or expensive. Throw in a dash of ethnicity, and even the most competent home cooks can become discouraged. Fear not: what *A Taste of Croatia* provides is a straightforward and easy way to celebrate a culture whose dishes can be created anywhere fresh ingredients can be found—all while capturing you with an inspiring story that will make you set out on your own adventure—without ever leaving your favorite chair.

I met Karen just after she and Bill returned from their seafaring adventure aboard the *Klatawa*. They were relocating to southern California's Ojai Valley, where the Mediterranean-like climate is similar to what they experienced in Croatia and where they could plant lavender, citrus and olive trees that would be constant reminders of the land and the people they had come to love along the Adriatic. This book, although it pays homage to the culinary traditions and flavors of a culture halfway around the world, is a gift to those of us who care about authentic foodways and culinary traditions and who love delicious, seasonal food.

A Taste of Croatia is really the best kind of book—travelogue, memoir and easy-to-use cookbook. The only step you need to take in order to enjoy all that it offers is one into your pantry or garden.

Tracey Ryder
Santa Fe, New Mexico
October 2007

Tracey Ryder is the president and CEO of Edible Communities, Inc.,
a network of over 50 regional food magazines that celebrate the local bounty
of distinct culinary regions throughout the US and Canada.

Introduction

Croatia is seductive. Gnarled olive trees cling precariously to rocky limestone hillsides. Crystal-clear and multi-hued blue waters shimmer in the summer sun. Rivers rush suddenly and forcefully from the rocky limestone faces of dramatic windswept mountains. Small, tidy and well-managed front yards produce a feast of table crops and at the local *konobas* (small, traditional restaurants) tasty, time-honored family dishes are accompanied by plenty of *vino locale*. Toss in a centuries-old respect for ethnic costumes and dances, happy and hearty folksingers, symphony orchestras performing in 16th century venues, community festivals celebrating secular and religious holidays and an intriguing diversity of local markets and it is tempting to stay forever. Especially if you come equipped with your own floating kitchen.

To be honest, by the time we arrived in Croatia, I was beginning to think about abandoning our cruising lifestyle and heading back to life on land in America. Bill, my blissfully retired sailor husband, and I, the reluctant and somewhat fearful first mate, had already spent more than three years sailing the coastlines and exploring the interiors of France, Italy, Greece and Turkey. Our life of constant movement, coupled with my never-ending trepidation over the possibility of stormy weather, was getting old. I was fantasizing about a home where I could plant my own garden and a community where the faces would remain the same. So on that day in June 2000 when we took our first steps on Croatian soil and savored our first tastes of her simple tradition-laden foods, I would never have predicted that we would linger and spend the better part of the next three years wandering the nooks and crannies of the fabulous Dalmatian coastline … a destination dubbed "The New Riviera" by the *New York Times*.

I had been enticed into the Mediterranean cruising adventure by my passion for food. For no matter where I have lived or traveled, I have always thrived on opportunities to explore new markets, to cook and experiment with new ingredients and techniques and to taste new dishes. So when I had the chance to join my recently retired husband aboard his sailboat in the Mediterranean—a lifestyle I had never dreamed—I eventually said (with a large dollop of trepidation) "yes." What sealed the deal was the idea of being a nomadic foodie traveling with her own kitchen. I could explore local markets, purchase new or familiar ingredients *and* I could come back "home" and cook.

Our welcome to Croatia was warm. We arrived in Dubrovnik where the customs and immigration officials (usually a cold and officious lot) greeted us with smiles, good humor and even a few restaurant recommendations. In near-record time, we had completed the customs procedures and were moving up the river to a nearby marina. As we approached the marina, shouts of *"dobro jutro"* (good morning) rang through the clear, cool early morning air. Smiling and ready to assist, we were greeted by several *marineros* who, in broken English and descriptive hand signals, guided us to an open space along the dock. Once the *Klatawa* was securely tied, those helpful dockhands directed us to the nearby marina café where two gregarious multilingual baristas served us a couple of the world's best cappuccinos.

In 2000, Croatia was just beginning to emerge from the traumas of a painful and destructive war of independence. Croatians were proud of their new nation and they were anxious to begin to rebuild their once-thriving tourist industry. *A Taste of Croatia* recounts our time in this recently rediscovered and rapidly changing Mediterranean hot spot. It describes our challenges with a very different and difficult language, our emotions stirred by the scars of war, our glorious sails through the seemingly endless channels that surround the nearly 1,200 stunningly picturesque islands, our visits to local markets, our experiences cooking and sharing Croatian recipes with friends and our wonderful restaurant outings on isolated islands and in crowded historic villages. It is the story of the people we met, the lives they lead and the food they eat.

▦ ▦ ▦

CROATIA

Croatia's history dates back to around 100,000 B.C., when Neanderthal man roamed portions of this land. Then for many centuries the details are sketchy as multiple streams of Indo-European tribes prowled and populated the region. It was at the beginning of the second century B.C. that invasive activity began to mount. The Romans arrived. From that time forward, this region has been invaded and conquered (and occasionally re-conquered) by multiple nations. Today's Croatia reflects the occupation by the Greeks, Romans, Turks, Venetians and Austro-Hungarians. Each nation has left its mark: architecture, language, beliefs, culture and, of course, food.

In June 1991 Croatia declared its independence from Yugoslavia. The following months and years saw horrendous bloodshed as battles were fought to secure and maintain that independence. Some regions of the country were virtually destroyed. Others, notably the offshore islands, remained largely untouched. Since the signing of the Dayton Peace Accords in 1995, Croatia has worked hard to focus her energies on reconstruction and economic development. With her natural gifts of intriguing geography and a holiday climate, tourism has, once again, begun to thrive as the primary industry.

▦ ▦ ▦

CROATIAN CUISINE

Forty years of Communism followed by a number of war-torn years combined to isolate Croatia from the influences of the "international cuisine" movement that shaped many Western palates throughout the 20th century. As a result, the adage "what grows together goes together" still describes Croatian cuisine, much as it did a century ago. Recipes seem to emerge from the garden with occasional supplements from the sea or nearby grazing land.

The region along the Adriatic coast is distinctly Mediterranean: abundant sunshine, rocky and often hilly soil, short winters, relentless winds and limited rainfall … perfect conditions for maintaining the centuries-old terraced vineyards and olive groves. Add a little water and Mediterranean kitchen crops thrive. Almost every front yard boasts a seasonal selection of red, juicy tomatoes, colorful peppers and eggplants, dusty green mangold (a spinach-like vegetable), creeping vines loaded with bright yellow zucchini blossoms and shiny green zucchinis, aromatic rows of onions and garlic, and red and green cabbages whose giant leaves sparkle in the morning dew. And if space is available, fruit and nut trees are planted for production as well as shade: pomegranates, olives, figs and walnuts on the dry land and cherries, lemons or oranges where irrigation is available.

Seafood plays a crucial role in this coastal diet. It seems like every family has access to a traditional, generations-old wood-planked fishing boat. Unfortunately the Mediterranean Sea has been over fished and quality fish are small, elusive and expensive. As a result, most seafood dishes now feature octopus, squid, farm-raised mussels, small fish or salt cod.

Inland the diet is also determined by the soil, the climate and the availability of water. In some areas, the land is windswept, barren and desolate. Growing crops is painfully difficult: a few rows of potatoes, a scraggly fruit tree, a couple of chickens and a lonesome goat or two. Diets are limited and the population is predictably small. In other inland regions, where the soil is richer and the climate is kinder, the eating habits are more Central European: dairy products and animal fats; corn, cabbages and carrots; apples and pears. You won't find an olive tree but there are often vineyards to keep the wine casks full.

That said, Croatia's food supply system is slowly transitioning. In larger towns and cities, supermarkets are becoming more common but they have not yet replaced the independent small shops: bakeries, green grocers and butcher shops (where it is not unusual to see the side of a cow, a pig and a lamb proudly hung for inspection in the window) still provide much of the daily menu. But in rural and remote areas there are no butcher shops or supermarkets. Almost all the food is cultivated, raised and preserved locally; what you see growing in the garden or grazing in the fields is what appears on the dinner table. The lives of these hard-working and independent peasant families who rigorously tend the land are as challenging today as they were centuries ago. There is little or no time to create complex sauces or multi-course meals. The traditional foods of Croatia are simple, satisfying, economical and nutritious, and they proudly echo the customs of previous generations.

▩ ▩ ▩

KLATAWA

Klatawa, the name of our boat, is a Chinook expression that means "to travel." And travel we did. From her launching in August 1997 to the day we sold her in March 2004, she transported us safely across more than 6,000 Mediterranean miles … through France, Italy, Greece, Turkey and Croatia. She was our bright-white, easy-to-maintain, 50-foot Beneteau fiberglass home. Meticulously designed, the interior featured four cabins: a "great room," a master cabin complete with a separate shower and head, and two guest cabins, each with a private head. Her sloop rig, with a roller-furling jib and jiffy-reef main, made her easy to sail … with special credit to her one electric winch. Throughout our travels, *Klatawa* performed extremely well … in gentle breezes with calm seas or in near-gale-force winds and rough waters, she brought us safely and (usually) comfortably to our destinations.

The kitchen is my favorite room in any house and the galley is my favorite part of a boat. The galley aboard *Klatawa* was approximately 5 feet by 10 feet and was the heart of the vessel: the center of our living and dining space. I considered myself exceptionally lucky when compared to some of my cruising friends to have had an efficiently designed cooking area that provided a generous amount of counter space, adequate storage, a double-well sink (although petite by land-based standards), a propane stove with three burners and an oven, refrigerator and freezer.

Aboard *Klatawa,* as on most small boats, there was one significant difference between a floating galley and a land-based kitchen. That difference was the refrigerator, its location and its access. On most sailing vessels, the refrigerator does not stand upright against a wall. It does not have a front door. Instead, it is a large locker located below the work surface with access through a hinged hatch in the countertop. This meant that *always,* once meal preparations had begun and the ingredients had been assembled for action, someone would need something from the refrigerator. A guest might call for a cold beer or I would suddenly remember a key refrigerated ingredient. Regardless of the what or the why, everything had to be moved aside, the refrigerator had to be opened, the prize had to be located (not always an easy task when working in a multi-layered "cave"), and then the culinary project reassembled. Obviously, a sense of humor was a key ingredient in most recipes.

As the former owner of a kitchen store and cooking school, most folks expected me to have a wide variety of gadgets and plenty of fancy equipment. Not so. Too much equipment is impractical in small spaces and I prefer to limit myself to a few proven, high-quality tools. On board, I had a small selection of really good knives, several special-purpose gadgets (garlic press, an inexpensive yet very

efficient plastic mandolin, zester, kitchen rasp, vegetable peeler, whisk, high-temperature spatulas and, of course, a corkscrew), a limited assortment of quality pots and pans, and a collection of utensils, bowls and dishes. There were no electric appliances. With the possible exception of an occasional yearning for a food processor, I never wished for more.

And there was another bonus to my spartan simplicity. It encouraged me to think about my ever-changing "neighbors"… the women who worked in the nearby kitchens. Whether anchored near a tiny village of red roofed and white stone Croatian homes, an elegant Italian villa, a French farmhouse, a humble and isolated blue-shuttered house on a Greek island, or a Turkish fishing boat, I would imagine, and then try to duplicate, the local cooks' preparation methods and techniques. Basic tools. Basic ingredients. Traditional methods. These were my guidelines for tasty and satisfying meals … the same constraints that have brought sustenance and pleasure for centuries. Please join me for *A Taste of Croatia.*

Croatia

Dobar ∂an, Dobar ∂an ...
Welcome to Croatia

The ship's clock strikes twice. It is exactly 6 a.m. on Wednesday, June 21, 2000, and we have just finished tying the *Klatawa* to the "Q" (quarantine) dock in Dubrovnik, Croatia. According to international customs protocol, the Q dock, always identified by a large yellow flag, is reserved for vessels entering a nation for the first time. Likewise, following international protocols, we are flying our yellow Q flag on the starboard mast spreader, indicating that we require the services of the customs and immigration officials.

Bill and I are both a little nervous. We are not certain what to expect. Our excitement about visiting a new country is tempered by a stomach-rumbling sense of trepidation. Less than five years ago this nation, once a thriving tourist destination, was in the midst of a violent and devastating war. Dubrovnik had been extraordinarily hard hit. Like most Americans we had read many reports and seen horrorific photos of the damage done to this once-spectacular city.

What kind of experience awaits us? What kind of welcome will we receive? Will we find Croatia to be a safe haven, or will we be in constant fear for our safety and well-being? Will there be marinas and repair services available if and when needed? And, finally, underlying all these concerns and based on rumors of a recent drought, will there be sufficient produce and galley supplies available to make our cruising relaxed and enjoyable? Or will we be constantly in search of the basics that sustain our relatively simple lifestyle?

Within moments of securing our stern line, a smartly uniformed customs official approaches us. He smiles and greets us with a friendly "Good morning. Welcome to Croatia." Soon he is joined by an immigration official and a police officer. Warm handshakes and friendly greetings are exchanged. The ship's papers are examined, forms appear from each of the officials, questions are asked and the blank spaces filled in. Our passports and papers are stamped—each official applying his authoritative mark multiple times to the multiple copies of the entry documents.

Once the paperwork is completed, our next stop is the nearby bank machine. *Kuna*, the local currency, is required to purchase an annual cruising permit. We insert our plastic card and with the seemingly magical response of these almost universal icons we receive 3,000 Croatian *kuna*, about 370 U.S. dollars. We deliver the specified amount to the authorities, more papers are stamped, and we become official and legal visitors to Croatia.

With the formalities complete, Dragan, the friendly customs officer, shifts gears and leads us to a wall-mounted nautical chart of Croatia. Soon he is identifying family homes, favorite fishing holes and preferred anchorages. With all of his enthusiasm and willingness to share, I can't resist the temptation to ask about his favorite traditional Croatian food. Without hesitation he replies *"buzara."* With a couple more questions I learn that *buzara* is a typical method for preparing mussels or prawns. Each family's recipe differs slightly ... some include tomatoes; others may add a splash of wine. But the essential and basic ingredient in a true *buzara* is breadcrumbs. Breadcrumbs, Dragan informs us, add a distinctive flavor and they help thicken the sauce.

Bill and I are beginning to relax: the check-in procedures have been completed in near record time, we have enjoyed a friendly and courteous welcome and we have already gained insight into the local cuisine and the heretofore-unknown cruising opportunities. Soon we're motoring up the Dubrovacka River to the nearby ACI marina (Adriatic Croatia International, a Croatian chain of marinas). It is still early in the morning, barely 7:30, but once more we hear the pleasant words: "*Dobro jutro,* good morning, welcome to Croatia. *Dobar dan,* welcome to Dubrovnik." These greetings come from the friendly and helpful marina staff, who quickly inform us that *"dobar dan"* is the universal greeting in Croatia and means good day or hello.

While the dock staff help us secure the boat and connect our power line, we hear a cheerful "Hello, Karen. Hi, Bill." It is our American friend Lois, off the sailing vessel *Topaz*. An extrovert and an organizer, she quickly gathers her husband, John, along with Rob and Liz from *Autumn Dream* and Judy and John from *Lindesfarne* and we all head off to the marina café for an early morning cappuccino. Three American couples and one British couple—it is reunion time. We had gotten to know one another last winter while we were moored together in the hospitable and picturesque Italian town of Gaeta.

The eight of us sound like a bunch of caged chimpanzees all babbling at once. We are excited about being together, and we each welcome the opportunity to speak English and to be understood. Each couple wants to share its sailing and touring adventures since leaving Gaeta six to eight weeks ago.

Traveling independently, we have explored the south coasts of Italy, the Aeolian Islands and Sicily. On our own initiative, we have listened to other sailors and have been enticed to Croatia by their idyllic descriptions of the islands and the mainland Adriatic coast. None of us know what to expect, what we will see or how long we will stay. We share our uncertainties, and our friendly chatter helps to sooth our trepidations and relax our concerns.

Bill and I are still wired from our 20-hour crossing, of the Adriatic Sea and, with the second cappuccino, our tongues shift into high gear. We compete to describe the highlights of our last 24 hours, interrupting one another with essential details. However, we both agree that we could not have written a better script for an awesome summer solstice experience.

⚏ ⚏ ⚏

Yesterday morning in Brindisi, Italy, the weather forecast had finally changed. After almost a week, the Italian weather radio report was no longer predicting another 24 hours of gale force winds and rough seas. At long last, it was time to cross the Adriatic and head for Croatia.

Sorely suffering from the frustration of being weather-bound to the dock, Bill had calculated and recalculated the length of time it would take *Klatawa* to make the 125-mile crossing from Brindisi to Dubrovnik. Unless we met extremely adverse weather conditions, it would take no more than 20 hours. More likely, we would finish the trip in less than 18 hours. As we wanted to arrive in Croatia in daylight, we planned a noon departure.

However, after five days of frustrating delays, Captain Bill was anxious to move and by 10 a.m., we were on our way. We cleared the harbor at Brindisi, and, once in the open water we were greeted with choppy seas and 12-plus knots of wind blowing directly from the north—straight from Dubrovnik. I sighed and took a deep breath and we exchanged those familiar Captain and First Mate expressions that said, "This could be an uncomfortable trip." Determined to reach Croatia by the following day, we slogged and bounced along. Our resolve was rewarded. The wind began to shift and within an hour or two, we were actually enjoying our sail. The seas began to settle down and the sun was breaking through the seemingly interminable Mediterranean haze. It was exactly what the Italian weatherman had predicted. Throughout the day the wind continued to abate and by late afternoon we were relying on the engine.

The magical part of the trip unfurled as the seas began to calm. Bill was at the helm and I was comfortably stretched out in the cockpit reading *The Lonely Planet Guide to Croatia*. I was trying to grasp some of the basic facts about this land that lay straight ahead. Suddenly Bill pointed to activity, lots of activity, off the starboard bow. *Klatawa* was being chased, followed and played with by a large pod of dolphins. Soaring gracefully along our side, they seemed to be saying "Follow me, follow me. Catch me if you can!" For nearly an hour, we watched, laughed and tried to count their numbers. Using our best guessing skills, we had at least 14 dolphins as playmates.

As sunset approached, we were just finishing one of our favorite Mediterranean pasta dinners: mixed seafood tossed with sweet cherry tomatoes, crushed garlic, a hint of spicy red pepper, chopped parsley and a splash of wine, all tossed together with a fine Italian spaghetti. Now it was time to ready the boat for night cruising and prepare ourselves for our respective shifts at the helm.

This evening there was no need to make any sail adjustments. We had packed away the sails hours ago when the wind had died. Now, it was only necessary to make sure that the decks were tidy and that we were both familiar with our location, our course and our sailing plan. All was in order and I was just about ready to go below and try to fall asleep for a couple of hours when Bill pointed in the direction of the setting sun. There, between us and the giant, magnificent and lustrous orange orb of the setting sun was still another pod of dolphins—performing a beautifully choreographed ballet magically backlit by the glowing sphere's unhurried disappearance into the sea.

Tonight's sky was just too special to ignore and go to sleep. In this peaceful and calm setting, the midsummer magic of the concurrent setting sun and rising moon seduced me to remain on deck and watch the reflection from the sun's red-orange glow as it penetrated the slowly rising, almost full moon. For more than two hours, we watched as the moon gradually changed color ... first the color of a giant blood orange and finally the milky white tones typical of the Mediterranean moon in June.

By dark, I was ready to assume the first three-hour night watch and as the hours ticked away, the night remained calm and still. About 1 a.m. Bill took over at the helm and I slipped quietly below to rest. The night remained quiet, calm and uneventful. Throughout the crossing, neither of us saw another vessel. And yet the magic of this night was not over. Just before dawn, when I was once again on watch, the intoxicatingly sweet aroma of mock orange suddenly enveloped the boat.

We were nearing land. I slowed the engine to postpone our arrival until daybreak. Croatia was within our reach.

▧ ▧ ▧

And now we have arrived. Surrounded by friends, I look around at this secure and modern marina. Small and sturdy day boats, magnificent world cruisers complete with smartly uniformed crew, humble sailing yachts and classic motor vessels are moored along six sturdy piers. From my chair on the large café patio, I can readily identify flags from Austria, Germany, Italy, the United Kingdom, France and the United States. At nearby tables, owners, guests and crewmembers are gathering for their morning espresso, tea, cappuccino, fruit juice or beer. The choice of morning beverages is as varied as the languages spoken.

Once again, it is 10 a.m. Just 24 hours since we left the dock in Brindisi. The uncertainties of crossing the Adriatic are history. The warm smiles and the genuine welcome from the customs and immigration people, and the smiles and laughter shared with old friends, have helped to ease our concerns about this new land. Bill and I are ready to rest for a few hours, but before we head back to our boat, plans are made to gather for a late afternoon glass of wine aboard *Klatawa*. We'll supply the wine and our friends will bring a selection of "typical" Croatian appetizers ... *pršut* (air-cured ham), sheep's cheese, fish pâté and the always-irresistible Mediterranean favorite ... a selection of olives.

Croatia

Appetizers

Appetizers Fifty years of communism followed by a painful and destructive war did little to promote a culinary tradition of elaborate beginnings to fancy meals. Simply put, Croatia has no equivalent to French hors d'oeuvres, Spanish tapas or Greek and Turkish meze. Unlike their Mediterranean neighbors, Croatians do not focus on a generous and leisurely appetizer course. Instead, Croatian meals often begin with a simple soup … the first step in satisfying a ravenous, work-driven appetite.

But there are exceptions. There are special occasions. A spontaneous gathering of family and friends on a warm summer evening provides the perfect excuse to share a liter of homemade wine and serve up a tasty Tomato Bruschetta created from a few sweet and succulent sun-blessed tomatoes from the garden. When friends gather around the fire on a chilly, rain-drenched winter afternoon to share stories and gossip—that's the time to assemble a simple meat and cheese platter that features the Dalmatian ham known as *pršut* and *paški sir* or sheep cheese from the island of Pag. These regional specialties are served with pride all along the Dalmatian Coast. *Pršut,* similar to air-dried Italian prosciutto, achieves its unique flavor and texture from the brisk Croatian north winds known as the *bora,* while the signature sharp flavor of *paški sir* can be attributed to the intense-flavored milk produced by the hardy sheep that live and graze on the barren, rocky, salt-sprayed island of Pag.

And who could resist the extraordinary fresh oysters that are available on the Pelješac Peninsula, especially in the ancient, fortified towns of Ston and Mali Ston? These tasty and tender gems, served on a bed of crushed ice and accompanied by a simple Mignonette sauce (finely chopped shallot, red wine vinegar and freshly ground black pepper), are traditionally offered to honeymooners who flock to the peninsula to dine on these oysters which, according to legend, bring prosperity, long life and fertility.

These are all good reasons to slow down, share a glass of wine and enjoy being with friends and loved ones. *Dobar tek! Bon appétit!*

Appetizers
APPETIZERS

COLD APPETIZERS

HOT APPETIZERS

Fish Pâté
Serves 6 to 8

This tasty recipe is so versatile that you may never make the same version twice. It's a wonderful way to use up small chunks of leftover seafood, but you can also start from scratch with some almost-always-on-the-shelf canned tuna or salmon.

To jazz up the flavor, consider adding a combination of one or more of the following: cornichons, dill pickle, sweet pickle, shallots, parsley, garlic, basil, sun-dried tomato, Tabasco or Worcestershire. Just remember to use small quantities. In this recipe a little flavor goes a long way.

2–3 ounces cooked seafood

4 ounces butter, softened

6 ounces cream cheese, softened

2 large green olives, pitted and coarsely chopped

2 teaspoons anchovy paste

2 teaspoons tomato paste

Salt and freshly ground pepper to taste

Place all of the ingredients in the bowl of a food processor fitted with the metal blade. Pulse until the mixture is smooth and creamy, stopping occasionally to scrape down the sides of the bowl. Taste and adjust seasonings. Serve with warm toast triangles, crostini or crackers.

FOR MOST CROATIAN FAMILIES, eating out is an infrequent event. The culture, tradition and the economy necessitate that the majority of meals be eaten at home. That is not to say that Croatians do not love to gather at the end of the day to show off their children, to chat about the day's events or to catch up on the latest gossip. These gatherings with family and friends often occur before dinner at a neighborhood café or after dinner for a post-dinner *digestif*.

As a result dining out is a special occasion … from start to finish. When guests arrive at a restaurant, the maitre d' will frequently welcome them with a small token of appreciation from the chef … often a serving of fish pâté attractively garnished with a thin slice of cornichon and served with a basket of fresh bread or warm toast. The flavor and texture of the pâté will vary from day to day and from restaurant to restaurant—that's because it usually depends on what the chef has on hand.

Just as the evening starts with a special offering of pâté, the maitre d' will often conclude the meal with a complimentary glass of *rakija* (the Croatian equivalent to *grappa*, made from the grape solids that remain from the wine pressing). From beginning to end, restaurant guests are treated cordially by the entire restaurant staff. *Dobar Tek! Bon Appétit!*

Marinated Brussels Sprouts
Serves 6 to 8

Try to make these tasty morsels a day or two in advance so the flavors penetrate the Brussels sprouts. Be sure to refrigerate (they'll keep for up to two weeks in the refrigerator) and stir once or twice each day. Bring to room temperature before serving.

$1^1/2$ pounds Brussels sprouts, trimmed and washed
$1/3$ cup olive oil
2 tablespoons red wine vinegar
2 cloves garlic, minced
1 teaspoon Dijon mustard
1 teaspoon honey
$1/2$ teaspoon salt
$1/2$ teaspoon freshly ground black pepper

Steam the Brussels sprouts just until they are barely tender, about 10–15 minutes. Meanwhile whisk together the remaining ingredients. As soon as the Brussels sprouts are tender, remove them from the heat and transfer them to a small bowl. Toss immediately with the dressing and refrigerate for at least 1 hour. Serve at room temperature.

Cook's Notes:
• For a quicker version, use your favorite oil and vinegar type bottled dressing. Pour over hot Brussels sprouts, toss and cool.

MY FIRST INTRODUCTION to Marinated Brussels Sprouts was nearly 20 years ago when they were served with a hearty glass of red wine after a long day of skiing in the Pacific Northwest. Their slightly crunchy texture and nutty flavor, spiked with a tangy red wine vinegar dressing, made them so addictive that they became a household favorite for years. At that time, I never realized that an old Croatian recipe had more than likely inspired those tasty bits.

Marinated Olives
Yields about 2 cups

For a multi-flavored, multi-colored dish, select a variety of both black and green olives.

2 cups olives, mixed
$1/3$ cup extra virgin olive oil
2 teaspoons dried herbs, mixed (thyme, oregano, basil, and/or tarragon)
2 teaspoons fresh lemon or orange peel, finely julienned
$1/2$–1 teaspoon dried pepper flakes (optional)
2 large cloves garlic, minced

In a medium bowl, combine all of the ingredients. Mix well and place in a jar with a screw-top lid. Refrigerate and rotate the jar every day or so. Olives will keep for at least 3–4 weeks refrigerated. Serve at room tmeperture.

Cook's Notes:

• If you want a more intense flavor, warm the olive oil in a sauté pan and add the herbs, citrus peel and pepper flakes. Stir over medium-low heat until the aromas are released, about 3–5 minutes. Add the olives and stir for 10 to 15 additional minutes. Toss in the garlic and transfer to a jar. Keep olives refrigerated and bring to room temperature before serving.

UNLIKE MANY OF OUR land-based Croatian friends, we did not cure our own olives. Home curing is a tedious process of picking, sorting and carefully soaking the olives in a lye solution to remove the bitter flavor before placing them in a brine solution to cure. Instead, I chose to follow in the footsteps of a cruising friend who taught me long ago that many tastes could be satisfied by combining a variety of already-cured olives, mixing them with herbs and olive oil and storing them in the refrigerator. ▓

Miracle Spread (Imitation *Kajmak*)
Yields about 2 cups

"Kajmak"—*a type of clotted cream made by simmering unpasteurized milk—is traditionally served on dense, dark breads such as rye or pumpernickel. Equally smooth, rich and creamy but much easier to make is this recipe for imitation* kajmak.

Tightly wrapped, this spread will keep for one week in the refrigerator and up to one month in the freezer. It can be quickly transformed into a delicious appetizer when unexpected guests drop by. The variations are endless. Try combining imitation kaymak *with chutney or spice it up with Worcestershire or Tabasco and add some chopped olives. Let your imagination be your guide.*

> 8 ounces cream cheese
> 8 ounces unsalted butter
> 1/4 teaspoon salt

Bring cream cheese and butter to room temperature. Place one half of the cream cheese, one half of the butter and the salt in a medium bowl. Beat with a fork until well blended. Add the remaining butter and the cream cheese one at a time, mixing well after each addition. The spread should be light, smooth and fluffy.

Cook's Notes:

• This recipe can be made in a food processor fitted with a metal blade. Cut the cream cheese and the butter into chunks and combine with the salt in the processor bowl. Process until the *kajmak* is well mixed, light and fluffy.

Variation #1 Sun Dried Tomato Spread

1 cup *kajmak*
2 tablespoons sun dried tomatoes, finely chopped and rehydrated in a small amount of hot water
1 clove garlic, minced
2 tablespoons fresh basil, finely chopped
Salt and freshly ground pepper to taste

Combine all ingredients and serve with thin baguette slices or crackers.

See page 12 for more variations

WE FIRST TASTED *KAJMAK* while we were on a road trip exploring Croatia's interior and visiting the capital city, Zagreb. Since we were not equipped with restaurant recommendations, we chose to follow the locals as they headed to an obviously popular lunchtime destination. The menu, the décor and the wait staff confirmed our impressions that we had left the Mediterranean coast and were rapidly moving toward Central Europe. The culinary traditions of Austria, Germany and Hungary were replacing those of Turkey, Greece and Italy. Butter, cheese, meat and game had replaced olive oil, citrus, lobster and squid.

The authentic version of this rich and creamy spread was served along with a basket of chewy, moist dark breads. Despite multiple "smears," we were mystified. Was it butter or was it cheese? Many tasty "smears" later, we learned that *kajmak* is the cream from cooked milk. This recipe, gleaned from a Croatian-American friend, offers a quick and easy substitute for the genuine product; and with its adaptable nature, it was dubbed Miracle Spread.

Miracle Spread (Imitation *Kajmak*)
Yields about 2 cups

Variation #2 Summer Herb Spread

1 cup *kajmak*
$1/2$ cup mixed, chopped fresh herbs: basil, parsley,
    rosemary, oregano, thyme or marjoram
Salt and freshly ground pepper to taste
1 clove garlic, finely minced (optional)

Combine all ingredients and serve with thin baguette
slices or crackers.

Variation #3 Cinnamon-Raisin Spread

1 cup *kajmak*
2 tablespoons raisins, chopped
$1/2$ teaspoon cinnamon
1 tablespoon honey

Combine all ingredients and spread generously on
toasted bread or bagel. Great for breakfast.

Sataras
Serves 6 to 8 as an appetizer or a side dish

Throughout the Mediterranean, grilled and marinated bell peppers are often served as a tasty and colorful appetizer or side dish. This Croatian version eliminates the time-consuming need for roasting the peppers and it boasts a slightly sweet and sour flavor. Feel free to experiment with your own variations. You may choose to roast and peel the peppers, eliminate the tomatoes and/or the onion, or add more garlic.

4 large bell peppers (about 2 pounds), preferably
   a combination of red, green and yellow
$1/4$ cup olive oil
1 medium onion, peeled, cut in half and sliced into $1/4$-inch slices
6 cloves garlic, thinly sliced
4 Roma tomatoes, diced
2 teaspoons honey
$1/2$ teaspoon salt
$1/2$ teaspoon freshly ground pepper
1 tablespoon balsamic vinegar

Cut the peppers in half. Remove the seeds and all the white membrane. Slice the peppers lengthwise into $1/4$-inch strips.

Heat the olive oil in a large frying pan over medium heat. Add the peppers and the onions and sauté for 10 minutes, stirring frequently. Add the sliced garlic and continue to stir-fry over medium heat until peppers begin to soften and onions begin to turn translucent, about 10 minutes.

Add the tomatoes, honey, salt and pepper and continue to stir-fry for 10 more minutes. Peppers and onions should be soft but still retain their color. Add the balsamic vinegar. Taste and adjust seasonings. Serve at room temperature with thinly sliced country bread or crackers or as a side dish to accompany your favorite grilled dish.

SATARA IS A TURKISH word that means meat cleaver or sword. It is said that the vegetables for this dish were originally chopped with a special knife known as a "satara."

Sliced Eggplant in Olive Oil
Serves 8

2 large eggplants, washed and cut horizontally into 3/4-inch slices
Salt
Olive oil
5 large garlic cloves, peeled and thinly sliced
2 bay leaves
2 8-inch sprigs of rosemary
Additional rosemary sprigs for garnish (optional)

Generously salt the eggplant slices, place in a colander and allow to drain for 15 minutes to 1 hour. Gently rinse and pat dry. Brush the slices with olive oil and grill over an open fire or on a non-stick pan for 4–5 minutes per side, until the eggplant is browned and the flesh is soft. Layer the eggplant slices in a ceramic or glass dish, sprinkling each layer with garlic and drizzling each layer with olive oil. Continue to arrange in layers and pour sufficient olive oil over all to completely cover. Tuck bay leaves and rosemary into the oil, cover tightly and refrigerate for at least 2 hours or until ready to use.

A SIMILAR VERSION of this dish is found on tables throughout the Mediterranean, a fact that confirms the strong influence of ancient traders on international culinary trends. This version was inspired by my friend Jany, founder of the women's refugee organization in Dubrovnik known as DESA.

DESA came to life as the Yugoslav Army was shelling the ancient city of Dubrovnik during the 1991–92 war and refugees were being housed in the large conference hotels that had been a mainstay of the Yugoslav tourist economy. The refugees, mostly women and children, received shelter and food ... but they had nothing to occupy their thoughts, except their nightmares. They were miserable, lost, and disoriented. DESA sought to give the women refugees the tools to stimulate their own creative powers and to enable them to be functional members of a society in a state of emergency.

Humanitarian aid poured in: food, medicines and mountains of used clothing. Using old scissors, a dedicated nucleus of women encouraged the refugees to set to work and create new works out of those clothes. They sewed blankets and shoes, created puppets and dolls, and eventually they began to weave. It was of little importance what these items looked like; what was important was the distraction this project provided to women experiencing deep psychological distress. The women were employing their hands to turn off their minds. As they sewed, they began to talk. As they began to talk, they began to laugh again. Once more these women had a purpose; they were inventing and creating.

For more than a decade, DESA has guided women through the challenges of war and the restoration of their heritage. Today, the organization focuses on providing women the tools for economic success in their developing economy. Computer and business classes are offered, and tools for strengthening rural tourism are being developed. ▨

Tomato Bruschetta
Serves 6 to 8

This dish is best when made with summertime fresh-from-the-garden, vine-ripened heritage tomatoes. To make it eye-catching spectacular, use a variety of brightly colored red, orange and yellow tomatoes. Cut the bread slices slightly thicker than normal to soak up some of the flavor-packed juices.

> **1 baguette, cut into medium-thick slices**
> **Olive oil**
> **6 medium to large vine ripened tomatoes**
> **2–3 cloves garlic, minced**
> **3 tablespoons extra virgin olive oil**
> **2 teaspoons red wine vinegar**
> **$1/4$–$1/2$ cup fresh basil, finely sliced**
> **Sea salt to taste**
> **Freshly ground pepper to taste**
> **Whole basil leaves for garnish**

Preheat the oven to 375 degrees. Brush the baguette slices with olive oil and toast the bread slices until just crisp and golden, about 10 minutes. Core the tomatoes and cut them in half vertically and squeeze out seeds and excess juices. Chop the tomatoes and place them in a bowl. Stir together with the garlic, olive oil, wine vinegar, basil, salt and pepper and allow the flavors to blend for about 10 minutes. Drain excess juices, garnish with basil leaves and serve with toasted baguette slices.

THE TOMATO IS NATIVE to the Americas, and is known to have been cultivated as early as 700 A.D. by the Aztecs and Incas. The seeds were first taken to Europe by the Spanish Conquistadors in the 16th century and cultivation began in the Mediterranean countries in the 1540s.

Bakalar

Traditionally made with salt cod and potato, this version substitutes high quality canned tuna for the often difficult to find traditional salt cod. Light, fluffy and fragrant with garlic and olive oil, bakalar is a popular appetizer. Spread on crusty bread or crostini or use as a dip for fresh vegetables.

1 large russet potato, peeled and cut into 1-inch cubes (1^1/$_2$ cups)
^{1}/$_2$ teaspoon salt
Freshly ground black pepper
1 (6-ounce) can oil-packed tuna, drained and flaked
4 cloves garlic, finely minced
^{1}/$_4$ cup cream
^{3}/$_4$ cup extra-virgin olive oil, divided
Additional extra-virgin olive oil for garnish (optional)
2 tablespoons chopped parsley

Cover the potatoes with water and cook in a small saucepan until tender. Drain and place in a medium-sized mixing bowl. Add the salt, pepper, flaked tuna, garlic, cream and ¼ cup of the olive oil.

Using a hand-held electric mixer, beat the tuna/potato/oil combination briefly—until the tuna and potato are mixed together and they are just beginning to break up. The combination should be soft and moist. If it appears to be too dry, add more cream in small increments. With the beaters running, add the remaining olive oil in a steady, slow stream. Continue to beat until the mixture is light and fluffy. Taste and adjust the seasonings. If desired, drizzle with additional olive oil, sprinkle with parsley and serve warm or at room temperature.

Cook's Notes:
• *Bakalar* can be made in advance and refrigerated. Cover and re-heat in a 375-degree oven for 15 minutes. Stir well with a fork and garnish with chopped parsley.

THE COD FISHING INDUSTRY began late in the 15th century, when abundant quantities of cod were discovered off the Grand Banks of Newfoundland. Salted and dried, these preserved North Atlantic catches rapidly became a part of the diet in England and the Mediterranean nations where fresh fish was often scarce and expensive.

Known as *bakalar* in Croatia, *brandade* in France and *baccala* in Italy, this cod and potato combination is popular throughout the Mediterranean. My first introduction to *bakalar* was at a pre-symphony dinner in Dubrovnik in the company of some good sailing friends at restaurant Dundo Maroje. Tucked into a narrow cobbled stone alley off the busy *Placa* in Dubrovnik, Dundo Maroje was originally recommended to us by the customs officer who cleared us into Dubrovnik in 2000. The rich, creamy and garlicky flavor of this traditional dish made it a favorite appetizer to share.

Baked Clams or Mussels
Serves 6 to 8

This dish is perfect for entertaining. The mussels or clams can be prepared 2–3 hours in advance. Just cover and refrigerate until ready to bake and serve.

> 40 large clams or mussels
> 1¹/₂ cups fresh breadcrumbs
> 2 tablespoons parsley, chopped
> 8 cloves garlic, minced
> Salt and freshly ground pepper to taste
> 6 tablespoons olive oil
> 2 tablespoons cream
> ¹/₄ cup Parmigiano Reggiano, grated
> 3 tablespoons cold butter
> 1 tablespoon parsley, finely chopped
> 1 lemon, sliced into wedges

Wash and scrub the clams or mussels and de-beard the mussels if necessary. Place the shellfish in a large sauté pan and add a small amount of water (about ¹/₂ cup). Cover and place over high heat and cook, stirring occasionally, until all the shellfish have opened, about 5 minutes. Remove the shellfish from the pan and allow to cool. Discard any clams or mussels that do not open.

Remove the meat from the shells and break shells in half. Reserve the best looking half and return the seafood to the reserved shells. Mix together the breadcrumbs, parsley, garlic, salt and pepper. Stir in the olive oil, cream and the Parmigiano Reggiano.

Preheat the oven to 450 degrees. Divide the topping among the shells and top with a small sliver of butter. Place the filled shells on a rimmed cookie sheet and bake for 4–5 minutes, just until the topping is crisp and golden. Sprinkle with parsley and serve with lemon wedges.

Savory and Sweet Spinach and Onion Pie
Serves 4 to 6

The unique combination of savory and sweet flavors blends together to create a dish that is as delicious as it is distinctive. Served at room temperature, it can be prepared in advance … ready whenå the guests arrive.

4–7 inch flour tortillas
FILLING:
$1/2$ pound spinach leaves, chopped
$1/2$ medium onion, thinly sliced
1 tablespoon olive oil
$1/3$ cup raisins
$1/2$ teaspoon cinnamon
$1/4$ teaspoon salt
TOPPING:
2 tablespoons olive oil
1 tablespoon sugar
1 large clove garlic, minced
Freshly ground sea salt

FOR THE FILLING: In a large open pan over medium-high heat, quickly braise the spinach in $1/2$ cup of water, tossing the spinach as it wilts and cooks. As soon as all the spinach is completely wilted, transfer it to a heavy-duty strainer or colander and press out as much liquid as possible. Transfer to a medium bowl and using a fork, separate and fluff the spinach. Add the onion, olive oil, raisins, cinnamon and salt to the spinach. Continuing to use a fork, toss and combine these ingredients until well blended.

FOR THE TOPPING: Combine the olive oil, sugar and minced garlic in a small bowl.

Preheat the oven to 400 degrees. Lightly oil a 10 x 15-inch cookie sheet. Place 2 tortillas on the cookie sheet and spread half of the filling over each tortilla, keeping the filling $1/2$ inch away from the edge. Top with the remaining tortillas and press the edges firmly together. Brush the tops of the "pies" with the olive oil mixture and sprinkle lightly with sea salt. Put another cookie sheet, bottom side down, on top of the tortillas and place in the preheated oven. Bake for 10 minutes.

Remove the pans from the oven and holding the 2 cookie sheets firmly together, carefully flip them over. Return the pies to the oven and bake for an additional 3–5 minutes.

Remove the pies from the oven and carefully flip them over once again. The salt side should now be up. Whisk the topping ingredients together and brush the mixture on each pie. Cover with a clean cloth and allow to cool. Cut each pie into 8 triangles and serve.

Cook's Note:

• One 10-ounce package of frozen, chopped spinach can be substituted. Defrost and squeeze out any excess moisture. Spinach can be drained and squeezed dry by placing it in a compact pile on a clean towel. Roll the towel and, holding the towel over the sink, squeeze out excess moisture.

• Do not expect the edges to seal tightly when pressed together.

A SIMILAR RECIPE in *The Art of Croatian Cooking* by Anna Bozin intrigued me. In her version, the pastry dough was made from scratch. Although the results were delicious, the process was time consuming—a drawback that was noted by several volunteer testers around the world. I struggled with the possibility that this recipe should perhaps be deleted from the book as I was trying to emphasize simplicity in most of the dishes. Then in 2003, a new *supermercato* opened outside Dubrovnik; and there, staring out at me from the shelves, were packages of pre-made flour tortillas. Within hours, this dish was reborn into this simpler, easier-to-prepare version. 🔲

The Klatawa

Springtime Frittata

Serves 4 to 6 as an appetizer or 2 as a main course

The colors in this easy-to-make recipe will look as springtime bright as you choose. Add some thinly sliced red pepper; leave the bright skins on small new red potatoes or garnish with fresh chopped basil and/or parsley. The bright colors and distinct flavors are guaranteed to make this dish a springtime favorite.

1 tablespoon olive oil
2 cloves garlic, minced
3 small new potatoes, scrubbed and thinly sliced
2 tablespoons water
2 small zucchini, thinly sliced
6 green onions, mostly white part, thinly sliced
6 eggs, whisked
1/3 cup Parmigiano Reggiano, freshly grated
Salt and freshly ground pepper to taste

Over medium heat, warm a 10-inch non-stick skillet. Add olive oil and garlic and sauté until the garlic is soft, about 2 minutes. Add the potatoes and 2 tablespoons water. Stir, cover and let the potatoes steam for 4–5 minutes, stirring occasionally.

Remove the cover and stir in the zucchini. Cook for 2 minutes. Stir in the green onions and cook this mixture for an additional 2 minutes. Combine the eggs with the cheese, salt and pepper. Stir this mixture into the vegetables and cook, covered, over medium low heat for 10–15 minutes, gently lifting the edges from time to time to allow the uncooked eggs to slip to bottom of the pan.

When the frittata is nearly cooked through and lightly golden on the bottom, remove from heat. Carefully cover with a plate and flip upside down. Slide the frittata back into the pan and cook for 2–3 more minutes. Slip onto a serving plate, cut into wedges and serve.

Cook's Notes:

- When creating a frittata, the choice of vegetables as well as the ratio of vegetables to eggs can vary. Feel free to experiment. In addition to or in place of the potatoes, zucchini and green onions, try red or green bell pepper, mushrooms, and broccoli.

- If you prefer, the frittata can be finished in the oven. Just be sure that the pan handle is oven safe. Preheat the oven to 350 degrees. Once the eggs begin to set on the bottom, transfer the pan to the oven and bake uncovered for 20 to 25 minutes or just until the frittata is fully set and a knife inserted in center comes out clean. Slip onto serving plate, and cut into wedges and serve.

On a warm and sunny spring day, I joined my friend Jean from the sailing vessel *Sheba Moon* and Tugger, her faithful Chow, for a hike through the hillsides surrounding the Dubrovnik ACI marina. As we wandered and chatted, we came upon a narrow valley dotted with little farms. Tidy Croatian limestone homes, complete with brown shutters, were surrounded by gently rolling green fields bursting with the bounty and energy of springtime. At the end of the road, we stopped to chat with a Croatian couple as they sat in the cool shade of their neat and tidy garage. As we visited, their hands remained busy tying red plastic "ribbon" around each perfect bunch of spring onions before gently placing it in the well-used wooden crate that they would carry the next morning to the farmers' market.

We struggled to communicate. But a few Croatian words from us, a few English words from them—along with creative hand signs, lots of pointing and a generous dose of smiles and laughter—and we soon learned that "Mama" goes to the market twice a week to sell the extra produce from the family garden. This week there would be cherries, potatoes, zucchini, spring onions, parsley, peas, lemons and fresh eggs. And how lucky we were. Before we left this warm and charming couple, they presented us with generous samples from their garden. We headed back to *Klatawa*, gathered a few more friends and created a wonderful dinner: Springtime Frittata and Bowtie Pasta with Peas.

Dubrovnik ...
Our Croatian Homeport

For more than three years, the ancient city of Dubrovnik was *Klatawa's* homeport and the ACI Marina, situated in the worn and war-torn yet still-elegant grounds of a former summer villa, was our neighborhood. It was within this stone palace and modern marina setting that we got to know our cruising neighbors from England, Scotland, Austria and America. And it was here that we formed lasting friendships with Croatians who helped and directed us through the seemingly endless but rewarding challenges of living in a country where we did not speak the language or understand the local customs.

The decision to stay in Croatia and base ourselves in Dubrovnik had been easy. Within weeks of our arrival in Croatia, we had become smitten with the people, the land, the architecture, the history and, of course, the food. The marinas had reasonably priced space available and the anchorages were quietly pastoral and secluded. Maintenance services for the boat were accessible and simple provisions were obtainable. In 2000, Croatia was just beginning to recover from a disastrous war and visitors were warmly welcomed.

Once we had made the commitment to stay, our roles changed—we were no longer considered "visitors" but instead we were residents; clearly temporary residents but nevertheless we were folks who would be around for a while. We quickly learned that visiting a place is very different from living in a community. As a visitor, a guidebook is your primary source of information; as a resident, the locals become your guide.

A visitor sees the sights, eats in restaurants, writes a few postcards and moves on. But a resident takes the time to absorb the surroundings, shop in the local markets, develop personal relationships and participate in community events. And if food is a passion, there is almost always someone who will share information about a local *konoba* (a small restaurant that specializes in serving homemade dishes) or reveal a favorite family recipe.

Each year, as the cruising season ended and winter storms threatened, we returned home to slip B27. There I relaxed—I did not need to worry about the weather or about the challenges of reaching our next destination. From late October to early May, when we were aboard *Klatawa*, we were securely tied to a sturdy and beautifully situated dock—surrounded by vertical limestone mountains and centuries-old buildings. Our days were spent developing friendships and learning more about our host city and country. Throughout those months, our daily routines became as vital as our opportunities for new adventures.

I liked to begin my day with an early morning walk. But before I got started, I had to decide what path I would take. Should I pick up my three-pound, bright pink weights and walk briskly out of the marina to follow the shoreline of the fast-flowing Ombla River? Or should I remain within the ACI grounds and do "laps" through the sadly neglected yet still-magnificent formal gardens adjacent to the old abandoned palace? As much as I liked to think that I walked just as fast on the open road, I knew that if I left the marina grounds, I would be tempted to dally ... to slow down and snap "just one more" photo of the lively, noisy and ever-expanding family of black and white ducks that dwelled along the river's edge. Or I might be lured to linger for an early morning chat with my friend Anna as she climbed into her elderly and well-used yellow VW to head off for work.

However, if I decided to remain within the palace gates, I could pursue my workout with determination. On familiar ground, I would concentrate my energy on exercising and focus on the smaller details of my environment. I could stretch and bend while I analyzed the old stone carving of Aeolus as he spewed water from the weathered palace fountain, and I could continue my brisk walk along the graveled palace paths as I imagined myself in attendance at one of the summer garden parties that took place centuries ago on these very grounds. I could almost hear the chamber music playing in the background as the well-dressed and carefully coiffed ladies gathered to gossip about their children's academic achievements and their husbands' trading or ship-building successes.

But then, five or six laps later, reality would settle upon me and I would simply try to conjure up one more recipe in which to use some of the endless supply of rosemary that lined the garden path. Without a doubt, what I liked most during my garden workouts was the invigorating yet soothing Mediterranean aroma in the air ... the scent of rosemary warmed by the morning sun mingled with the sweet and tangy aroma of ripe citrus clinging to the nearby trees.

Whatever my choice, I was sure to be inspired by my surroundings. The centuries-old palace grounds, a legacy from an affluent and peaceful period of the Dubrovnik Republic, had been designed as a summer home for the family of the reknown Croatian poet Ivan Gundulic. This riverfront location had been selected as an escape from the stifling summer heat of Dubrovnik, heat that spread like a heavy, oppressive blanket and remained trapped within the massive walls that surround the city. But here, just a few miles away from the *stari grad* (old city), was a totally different microclimate, a place where the fresh northerly winds blew down from the towering limestone hills and mingled with the cool air wafting from the chilly river waters.

When we arrived in June 2000, we immediately realized that we had found a special place. The marina felt like a luxury resort, complete with restaurant, café bar, showers, laundry, grocery store, clay tennis courts and a beautiful swimming pool that overlooked the river valley. And we appreciated the modern marina amenities, the well-built docks and the competent marina staff. These were the features that enticed us to spend our first several days. But soon we began to recognize the matchless merit of our environment—the new and the old set against a background of incredible natural beauty. Throughout our years in Dubrovnik we were soothed and nurtured by the large, symmetrical formal gardens, the elaborate fishponds and the handsome limestone villa.

Known in Croatian as Rijeka Dubrovačka (Dubrovnik Riviera), our Dubrovnik neighborhood was located near the head of the mile-and-half long bay created by the River Ombla. The Ombla was not a conventional river that gains size and strength as it merges with smaller streams on the way down to a lake or an ocean. Rather, it was a cool, wide, crystal-clear river that suddenly and breathtakingly emerged from a buried spring at the head of the bay. It was one of those amazing Croatian karst phenomena where chilling waters suddenly erupt from a vertical mountainside.

On those days when I decided to leave the marina grounds and walk along the river's edge, my path took me across this fast-moving waterway via a highway bridge. It had been constructed about 100 yards from the powerful waterfalls that formed the head of the river, just where it surfaced from its underground route. On my walks, I had a close-up view of this awesome natural wonder and I never ceased to be amazed.

Once across the bridge, I headed toward the limestone church and the Franciscan monastery in the tiny village of Rožat. Built in 1393, this classic, beautiful old parish church anchors a small group of ancient church buildings—all perched near the river's edge. Both the church and the adjacent tall and stately campanile are capped with mellow, well-weathered red roof tiles. On Sunday mornings, the finely tuned bells rang out to call the villagers to prayer, and sometimes on weekdays those bells would chime to signal the beginning of the funeral procession for a departed congregant. On those occasions, I would stop and watch the mourners as they wound their way slowly and sometimes painfully up the steep and rocky path to the hilltop cemetery.

Completing the religious complex were three or four seemingly contiguous buildings, all part of an ancient, continuously operating monastery. Centuries ago, these buildings had been walled off for privacy and seclusion. Since this was my turn-around point, I would stop, give thanks and head back home ... but only after I had taken a quick peek through a knot-holed wooden fence to peer in on the well-tended vegetable and flower gardens hidden behind the walls.

⊠ ⊠ ⊠

Throughout the years, there were times when I yearned to be a part of a church community. On those occasions I would head across the river for a Sunday morning service at the parish church. On one such Sunday in early October, I arrived well before the start of the service. I sat alone in a pew near the rear of the sanctuary and watched quietly as a youthful nun organized the altar for the day's special harvest celebration. As she covered the sacred table with autumnal chrysanthemums, a variety of squashes and aubergines, and beautiful homemade breads, sister fussed over the artistic details. She bustled about, making certain that the very large, round and elaborate loaf of bread (complete with a beautiful braided edge and a perfectly executed center cross formed from the bread dough) was visible from all directions. Once satisfied that her decorating responsibilities were complete, she turned her attention to the 15 or so polished and well-disciplined members of the pre-teen youth choir as they slowly wandered in for this service of thanksgiving.

One spring, we attended Mass on Easter Sunday. The church was tightly packed as families and friends gathered for the traditional service in this largely Catholic nation. Squeezed by my side was an older woman, probably in her 70s. It was obvious from her firm, calloused hands and sun-darkened and wrinkled face that she had spent many years working the land. On this holiday Sunday, she was dressed in her very best: a long, dark, navy blue skirt; a well-tailored, dark, almost-black, buttoned jacket with velvet cuffs; a clean and crisp black apron decorated with a tiny, cream-colored geometric pattern; a scarf around her neck, a shawl around her hips and a *babushka* on her head. Every piece of clothing was either black or navy with just an occasional sprinkle of white or cream.

As I sat silently and contemplatively beside her, I could not help but compare her life to mine. Throughout the service, I gave thanks for my life, a life that had been blessed with incredible and seemingly endless travel opportunities, and I considered with great admiration her life, one that I imagined had been filled with hard work and toil. After the Mass, I realized from the genuinely warm smiles and the greetings she received from the children, grandchildren, neighbors and friends who gathered at her side that her life was also blessed; her hard work and her commitment to family, friends and the land had earned her love, respect and companionship.

▩ ▩ ▩

All it took was a quick 15-minute bus ride and we were in a totally different environment ... the old walled city of Dubrovnik, "the Pearl of the Adriatic." Entrance into this living museum was through one of two gates and, since there were no vehicles allowed, residents and visitors alike became pedestrians. The more convenient and busier gate was the picturesque Pile Gate. Dwarfed and overwhelmed by the massive stone walls, the gate was a beautiful 16th century Renaissance arch, topped with a statue of Saint Blaise, the patron saint and protector of Dubrovnik. The steady stream of residents and visitors that passed through this gate funneled across the moat via a sturdy, wooden drawbridge. Seasonally, especially during the summer tourist months, the stone benches that lined the gate's entrance were filled with Croatian ladies of all ages, calling out politely to passersby to take a moment, examine their fine and colorful needlework and make a purchase to "remember Dubrovnik."

Once through the gate, it took just a few moments to walk down a set of well-worn marble steps and emerge onto the *Placa*, Dubrovnik's pedestrian main street. The *Placa*, paved with almost-pure white limestone and polished by hundreds of years of endless footsteps, seemed to glow in any light—the sunshine of midday or the moonlight at night. Lined with lovely old churches, public buildings and green-shuttered shops, it was impossible not to slow down and exclaim a quiet "wow."

But our favorite view of Dubrovnik was from above—from the top of those massive, 80-foot-high stone walls. Reached by climbing a narrow, irregular and sometimes steep set of stone stairs, we could walk the full mile-and-a-half-long stretch of protective walls and peer down upon the small peninsula that is old Dubrovnik. With this bird's-eye view, we could identify all the historical buildings and watch the activity throughout the city, both on the *Placa* and along the narrow, twisting side streets. From above, we could capture the picture that has come to symbolize Dubrovnik ... the collage-like assembly of rosy and irregular roof tiles perched on top of the light gray, almost white, limestone buildings.

For centuries, those roof tiles were handmade, formed by molding clay over a craftsman's thigh. The city's distinguishing, ancient roof tiles had been created from a unique type of clay excavated from nearby pits, their rich color a distinctive mellow blend of coral, gold and rose hues.

Unfortunately, that clay was depleted and since the 1991-1992 war that destroyed many of Dubrovnik's historical buildings, it has been impossible to ignore the difference between the vivid new factory-produced tiles and the mellow old handcrafted tiles. Those brighter, newer tiles will long serve as a painful reminder of the damage created by that war.

And we loved looking down on familiar landmarks like the elaborate Onofrio's Fountain. This classical central water source for the city was also damaged during the war with the Serbs. Now repaired, it spews fresh, cold and delicious water from the metal spouts that emerge from each of the 16 decorative stone masks that ring the fountain. Since 1438, this architectural treasure has continuously provided fresh water from the River Ombla to the residents of Dubrovnik. It is little wonder that Dubrovnik residents are very proud of their ancient water system.

Back down on the ground, we could never shake the feeling that we were in an outdoor museum. Nearly every building was a historical structure that provided an important link to Dubrovnik's past. The options for tours seemed endless, but we never tired of visiting a few of our favorites: the 14th century Franciscan monastery that housed the third-oldest functioning pharmacy in Europe, and the early 18th century Cathedral of the Assumption of the Virgin with Titian's painting, The Assumption of the Virgin. This cathedral also housed an extensive treasury that included numerous gold and silver reliquaries. For years, I was uncertain about the term *reliquary*—what did it mean? One day, thanks to a fortuitous meeting with a local nun, I learned that it is a receptacle designed to hold sacred relics, often pieces of bone alleged to have belonged to a deceased saint. Here in this cathedral treasury, there were several elaborate gold, silver and bejeweled reliquaries of Saint Blaise.

Whenever possible, we tried to be in Dubrovnik on Thursday night for the symphony performance. We often combined the pleasure of watching and listening to the wonderfully talented small orchestra with a pre-symphony dinner of *bakalar* and mussels *buzara* at Dundo Maroje. This restaurant, originally suggested by our friendly and welcoming customs inspector, had become one of our favorite Thursday night rituals. After dinner, we would head to the performance. Its location would rotate throughout the seasons, but we were thrilled when the orchestra played in the partially enclosed, stone-walled atrium of the old Rector's Palace.

Originally built during the 15th century for the governing rector of Dubrovnik, the setting was splendidly suited for a concert. A magnificent baroque staircase led up to an open balcony where ornately carved capitals topped the numerous supporting columns and a bronze bust of Dubrovnik's benefactor, Miho Pracat, helped set the stage for a unique and intimate performance center. The acoustics were marvelous, and we loved the intimacy of a setting that allowed us to watch and recognize the performers from our seats. What other symphony hall would allow you to make frequent and appreciative eye contact with a favorite violinist or an exuberant bass player?

❖ ❖ ❖

We loved our lives in Dubrovnik—the land, the architecture, the history and the food. But what made us feel most at home were the people, their smiles of welcome and their inclusiveness. And there was no place where we felt more at home than at the restaurant/café Buzan, located in the marina. It was here that we were introduced to many Croatian foods and many became our favorites: fish pâté, thinly sliced *pršut*, fish soup, grilled fish and *rožata*. Café Buzan was also where we would go for arguably the best cappuccino in Croatia. The intensely flavorful and richly foamed cappuccinos were made by our good friends Ivo and Stefan, and this marina café was the closest we have ever come to having a Cheers-type pub as part of our daily lives. Here the *baristas* knew us, joked with us and shared our daily life events. And as a special sign of friendship, they developed a ritual of using chocolate syrup to decorate the foam atop our cappuccino cups with a message for the day: happy faces, sad faces, political/national comments and modern art.

Each *barista* had his own "chocolate paint" style. On one visit, our friends Darryl and Jean from *Sheba Moon* and their Chow, Tugger, joined us. Tugger, as usual, was barking loudly and obnoxiously at the motley collection of local cats. When our next round of cappuccino was delivered, each cup was topped with *"av, av."* We scratched our heads, we wondered aloud, we could not figure this one out. Finally I went to the source and asked Stefan what *"av av"* meant. He readily replied: *"av, av*—you know, like the dog." Obviously, Croatian dogs bark with a bit of an accent ... "arf, arf" had become *"av, av"* in Croatian. We loved those friendly efforts and when a barrista would ask if we wanted our cappuccino with or without chocolate graffiti, we would reply *"Da, molim."* (Yes, please.)

Soups

Soups Many Croatian meals begin with a bowl of hot broth enhanced with a small amount of rice or a few flakes of fish. This tradition probably traces back to Croatia's land-based peasant culture when, after a backbreaking day in the field, family members would arrive at the table bone-tired and hungry. Since crop yields in the wind-swept, often-arid Mediterranean climate were sometimes sparse, housewives were forced to become efficient stewards of their meager stores: They learned that a light soup staved off hunger and reduced the craving for large servings of precious proteins and carbohydrates.

From this same tradition of frugal stewardship came hearty versions of soups and stews—one-pot meals that were the focal point of a rural supper. Healthy and satisfying, these substantial soups had other advantages: they could be thinned to feed unexpected guests, they helped stretch the scarce food supply, and they could be left unattended to simmer for hours in a large iron pot over an open fire while the housewife joined the rest of the family to work in the fields. At the end of the day, the rich aroma welcomed the family home … for centuries, hearty one-pot meals have been recognized as nourishment for the soul as well as the body. ▓

Soups
SOUPS

Country Bean, Cabbage and Potato Soup
Serves 8

This recipe is meant to serve as a foundation for creating your own hearty soups. Experiment with the vegetable combinations: add tomatoes, or a turnip, or a cut-up chunk of squash. Eliminate the ham-bone and substitute diced and fried bacon and/or sausage. On the second day, add some pasta. No two meals served from the same pot need to be the same.

A batch of this soup will make enough to serve a very hungry gathering of eight. Make it all. It keeps well in the refrigerator for up to three days (it tastes even better after a day or two) and stores in the freezer for up to one month.

Although this recipe takes about 4 hours from start to finish (not including the time to soak the beans), most of that time is simmer time—the active time is only $^1/_2$ hour.

$^1/_3$ pound dried beans (red kidney, pinto or great northern)

1 smoked ham-bone, preferably with some meat still intact

2 medium onions, peeled and diced (about $1^1/_2$ cup)

3 medium carrots, peeled and diced (about $1^1/_2$ cups)

1 stalk celery, diced

4 cloves garlic, sliced thin

1 teaspoon freshly ground pepper

3 medium potatoes, peeled and diced (about 1 pound)

2 bay leaves

$^1/_2$ large head of cabbage, cored and coarsely chopped

$^1/_4$ cup parsley, finely chopped

Salt and freshly ground pepper to taste

Beginning the day before you plan to serve the soup, pick over the dried beans and remove any small twigs or stones. Rinse the beans well and cover with water, allowing at least 4 inches of water on top of the beans. Let stand over-night. Drain and rinse the beans.

On the day you are preparing the soup, place the ham-bone, along with the beans, in an 8-quart stockpot and cover with cold water. Quickly bring to a boil, reduce the heat and simmer slowly for 1 hour. Add the onions, carrots, celery, garlic and pepper, and simmer for another hour. Add the potatoes, bay leaves and cabbage, and simmer for an additional hour. About 20 minutes before serving, remove the ham bone and allow it to cool. Remove the bay leaves and add the parsley. Taste and correct the seasonings. Remove the meat from the ham bone, coarsely chop and return to the soup pot. Stir and simmer for an additional 5 minutes.

Cook's Notes:

• Do not worry if you have not soaked the beans overnight. You can achieve very good results by washing the beans, placing them in a pot and covering them with 4 inches of water above the beans. Bring the beans to a boil, turn off the heat and allow them to rest for 1 hour. Drain and rinse the beans and proceed with the recipe.

• Some experts recommend that when cooking dried beans, you should resist the temptation to salt early in the soup making process. They say that salt tends to toughen dried bean. Others will argue that it is acid (lemon, tomatoes, vinegar, etc.) that will make the beans tough. It's your call!

• For a thicker soup, mash some of the beans and/or potatoes.

Istrian *Jota* (Bean and Sauerkraut Soup)
Serves 6

Rich with the Austro-Hungarian flavors of sauerkraut and smoked ham, this dish is popular in the inland portions of northern Croatia. An extra zap of flavor comes from the pesht, *a traditional blend of bacon, garlic, parsley and salt that serves as a seasoning, a minor thickening agent and a delightful appetite stimulator. The wonderful aroma that fills the air when the* pesht *is added to hot soup is the call to dinner.*

$1/2$ pound beans

$1/4$ pound bacon, chopped

4 cloves garlic, peeled

$1/2$ cup parsley leaves

$1/4$ teaspoon salt

1 ($14^{1}/2$ ounce) can sauerkraut

1 pound smoked ham, cut in $1/2$ inch cubes

Salt and freshly ground pepper to taste

3 bay leaves

1 pound potatoes, peeled and cubed

Beginning the day before you plan to serve the soup, pick over the dried beans and remove any small twigs or stones. Rinse the beans well and cover with water; allowing at least 4 inches of water on top of the beans. Let stand over night. Drain and rinse the beans.

On the day that you are preparing the soup, cover the beans with fresh water and bring to a boil. Reduce the heat and simmer over medium low heat for 1 hour.

Meanwhile, make the traditional Croatian pesht:

In a food processor fitted with the metal blade, combine the bacon, garlic, parsley and salt. Pulse together until nearly paste-like in consistency.

Wash and drain the sauerkraut and then add it to the beans along with the ham. Add the bay leaves, half of the *pesht*, salt and pepper. Simmer for 30 minutes. Add the cubed potatoes and cook until everything is tender, about 45 minutes. Stir in the remaining *pesht*, taste and adjust the seasonings. Serve steaming hot from the pot.

Cook's Notes:

• If you have not planned ahead and soaked the beans overnight, do not worry. You can achieve very good results by washing the beans, placing them in a pot and covering them with 4 inches of water above the beans. Bring the beans to a boil, turn off the heat and allow them to rest for at least 1 hour. Drain and rinse the beans and proceed with the recipe.

• I like to double the recipe for *pesht*. That way I can add the recommended amount to the pot and pass the extra at the table.

Pasta *Fazoli*
Serves 8

If you are not going to consume all the soup in one sitting, it is best to cook the pasta separately and add it to the soup as it is served. Otherwise, the pasta will continue to cook in the hot soup and will loose its firm texture.

1 pound red kidney beans
2 tablespoons olive oil
1/2 pound pancetta or thick sliced bacon
1 large onion, peeled and finely chopped
1 stalk celery, finely chopped
2 carrots, peeled and finely chopped
1/2 cup parsley, minced
6 cloves garlic, minced
4 Roma tomatoes, finely chopped
2 teaspoons paprika (hot, mild or a combination of both)
2 bay leaves
Salt and freshly ground pepper to taste
1/2 pound macaroni

Beginning the day before you plan to serve the soup, pick over the dried beans and remove any small twigs or stones. Cover the beans with at least 4 inches of water and allow to soak overnight. Drain and rinse the beans.

In an 8-quart stockpot, cover the beans with water and simmer the beans until nearly tender, about 1 hour. In another pan sauté the pancetta and onion in the olive oil until the onion is transparent, about 10 minutes. Add the pancetta and onion mixture to the cooked beans followed by the celery, carrots, parsley, garlic, tomatoes, paprika, bay leaves, salt, pepper and enough water to generously cover all of the ingredients. Stir together and simmer for 1 hour. Add the pasta and cook for an additional 20 minutes or until the pasta is tender, adding more water if needed or desired. Taste, adjust the seasonings and serve with a loaf of hearty bread to mop up the juices.

Cook's Notes:
• Do not worry if you have not soaked the beans overnight. You can achieve very good results by washing the beans, placing them in a pot and covering them with 4 inches of water above the beans. Bring the beans to a boil, turn off the heat and allow them to rest for at least 1 hour. Drain and rinse the beans and proceed with the recipe.

THIS DISH, A STAPLE in Italian cuisine, is popular throughout the Istrian peninsula. Located in northwest Croatia, Istria traces its strong Italian influence to the days when it was a part of Italy. It was not until a post-World War II treaty was signed that Istria became a part of the former Yugoslavia.

Then, in 1990, when Croatia voted its independence from Yugoslavia, residents of this region became Croats. Today, Istrian citizens who have lived through those confused times have held Italian, Yugoslav and Croatian passports. Historically rich and geographically beautiful, the traditions of good, hearty Istrian food have managed to thrive throughout the political turmoil.

Winter Warmer: Barley and Lentil Soup
Serves 8 to 10

In today's often-crazy world, we rarely have the time to simmer a ham-bone for several hours to produce a rich and satisfying stock. However, that is no reason to ignore recipes that are built upon rich smoked-pork flavors. Using smoked bacon, smoked sausage or a combination of both can create a satisfying alternative.

This recipe creates a rich, thick and hearty soup that is on the table in less than 2 hours. It is also the perfect "leftover" dish. As with most hearty soups, the flavor improves the second (or even the third) day, and it freezes well.

1^1/$_2$ cups barley
1^1/$_2$ cups lentils
8 ounces thick-sliced bacon, cut in ^{1}/$_4$ inch strips
3–4 quarts water
2 tablespoon olive oil
1 large onion, chopped fine
2 cloves garlic, minced
1 potato, coarsely chopped
2 carrots, coarsely chopped
1 (14^1/$_2$-ounce) can chopped tomatoes
^{1}/$_2$ cup parsley, chopped
1 tablespoon paprika (hot or mild or a combination of both)
Salt and freshly ground pepper to taste
1 long link kielbasa, cut in ^{1}/$_2$-inch cubes

Wash the barley and lentils, drain and set aside. In a large stockpot, sauté the bacon until it just begins to get crisp. Add the water, barley and lentils and simmer for about 45 minutes.

In a separate pan, over medium heat, sauté the onions and the garlic in the olive oil until the onions become translucent, about 5 minutes. Add the potato and carrots and cook for 10 minutes, stirring frequently. Transfer the vegetables to the barley and lentil pot and stir in the tomatoes, parsley, paprika, salt and pepper. Simmer until the vegetables are tender and the flavors well blended, about 45 minutes.

As the soup simmers, sauté the sausage until lightly browned. Add the sausage to the soup and cook for 10 more minutes. Ladle into large, individual bowls and serve with a crusty loaf of bread.

Dalmatian Creamy Tomato Soup
Serves 8

This recipe is a summertime favorite. Made with vine-ripened heritage tomatoes, the flavors explode with garden-fresh goodness. On the other hand, it tastes pretty darn good in the middle of winter when made with canned tomatoes.

1 pound potatoes (2 large), peeled and cut in 1-inch cubes
6 medium tomatoes, chopped; or 1 (28-ounce) can of tomatoes
2 cloves garlic, minced
1/2 teaspoon freshly ground black pepper
1 quart chicken stock
1 1/2 cups whole milk
1/4 cup chopped parsley

In a large pot, combine the potatoes, tomatoes, garlic, pepper and chicken stock. Bring the ingredients to a boil and reduce the heat. Simmer for 20–30 minutes or until the potatoes are very tender.

Working in small batches, carefully ladle the vegetables into a food mill, blender or food processor and purée. Return the puréed liquid to the pot and add the milk. Heat just to boiling and serve. Garnish with chopped parsley.

Cook's Notes:
• For a tasty, attractive and aromatic variation, garnish the soup generously with freshly chopped basil.

The pool at the ACI Marina - Dubrobnik

Wild Mushroom Soup
Serves 8

Although the recipe calls for a combination of 4 or 5 different mushrooms, don't let a lack of variety deter you from preparing this delicious, healthy soup. A simple combination of dried porcini mushrooms with white and/or crimini produces a worthwhile combination.

1 ounce dried porcini mushrooms
1/4 cup olive oil
2 slices bacon, chopped fine
1 medium onion, chopped fine
3 cloves garlic, minced
2 medium potatoes, peeled and diced fine
2 medium carrots, peeled and diced fine
2 quarts chicken stock
2 tablespoons butter
1 1/2 pounds mixed fresh mushrooms, cleaned and chopped
  (preferably 4–5 different varieties)
Salt and freshly ground black pepper to taste
1/2 cup chopped parsley, plus extra for garnish

Place the porcini mushrooms in a 2-cup glass measure and fill with boiling water. Allow the mushrooms to soak until they have softened, 15–20 minutes. Lift the mushrooms out of the liquid and squeeze out the excess liquid. Reserve the liquid. Coarsely chop the porcini mushrooms.

Meanwhile, in a large stockpot, heat the olive oil and stir in the bacon and onion. Cook over medium heat until the onion is soft and translucent, 7–8 minutes. Add the garlic and stir for 1 minute. Stir in the potatoes, carrots and chicken stock, and simmer over low heat for 30–45 minutes or until the vegetables are tender.

As the vegetables simmer, melt the butter in a large sauté pan and stir in the fresh mushrooms, working in batches if necessary. Cook, stirring occasionally, until the mushrooms have released most of their juices. Add the sautéed mushrooms, salt, pepper, parsley and the reserved juice from the dried mushrooms (taking care not to pour in any sediment that remains in the bottom of the cup) to the soup pot and simmer for an additional 15 minutes. Skim the foam from the top several times. Taste and adjust the seasonings. Serve piping hot with a garnish of fresh parsley.

THIS IS DEFINITELY a dish from Croatia's northern interior. The porcini mushrooms that provide so much of the flavor were, in the past, rarely available in southern Croatia. Today, however, dried porcinis are available in many Dalmatian coast *supermercatos* and in most U.S. markets as well. ▓

Zelena Manestra (Green Soup)
Serves 6 to 8 for two meals

Since the flavors in this dish improve after several days, having leftovers is part of the plan. This recipe actually creates 2 meals. Zelena Menestra—Meal #2 with polenta offers an entirely new dish with very little effort.

> 1 pound smoked ham, cut in chunks
> 1 pound bacon, sliced very thick and strips cut in half
> 1 pound smoked pork sausage
> 1 head green cabbage, cut in chunks
> 1 head red cabbage, cut in chunks
> 1 head savoy cabbage, cut in chunks
> Salt and freshly ground pepper to taste
> 4 large potatoes, peeled and each cut into 4 wedges
> 1¹/₂ cups dried polenta

In a 10–12 quart soup pot, layer the meat alternately with the cabbage, being careful to keep the different kinds of meats and different cabbages separate. Add salt and pepper and cover with water. Cover and simmer for several hours.

About one hour before serving, add the potatoes and continue to cook until tender. Remove the pot from the heat and attractively arrange the cabbage and the meat around the edge of a large oval platter. Place the potato quarters like a flower in the center and pour some broth overall. Invite diners to help themselves.

Meal #2: When everyone has eaten to his or her satisfaction, make the polenta, according to package directions, using some of the liquid from the soup. Pour the polenta onto an oiled plate, cover and refrigerate overnight. The next day, when ready to serve, bring the polenta to room temperature and cut into attractive shapes. Serve with the leftover soup.

THIS RECIPE CAME FROM my friend Marina, who together with her sister, maintains a strong commitment to their family's culinary traditions. Family events and holidays are always celebrated with traditional foods and prescribed menus.

This recipe is one of their favorites. Tradition dictates the key ingredients: 3 different kinds of smoked pork and 3 different kinds of cabbage. If you were to follow Marina's grandmother's method, you would need a smoked pig's snout, a smoked pig's ear (from which the hair had been carefully singed) and smoked ribs. Although these ingredients are still available in rural Croatia, urban dwellers may find it necessary to substitute bacon and sausage for the snout and the ear. However, a tasty *Zelena Manestra* does require an assortment of meats. Three varieties of cabbages are also essential: green cabbage, red cabbage and savoy cabbage work well.

Note: The first time I made this recipe, I was able to buy a pig's ear from a local butcher. Armed with a candle and matches, I set to work on our concrete dock, trying carefully to singe the hair from the ear without burning the flesh. High winds provided challenges with the candle flame, and as I stood there surrounded by the steep karst mountains and centuries-old buildings, I was overcome by a sense of total disbelief that I was actually going to use a pig's ear in a recipe. There was no question that our first *Zalenea Manestra* would provide us with many lasting memories. ▓

Chicken Soup with Dumplings
Serves 6 to 8

This is one of our favorite comfort foods, and it can be easily stretched to serve a larger gathering by using all the chicken and adding another carrot or two. Just be sure to double the recipe for dumplings. Although this recipe takes close to 2½ hours from start to finish, the active time is just 30 minutes.

1 whole chicken
1 large onion, cut in quarters
3 large carrots, peeled and cut in half
1 stalk celery, halved
Salt and freshly ground pepper to taste
¼ cup chopped parsley

Wash the chicken inside and out and place in an 8-quart stockpot. Add the remaining ingredients and cover with cold water. Simmer over low heat until the chicken is cooked through and begins to break away from the bones, about 90 minutes.

Strain the soup and return the stock to the pot. Set the chicken and vegetables aside until cool enough to handle.

Dice the onion, carrots and celery into ½ inch pieces and return to the stock. Remove the chicken from the bones and dice about half of the meat and return to the stock. Reserve the remaining meat for another use.

DUMPLINGS:
2 eggs
6 tablespoons farina (Cream of Wheat)
1 tablespoon flour
½ teaspoon salt

Whisk together the eggs, farina, flour and salt. Let stand for 10–15 minutes. Return the soup to a simmer and drop the dumpling mix by the half-teaspoon into the broth, being careful to drop in different positions in the pot so the dumplings do not stick together. Cook about 5 minutes or until dumplings are cooked through. Stir in the chopped parsley and ladle into soup bowls and serve.

Cook's Notes:
• Dumplings do not freeze well. If you are planning on freezing the soup, plan to make a fresh batch of dumplings when the soup is reheated.

• The farina dumplings are quick, tasty and easy to prepare. Farina (rich in protein and easy to digest) is often used as baby food throughout Europe. It is a bland flour or meal that is made from cereal grains.

THE LONG HOT SUMMER of 2003 began earlier than normal and continued with record-breaking temperatures through June, July, August and well into September. With almost no rain, water supplies were very limited, especially in the islands. Crops everywhere seemed to wither in the intense heat. By early September, the locals were all hoping for a cool and wet fall. On the last Monday of September, those who dreamed of heavy rain got their wish … along with some very strong southeasterly winds.

Bill and I were aboard *Klatawa*, anchored in Sipan harbor. A picturesque horseshoe shaped harbor, it is relatively well-protected from southerly winds. Nevertheless, we stood careful watch as winds reached close to gale force and rain came down in solid horizontal sheets. Visibility at times was reduced to less than a 100 feet. Our attentiveness paid off because late in the afternoon, we dragged anchor and had to fight the winds to keep *Klatawa* offshore and to relocate and reset the anchor. The good news was that it was not the middle of the night and miraculously the rain was only moderately heavy during this exercise.

This was a time when genuine comfort food was required. Fortunately, I had a whole chicken on board and I quickly tossed it into the pot. The tasty and easy-to-make dumplings became a favorite—a quick and satisfying alternative to the all-American favorite, chicken noodle soup.

Dalmatian Fish Soup
Serves 8 as a first course

Try to make this soup with at least 4 different kinds of fish. The variety in flavor and texture is part of what makes this quick and simple dish extra tasty. The addition of rice gives extra body to the broth, guaranteeing that every last spoonful will be lapped up.

1 small onion, minced fine
2 tablespoons olive oil
2 cloves garlic, minced
1 quart water
2 cups clam nectar
$1/2$ cup rice
4 Roma tomatoes, diced
$11/2$ pound combination salt-water fish, cleaned and cut in 1-inch cubes
  (salmon, halibut, cod, squid, scallops, prawns, etc)
$1/2$ cup white wine
$1/4$ cup parsley
Salt and freshly ground pepper to taste

In a large pot, over medium heat, gently sauté the onion in the olive oil until translucent and tender, about 5 minutes. Add the garlic and sauté for 1 or 2 minutes longer. Add the water and the clam nectar and bring to a boil. Add the rice and the tomatoes and simmer for 20 minutes. Add the fish and white wine and return to a boil. Reduce the heat and simmer gently for 7 minutes or until the fish is cooked. Stir in the parsley, salt and pepper.

Cook's Notes:

• Most Croatians who live along the coast fish regularly and as a result have fish heads and bones to throw into a stockpot. Along with a few vegetables and herbs, they create a rich stock. Most Americans do not have access to such simple luxuries, so we resort to the use of bottled clam juice to enhance the flavor of our fish soups. If you happen to have fish heads and bones, by all means, make your own stock.

A CROATIAN FISH SOUP can be as straightforward or as complex as the cook and the available ingredients permit. The tradition of creating tasty fish soups from small amounts of a variety of fish, originated in the small fish markets commonly found along the Adriatic coast. What remained at the end of the day became known as "the last of the catch" and was shared amongst the fishermen or sold to local housewives. Dinner evolved from these bits and pieces.

Please note that the fish in this recipe is exceptionally generous. The most simple and humble fish soups would have only a few small pieces of fish in each serving.

Thick and Creamy Fish Soup
Serves 4 to 6

This is a simple, one-fish soup. There is no need to gather a variety of seafood ... one variety creates a tasty, satisfying dish.

2 tablespoons olive oil
1 large carrot, peeled and diced
1 small onion, peeled and diced
1 stalk celery, diced
2 garlic cloves, minced
1 large potato, peeled and chopped
2 Roma tomatoes, chopped
2 bay leaves
2 tablespoons chopped parsley (divided)
1/2 cup dry white wine
Salt and freshly ground pepper to taste
5 cups water
1 pound boneless white fish
1/2 cup heavy cream (optional)

In a large pot, heat the oil over medium heat and sauté the carrot, onion, celery, garlic and potato until the onion is transparent and the vegetables begin to soften, about 7 minutes. Stir in the chopped tomatoes, bay leaves and 1 tablespoon of chopped parsley. Add the wine, salt and pepper and pour in the water. Simmer for 15 minutes or until the vegetables are tender. Add the fish and simmer over low heat until the fish is cooked through, about 15 minutes. Remove the fish from the pot and set aside. Remove the bay leaves from the pot and discard. Working in batches, carefully puree the stock and vegetables in a Mouli food mill, blender or food processor.

Return the pureed stock to the pot and, if desired, stir in the cream. Meanwhile, cut the fish into small pieces and return to the pot along with the remaining tablespoon of minced parsley. Ladle into warm bowls and serve topped with garlic-flavored croutons.

GARLIC FLAVORED CROUTONS:
2 tablespoons olive oil
1 clove garlic, minced
3 slices country bread

In 10-inch sauté pan, warm the garlic in the olive oil over low/medium heat. Remove most of the crust from the bread slices and cut into 1-inch cubes. Add the bread to the pan and toast over low/medium heat for 10–12 minutes, stirring frequently, until the cubes are crisp and golden. Croutons may be made several days in advance. Cool and store in Ziploc bag until ready to use.

From Field to Fork ...
the Market at Trogir

Friendships form quickly within the international cruising community. Live-aboard sailors share a passion for sailing, travel, adventure and, more often than not, for good food and wine. These mutual interests, combined with a sometimes-desperate yearning to carry on a conversation with someone other than your own boat-mate, spawn frequent, spur-of-the-moment invitations ... for a shared glass of wine or even a full meal. Therefore, when a boat arrived in a harbor or an anchorage flying the flag of an English-language nation, we would often extend an invitation with our introductory greeting. That's how we met Ian and Pippa one midsummer evening as they arrived in Trogir aboard *Arriba*.

A vigorous, fun-loving British couple, we quickly discovered that we had much in common—previous lives lived overseas as professional expatriates, adult children pursuing their careers and a shared interest in the foods of the land. Our invitational glass of wine quickly became a second pour, and with the third, came an invitation to stay for dinner. (Fortunately we had leftover Dalmatian Vegetable Casserole in the fridge ... just enough to toss with pasta and serve with a fresh green salad.)

Since this was Ian and Pippa's first visit to Trogir, Bill and I jumped at the opportunity to share our enthusiasm and pleasure for this jewel of a walled town. A UNESCO Heritage City, Trogir is a hospitable place that boasts many buildings dating to the 13th century. With narrow cobbled streets and twisting alleys it is perfect for "photo-op" strolling—distinctive doorways, unique windows, intricate stone carvings and wrought-iron ornamentations. Nearly every structure boasts something special: a weathered stone fountain, a slightly warped old wooden shutter whose centuries of service are revealed in the multiple hues of peeling paint, and a large number of considerably shorter-than-six-foot intricately carved wooden doorways. (We all chuckled at the image of Ian, a large, significantly taller-than-six-foot man, trying to negotiate his way through some of these midget-sized entrances.) And for many Trogir residents their interest in their surroundings extends beyond the hardscape. There are carefully tended and well-placed garden pots everywhere. Bursting with healthy, lush greenery and seasonal color, these miniature gardens do much to soften and balance the monochromatic gray surfaces of the stone buildings and marble streets.

Throughout our inaugural dinner, the four of us talked about our cruising lifestyle and the almost endless adventures it provides. We shared our appreciation for the abundant opportunities to peek into the routines of daily living in so many different cultures. Our laughter-filled conversation was sprinkled with memories of early morning walks through centuries-old European villages—the aroma of freshly baked bread seeping through tightly shuttered windows and doors, small groups of uniformed children burdened with backpacks giggling their way to classrooms, and young mothers busily gossiping as they gathered in local parks to supervise the play of their toddlers.

Over espresso prepared in our stovetop Bialetti, Bill and Ian talked about their respect for the elderly Mediterranean fishermen, dedicated weather-worn men who spend hour after painstaking hour chipping away to repair or replace rotted planks and repaint their old wooden fishing boats. Along these coasts, there are almost no new, easy-to-care-for fiberglass fishing vessels. In Croatia, as throughout much of the Mediterranean, there are meticulously maintained relics, family treasures that are passed down from generation to generation.

As the guys talked about boats, Pippa and I chatted about how much we have learned by simply watching and listening to the local housewives as they go about their daily routines ... selecting produce in the marketplace or directing the butcher on the precise way to cut and trim their selection of meat. We also discovered that we share a passion for dining in the local *konobas* (small restaurants that specialize in serving homemade dishes) rather than eating out in the larger and newer restaurants that have been developed to attract the tourist trade. Our *konoba* meals spent tasting and analyzing regional dishes armed us with basic knowledge ... providing us with the tools to head back to our own galleys and attempt to replicate a local dish.

Our lively conversation continued for hours and by the time we said goodnight, the harbor was quiet and an almost-full moon glistened down upon the multitude of gently swaying masts. We agreed that there were many conversations in our future and that we would meet for a midmorning cappuccino before heading off to our next, but independent destinations.

▦ ▦ ▦

I rose early to pursue one of my very favorite activities ... a morning visit to the Trogir market. In my experience it is one of the best little markets in the Mediterranean. Rows of concrete tables are colorfully heaped with the freshest seasonal fruits and vegetables, homemade cheeses (just nod hello to the smiling, round-faced farm woman and you'll soon have a taste), locally smoked *pršut*, freshly butchered chickens, long garlands of dried figs strung alternately with aromatic bay leaves, fruit jars filled with honey, locally grown and pressed olive oil, traditionally blended herbal vinegars and homemade herbal-flavored schnapps (the oils, vinegars and schnapps are resourcefully packaged in recycled plastic water bottles.) And like frosting on a cake there is always a colorful and spectacular selection of seasonal fresh flowers ... I love bringing home a garden-fresh bouquet of daisies, mums, statice or roses.

You simply cannot buy produce that is any fresher than what is offered at Trogir. Most of it is grown within a five-minute walk from the market in a community of tidy homes with small plots of rich land. Just about every front yard is thoughtfully planted and carefully tended. Bright, flavorful and at their peak, fruits and veggies are harvested late in the evening or very early in the morning for near-dawn delivery to the mostly open-air market. In Trogir, the time from field to fork is measured in hours, not in days.

I love this connection of food to the land. There is something very special, very simple and very pleasurable about watching a proud and productive gray-haired, sun-tarnished farm lady dressed in her simple, well-worn dark cotton dress head to the market pushing an ancient wheelbarrow. And I know with confidence as I watch her carefully negotiate the narrow, potholed paths that her wheelbarrow has been painstkingly packed with the very best fruits and vegetables that her garden has to offer.

On this morning, I was well into my shopping expedition when a miniature pile of small and perfectly formed eggplants suddenly caught my eye. I must have missed them on my first pass through the crowded aisles because suddenly they appeared, so very tempting and appealing, just four or five inches long with a shiny deep purple armor and bright green, freshly-cut fuzzy and prickly stems. Instantly my mouth began to water as I pictured these little gems braised in a fresh tomato sauce, sprinkled with fresh basil and topped with a thin slice of fresh mozzarella. They would be the perfect accompaniment to the rotisserie chicken that was already in my rustic straw French market bag.

There was only one problem. I had spent my last *kuna* and it was a long walk back to the boat. Once more I admired the eggplants, mumbled my disappointment to the lady behind the stand, and started to turn away. But as I turned, there was Pippa smiling an early morning greeting. Without hesitation, I asked to borrow about one dollar's worth of *kuna* and without question the money was in my hand. It took only seconds for me to scoop up six tiny gorgeous globes. Suddenly I was one happy lady ... with a new friend at my side and some of nature's most beautiful jewels to display in the fruit and vegetable basket aboard *Klatawa* before they hit the sauté pan for dinner.

❊ ❊ ❊

Almost all of the produce sold at the Trogir market is locally grown. Each crop is a product of the local terroir. My favorite time to visit is spring, when the earth's goodness begins to spill out upon the once winter-dreary and largely barren concrete produce tables and the smiles on the round-faced, sun-wrinkled peasant women are as big and bright as the new season's sun. In April, the tables suddenly ripen into an artist's palette of color: pencil-thin wild green asparagus, enormous and deliciously mild and succulent red spring onions, slight and slender green beans, tender pods of sweet peas and mounds of juicy-red strawberries. My smile broadens and my heart beats faster on those days when I arrive early enough to capture a "*po* kilo" (half kilo ... about one pound) of tiny zucchini with their tender bright yellow flowers still attached ... perfect for a simple springtime pasta. Even the red and green cabbages, available almost year round, seem to glow with a shinier, deeper and more intense color in the springtime sun.

But the personality of a farmers' market goes beyond the freshness of the produce, the mouthwatering aromas of the tree-ripened fruit, or the quality of the bread, or the cheese or the eggs. It includes all of the activities, conversations and subtle exchanges that help to create the ever-evolving saga of the lives and lifestyles of the people whose daily sustenance centers around the market activity: the vendors and their customers.

The Trogir vendors are mostly women and they are a seemingly happy lot. They smile and joke. They appreciate my stumbling efforts with their tongue-twisting language (any language in which the "R" is sometimes considered a vowel has to be a challenge); they help me pick the very best of what they have to offer and they all call out and greet me, hoping that I will buy something from each of them. And I do try to spread my purchases around, as they are each scrupulously honest. In Trogir, there is no effort to take advantage of the tourist, to charge more than fair market value or to short-weigh a bag of produce.

But my everlasting love affair with this market is based on more than the fresh and tasty fruits and vegetables. It is also built upon happy memories of little incidents that blend together to create my own private smiles and provide me with fuel for endless stories. One such memory is described in a May journal entry:

"Today, I wanted to buy a half-kilo of fresh, picture-perfect red spring onions. There were just the two of us on board and I had no specific plans as to how I would prepare them, they were simply irresistible. One half-kilo would surely be enough. However, when I described my desires to the proud peasant lady, dressed in a very dark and somber dress and well-worn apron, she burst into a huge grin, said "no, no, no" and waved the stub of some sort of ticket in front of me. Soon, with laughter and smiles all around, I was buying a full kilo of red onions. I paid her the negotiated five *kuna* (about 60 cents), she grinned broadly and immediately walked a few steps across the aisle. She tapped an elderly, nearly toothless gentleman on his shoulder, waved her five *kuna* piece and purchased another, what I now recognized to be, lottery ticket. My purchase of a full kilo of red onions helped to fuel her dream of being a big winner. I hope it worked!"

That Trogir market event is a little story that makes me smile. However, another journal entry, this one dated in July, describes a much larger event known as "Baking the Bull."

"Just mouthing the words *baking the bull* brings a huge grin to my face. This event is a Trogir festivity that we were lucky to share with American friends and guests aboard *Klatawa*, Lee and Karen. It is a unique festival that takes place annually at the end of the local soccer team's competitive season.

Our experience began at about 2 a.m., when we were awakened by a very loud siren. The disruption seemed to be coming from across the narrow river in the direction of the old town. The siren would pierce the night air and then would stop just as abruptly as it had begun. Bill and I groggily rolled over several times and mumbled to one another that we would have to check out the source of this disturbance in the morning.

Later that morning, as the four of us neared the completion of our marketing, we began to get a whiff of a wood fire accompanied by the scent of roasting meat. Our noses led us in the direction of the classic, gray-stone walls of the crumbling medieval Karmelengo Fortress and the adjacent green soccer field. As we neared the fort, the siren once again began its persistent screech. Now, our ears led us to the sound. To our surprise, the piercing noise was being generated by a very large and very old hand-cranked siren being powered by several young men.

We quickly learned that the soccer season had just come to a successful conclusion and that this "siren sounding" was one last opportunity for the members of the team to demonstrate their individual strength. The challenge in this competition was to determine who could make the siren perform with the greatest intensity, the highest pitch and for the longest duration.

On this day of festivity, the entire soccer field was alive with activity. Preparations were underway for a community-wide celebration. A large fire pit had been dug and here I emphasize and give new meaning to the term *large*. This pit was large enough to hold a full-sized bull! Mounted over this pit was a giant, hand-rotated spit piercing a very large, skinned, cleaned and trussed bull. Beneath the bull was a bed of very hot coals that was kept alive by a team of hearty middle-aged men. Their job, performed between frequent sips of midmorning beer, was to feed the fire with carefully selected pieces of firewood.

Distanced from the fire but gathered in friendly groups around the soccer field were teams of men and women of all ages. They were sitting on low, wooden, three-legged stools and peeling and cleaning the hundreds of pounds of potatoes, onions and carrots that had been spilled out of huge burlap bags. We were told that their job was to fill at least five or six humongous washtubs with a combination of cleaned veggies. This was definitely going to be a feast!

By late morning the four of us had turned down multiple offers of beer and wine and had heard several more explosive blasts from the siren. The locals were hard at work but were relaxed, happy and welcoming. As we moved around and watched each of the activities, we had frequent invitations to stay and spend the rest of the day and the evening and to participate in the feast. Regrettably, we had made a commitment to meet friends in a quiet nearby anchorage. We declined but offered our late-morning farewells with a toast to the team ... wishing them another successful season next year."

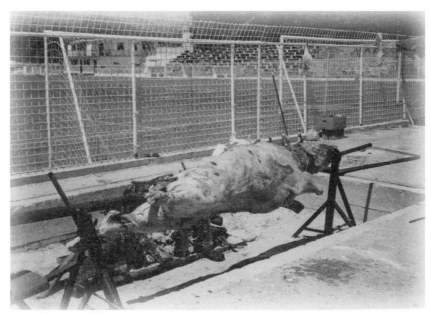

"Baking the Bull"

Salads & Side Dishes

A short stroll through Croatia's small towns and rural areas affirms the importance of the family garden. Nearly every front yard—no matter how small—is filled with tidy rows of carefully tended vegetables planted for seasonal use. To quote Dennis Valcich from his book, *Croatian Cookbook, A Walk Through Croatia:* "(in Croatia) vegetables are available all year round. For people living in a house with a back yard there is no excuse not to have some vegetables in their gardens for personal use as they are so easy to grow."

When it comes to vegetables in Croatia, the word *fresh* clearly implies local and in season. And like elsewhere in the world, nature's bounty often results in large quantities of seasonal produce, making a variety in preparation methods welcome alternatives. Croatian housewives have met this challenge: fresh-sliced summertime tomatoes are enlivened by the addition of a generous handful of chopped basil; extra-virgin olive oil, minced garlic and fresh lemon juice are added to sautéed fresh spinach to intensify the natural flavor of the spinach as well as add new flavor dimensions; and grated apple and thinly sliced red onion are combined with finely shredded red cabbage for a delicious hot slaw. These simple ideas, and many more like them, have been generated by a hard-working and creative peasant culture. What grows together goes together ... a simple mantra that guides everyday Croation life. ▨

Salads & Side Dishes
SALADS & SIDE DISHES

SALADS & SIDE DISHES

SALADS

SIDE DISHES

Bean and Bacon Salad
Serves 8 to 10

This tasty side salad combines two of Croatia's favorite ingredients: beans and bacon. Fresh green onions and fresh red pepper are added for color, flavor and crunch. Although the traditional Croatian housewife makes this salad with dried beans, a method that requires the beans to be soaked overnight, I have substituted canned beans so the salad can be prepared in less than 30 minutes—making it a perfect addition to the summertime barbecue menu.

8 slices bacon, cut into $1/4$-inch strips
1 medium onion, finely chopped
2 cloves garlic, minced
2 (20-ounce) cans beans (kidney, garbanzo or a combination of the two)
1 bunch green onions, trimmed and thinly sliced
$1/2$ red pepper, washed, seeded and finely diced
$1/4$ cup olive oil
$2^1/2$ tablespoons fresh lemon juice
Salt and freshly ground pepper to taste

In a medium frying pan, over medium-high heat, sauté the bacon until nearly crisp. Reduce the heat and add the finely chopped onion and the minced garlic. Stir until the bacon is crisp and the onion is translucent, about 5 minutes. Remove from the heat, drain the excess bacon fat and allow to cool slightly.

Meanwhile, rinse and drain the beans and place in a medium-sized bowl. Add the green onions and red pepper.

In a small bowl, whisk together the olive oil, lemon juice, salt and pepper. Add the bacon/onion mixture and stir to combine. Toss the bacon dressing with the beans. Taste and adjust the seasonings. Serve immediately or refrigerate for several hours to allow the flavors to blend. Bring to room temperature before serving.

THE TRADITIONAL CROATIAN FARM kitchen has a limited pantry. There are no exotic spices or ingredients for whipping up an Asian stir-fry or a Mexican burrito. Nearly every ingredient, whether fresh or preserved, was raised within sight of the kitchen door—planted, tended and harvested by the housewife's diligent labor. The list of ingredients may be restricted, but the creativity and ingenuity demonstrated by these stalwart peasant ladies is admirable.

Croatian Coleslaw

Serves 8 to 10

No Croatian cookbook would be complete without this staple dish. Crisp, crunchy and tasty coleslaw is often served as a part of a mixed salad but it's also great as a side dish for seafood, grilled sausages or just about any barbecued dish.

1 medium head of cabbage
1 small onion, peeled and thinly sliced
$3/4$ cup olive oil
$1/2$ cup white wine or cider vinegar
2 teaspoons sugar
Salt and freshly ground pepper to taste

Remove any damaged outer leaves from the cabbage. Quarter the head and remove the center core. Shred or thinly slice the cabbage, and place in a medium bowl and add the onion. Whisk together the olive oil, vinegar, sugar, salt and pepper. Pour the dressing over the cabbage and thoroughly toss the slaw. Allow to marinate for at least 1 to 2 hours, tossing occasionally, before serving.

THERE ARE NEARLY 1,200 islands and islets strung out along the Croatian coast. Some are flat, windswept and barren, some are rugged mountains that plunge deep into the sea, and some appear to be verdant and inviting havens of paradise. Just 66 islands are inhabited, but many of the inhabitants are often summertime-only residents. Like in so many Mediterranean communities, fresh water is often a limited resource.

Most island residents make some effort to collect water in private or shared community cisterns. Nonetheless, hot summers can dry up the supply. The good news is that the government will send a water barge to replenish the water supply to the stricken island.

This water is essential for these island residents, not just for drinking but also for nurturing their gardens. True to the tradition of conservation, an automatic sprinkler is almost never seen watering a family garden. Rather, it's more common to see a family member, frequently the grandfather, hand-water each plant with a bucket or can. Thanks to this careful and responsible stewardship, fresh vegetables are available throughout the dry and hot summer.

Cucumber Salad
Serves 4 to 6

The salt in this dish adds more than flavor; it helps to remove the excess liquid from the cucumber slices, and it helps to diminish some of the sharp, bitter flavor from the onion. This simple salad is sure to become a favorite—easy to prepare and easy to get hooked on its tangy, sweet-and-sour flavor.

2 medium cucumbers, peeled and thinly sliced
1 medium onion, peeled and thinly sliced
1 tablespoon salt
$1/4$ cup vinegar
1 tablespoon water
$1/3$ cup olive oil
2 tablespoons sugar
Salt and freshly ground pepper to taste
$1/2$ cup sour cream (optional)

In a medium bowl, toss together the cucumbers, onions and salt. Let rest for 30 minutes. Transfer to a colander and rinse, drain and squeeze excess liquid from the cucumbers and onions. In a small bowl, whisk together the vinegar, water, oil, sugar, salt, pepper and sour cream. Toss the dressing with the cucumbers and onions. Taste and adjust the seasonings. Refrigerate until ready to serve.

Cook's Notes:

• When preparing this dish, I like to use English cucumbers; they tend to be sweeter and less bitter. However, if you do use traditional cucumbers, cut the cucumber in half lengthwise and scrape out the seeds with a spoon.

• If you are using fresh and tender cucumbers, leave them unpeeled, or score them with the tines of a fork for a more colorful appearance. If however, the cucumbers have been oiled or if they have been sitting in the produce department for days, the skin is likely to be tough and bitter … get out the peeler.

THE CRYSTAL CLEAR WATERS of the Adriatic that settle in the warm Croatian coastal saltpans create a very special sea salt. Harvested commercially from the salt flats on the Island of Pag and in the town of Ston on the Pelješac Peninsula, these bright white crystals, each with their own distinctive crisp and lively taste, bring unexpected flavor to any dish.

In some of the smaller and more remote coastal towns and villages, residents carefully harvest their own salt from manmade or natural salt ponds. The salt is then left to dry in the sun and the wind. It is a traditional skill handed down from generation to generation and born from the necessity to preserve food in the days before canning or freezing. ▨

Dalmatian Summer Salad
Serves 4

In this recipe, cool, crisp cucumbers are paired with succulent sweet, just-picked tomatoes to provide a winning combination that helps to beat the summer heat and to satisfy light summer appetites. Just be sure on hot summer days that all of the vegetables are well chilled.

1 medium English cucumber, peeled and diced

3 vine-ripened tomatoes, washed, cored and diced

1 small green pepper, washed, seeded and diced

1 medium red onion, peeled and finely chopped

5 tablespoons olive oil

1$^{1}/_{2}$ tablespoons red wine vinegar

Salt and freshly ground pepper to taste

In a medium bowl, combine the cucumbers, tomatoes, green pepper and red onion. Drizzle with the olive oil and the vinegar. Season with the salt and pepper, toss and serve.

JULY AND AUGUST ARE HOT—often really hot — in the Mediterranean. Temperatures soar into the triple digits, and the scorching summer winds sweep away what little moisture clings to the land. The days for growing delicate plants such as lettuce are past. If any lettuce remains in the ground, it will more than likely bolt—sending up flower stalks and turning bitter. Consequently, summer salads tend to focus on summer-hearty vegetables like cucumbers, tomatoes and peppers ... what grows together goes together.

Fresh Green Bean Salad
Serves 4

The thinly sliced red onion adds a burst of color and the garlicky-rich vinaigrette provides a boost in flavor for plain steamed green beans. Since the dish is served at room temperature, it is the perfect company dish … you can make it an hour or so in advance and avoid last-minute preparation.

1 1/2 pounds green beans
1 small red onion, sliced thin
2 cloves garlic, peeled and minced
1/4 cup olive oil
2 tablespoons vinegar
1 teaspoon Dijon mustard
Salt and freshly ground pepper to taste

Cook green beans in boiling water until tender, about 8-10 minutes. Drain well and toss together with the red onion. Whisk the remaining ingredients together and toss with beans and onions. Serve at room temperature.

Green Salad with Candied Walnuts and Pomegranate Dressing
Serves 4 to 6

In this salad, bright red and tangy pomegranate seeds, sweet and crunchy walnuts, smooth and distinctive blue cheese and crisp salad greens are tossed together to provide a wonderful combination of contrasting color, texture and flavor.

Available from early fall through late January, pomegranates can be tedious to peel and separate; but the rewards are worth the effort. They are high in antioxidants and are a great source of potassium. Their bright color and tart flavor add interest to this and many other Mediterranean dishes.

CANDIED WALNUTS:
1 cup walnut halves
$1/2$ cup powdered sugar

Preheat the oven to 325 degrees. Line a cookie sheet with aluminum foil and lightly butter the foil. In a medium saucepan, bring 1 quart of water to boil. Add the walnuts, return to a boil and boil for 3 minutes. Drain immediately and return the walnuts to the saucepan. Stir in the powdered sugar and spread the coated nuts on the cookie sheet.

Bake for 15 minutes and then stir the walnuts. Return to oven and bake for an additional 10 minutes. Remove from oven and allow to cool. Remove the nuts from the foil and break the nuts apart if necessary.

DRESSING:
$1/4$ cup pomegranate juice (fresh squeezed or bottled)
2 teaspoons lemon juice
2 teaspoons honey
$1/3$ cup olive oil
Salt and freshly ground pepper to taste
Whisk all the ingredients together.

SALAD:
$3/4$ pound mixed salad greens
$1/3$ cup crumbled blue cheese
$1/2$ cup pomegranate seeds

Reserve 12 candied walnut halves. Toss the remaining walnuts together with the salad greens, blue cheese, pomegranate seeds and the dressing in a large salad bowl. Divide among 6 salad plates, top each plate with 2 of the reserved walnut halves and serve.

Cook's Notes:
• Pomegranate juice is available in many United States supermarkets. If you are unable to find the juice, press pomegranate seeds firmly through a strainer. About 1 cup of seeds will yield a quarter of a cup of juice.

- To seed pomegranates more efficiently, slice off the crown and cut the fruit vertically into sixths and place in a bowl of cold water. Working over a strainer, pop out the seeds by inverting the thick skin. Remove the white membrane and rinse.

- The method for making candied walnuts is not authentic Croatian but rather an easy version that I have favored for years.

- If you are making this salad when pomegranates are not available, a washed and thinly sliced crisp pear makes a good substitute.

INDIGENOUS FROM IRAN TO NORTHERN INDIA, pomegranates have been cultivated in the Mediterranean since ancient times. Known as *granada* in Spain and *grenade* in France, they are a common sight throughout the Mediterranean.

Along the Adriatic coast, some are cultivated in gardens and many grow wild along trails and roads. It is fascinating to watch the trees change throughout the seasons. Bright and glossy green pomegranate leaves are a sure sign that spring is on the way. Summer is heralded by dramatic and bold bright red-orange flowers. Throughout the summer, the fruit develops and continues to grow into large, dark crimson globes that are ready for harvest by early fall. By late fall, the fruit is so ripe that some will burst their tough, leather-like skin exposing hundreds of bright red seeds. All winter long, a few fruits will cling tenaciously to the branches, drying to shining resilient balls that are perfect for use in a harvest floral arrangement. 🏵

Mixed Salad (*Insalata Mista*)
Serves 6

A version of Insalata Mista, the classic Croatian dinner salad, is served in nearly every Croatian restaurant. The ingredients vary with the season and the geography, but you can always count on a bit of plain shredded cabbage or cabbage slaw to be included. If there is no fresh produce in season, Croatians turn to canned corn or beans to provide variety. The salad is always composed on the salad plate or bowl and is never tossed.

1 small head butter lettuce, cored, washed and dried

1 large tomato, washed, cored and cut into wedges

1/2 English cucumber, peeled and thinly sliced

1/4 head cabbage, cored and finely shredded

2 tablespoons red wine vinegar

6 tablespoons extra virgin olive oil

1/4 teaspoon sea salt

1/4 teaspoon freshly ground pepper

Gently tear the lettuce leaves and divide evenly between 6 salad bowls. Arrange the tomato, cucumber and the shredded cabbage in separate sections on top of the lettuce. Whisk together the vinegar, olive oil, salt and pepper and drizzle over the salad.

Cook's Notes:

• To keep this salad a year-round favorite, consider a selection of the following: rinsed and drained sauerkraut; canned or defrosted corn; washed and drained canned pinto or garbanzo beans; sliced beet; thinly sliced green and/or red peppers; cleaned and sliced raw mushrooms. Just be sure to use lettuce or cabbage as a base and include at least three additional toppings.

I LOVED IT WHEN GOOD LUCK came my way and I unexpectedly happened upon a small, local farmers' market … an occurrence that happened fairly often in Croatia. These "markets" ranged from small and informal weekly affairs with two or three peasant ladies gathered in the shade of a large old tree, selling their produce from a small cart or table to large daily events with permanent, conveniently located concrete tables, positioned in the center of town.

Whether the market was small or large, the local produce was carefully displayed and the sun-bronzed and weather-wrinkled women smiled their greetings and called out friendly words of encouragement … always trying to entice passersby to purchase their products. Produce changed with the seasons but regardless of the time of the year, I could usually find a few fresh ingredients to include in an *Insalata Mista*.

Sweet and Tangy Sauerkraut Salad
Serves 4 to 6

The thinly sliced red and green peppers add welcome color to what would otherwise be a lackluster dish. However, what this salad may lack in appearance is made up for by its wonderful tangy/sweet flavor. Good served with sausages, ham or most any grilled or barbecued dish, it is quick, easy to prepare and easily doubled. Guaranteed to become a favorite even with those who profess not to like sauerkraut.

1 32-ounce jar sauerkraut

$1/2$ cup sugar (white or brown or a combination)

3 tablespoons cider vinegar

1 teaspoon celery seed

$1/2$ teaspoon salt

$1/4$ teaspoon pepper

$1/3$ cup chopped onion

$1/2$ red pepper, sliced fine

$1/2$ green pepper, sliced fine

Using a colander, rinse the sauerkraut under running water and drain well. Combine the sauerkraut with the remaining ingredients in a large, non-reactive bowl. Toss occasionally while keeping refrigerated for several hours or overnight.

SAILING ALONG THE COAST and traveling inland, we learned to admire and respect the many different ways of Croatian rural life. There were those who resided on tiny islands with 40 full-time residents whose only contact with the rest of the world during the winter was a brief visit by a weekly ferry. There were those who dwelled in tiny farmhouses where three generations resided happily together. There were those who inhabited small villages where seasonal tourists frequently interrupted their daily chores to greet them as they worked in tiny, front-yard kitchen gardens.

We learned to admire the remarkable commitment Croatians make to responsible stewardship of the land. Eating local is a way of life in these small communities where feeding the family from the garden is not a hobby but a necessity. Pickling, salting, drying and canning are well-honed skills on which winter meals depend. Creativity abounds and this sauerkraut salad is a tasty example of that know-how.

Quick and Tasty Potato Salad
Serves 4 to 6

A tasty alternative to a mayonnaise-based potato salad, this sweet and tangy potato salad is the perfect accompaniment to just about every barbecued beef, pork or chicken dish.

2 pounds red potatoes, all about the same size
1 clove garlic, minced
3 tablespoons red wine vinegar
2 tablespoons honey
$1/3$ cup red onion, finely diced
$1/3$ cup olive oil
Salt and freshly ground pepper to taste

Scrub the potatoes and place in a medium saucepan. Cover with water and bring the potatoes to a gentle boil. Simmer until the potatoes are barely tender when pieced with a knife. Remove from the stove and drain. While they are still hot, cut the potatoes into $3/4$ inch cubes.

As the potatoes are simmering, whisk together the garlic, red wine vinegar, honey, red onion, olive oil, salt and pepper in a small bowl.

Toss the dressing with the hot potatoes. Taste and adjust the seasonings. Serve at room temperature.

Cook's Notes:
• The flavors in this dish improve if they are allowed to marinate for at least several hours and it is best if made a day in advance. Refrigerate overnight and bring to room temperature before serving.

POTATO SALAD IS A FAVORITE dish in nearly every European country and Croatia is no exception. This popularity may stem from the fact that it is the perfect accompaniment to Croatia's favorite fast food—rotisserie chicken. Available in many small towns and at village markets, these well-seasoned chickens are slow-cooked in full view of the customer. I considered myself very lucky to be lined up at the market when the chickens were being pulled off the spit. They usually sold as fast as the merchant could slip them into a bag. ▓

Bright and Scrumptious Broccoli Pancakes
Serves 6

Clifford Wright's A Mediterranean Feast *inspired this recipe, which provides a unique way to serve this nutritious vegetable. The color is incredible and the batter can be prepared in advance and refrigerated for up to one day. Stir thoroughly before spooning the batter onto the griddle.*

1$^{1}/_{2}$ pounds broccoli, florets and tender stem portions

$^{1}/_{3}$ cup flour

3 eggs

$^{1}/_{4}$ cup milk

$^{1}/_{2}$ teaspoon salt

$^{1}/_{2}$ teaspoon pepper

$^{3}/_{4}$ cup yogurt or sour cream (optional)

Bring a large pot of salted water to a boil. Add the broccoli and cook until barely tender, about 5 minutes. Drain immediately and allow to cool. Transfer the broccoli to a food processor and pulse until pureed, pausing occasionally to scrape down the sides. Add the flour, eggs, milk, salt and pepper. Process until all ingredients are thoroughly blended.

Preheat the oven to 250 degrees. Preheat a large griddle or fry pan until a drop of water sprinkled on the surface just begins to "dance." Lightly oil the surface of the griddle. Spoon $^{1}/_{4}$ cup portions of pancake mixture onto the griddle and cook for 4–5 minutes. Flip and cook for an additional 4–5 minutes. Pancakes should be golden brown on the outside and moist but not wet on the inside. Remove and keep warm until all the batter is cooked. Serve topped with a dollop of sour cream or yogurt.

BROCCOLI, A PART OF THE CABBAGE FAMILY, originated in Greece or Turkey and most likely made its first appearance in Croatia in the 17th century. The very early specimens did not resemble the tight and dense-headed version common in today's American markets. In fact, much of the broccoli sold today in the Croatian farmers' markets resembles the broccoli of the past: a thin-stemmed stalk, about 6 inches long, with a small floret at the top.

Dalmatian Vegetable Casserole
Serves 8 as a topping, side dish or a sauce

I like to take the time to dice the vegetables into 1/4 to 1/2-inch pieces. The result is more versatile and more attractive, particularly as a topping for bruschetta. However, if you're in a hurry or if you prefer a chunkier sauce, cut the vegetables into larger pieces. The flavor will be similar. Just be sure to keep all the vegetables approximately the same size. This dish keeps well for 3–4 days in the refrigerator and up to 1 month in the freezer.

2 medium eggplants, diced (about 2 1/2 pounds)

2 teaspoons salt

1/4 cup olive oil

1 large onion, diced

1 red or green pepper, diced

4–6 cloves garlic, minced

3 small zucchini, diced

Salt and freshly ground pepper to taste

1 (28-ounce) can tomatoes, diced

1/2 cup parsley, chopped

1 teaspoon thyme

1/4 cup basil, chopped

Place the eggplant in a colander, sprinkle with the salt and let it rest for 15 minutes. Meanwhile, heat the olive oil in a large sauté pan, over medium heat and add the onion, pepper and garlic. Sauté until the onion is translucent and the peppers begin to soften, about 7 minutes.

Rinse and drain the eggplant and pat dry with paper towels. Add the eggplant to the sauté pan and continue to sauté until the eggplant is soft and begins to turn golden, about 15 minutes.

Add the zucchini, salt and pepper and sauté for 5 minutes. Reduce the heat to low and pour in the tomatoes. Simmer, stirring occasionally, for 30 minutes. Stir in the parsley, thyme and basil and simmer for an additional 15 minutes. Taste and adjust the seasonings. Serve hot or cold as a side dish, as a topping for pasta or as a sauce for chicken or chops.

Cook's Notes:
- Feel free to alter proportions and quantities; this is a very flexible dish. For a bolder flavor, try adding one or more of the following: a dash or two of balsamic vinegar, 1/2 cup of pitted and chopped Kalamata olives, 2 tablespoons of capers, 6 coarsely chopped anchovy fillets.

As we sailed about the Mediterranean, friends came to visit and to share in our adventures. Some stayed for just three or four days while others would be with us for a week or longer. Some arrived direct from an overseas flight while others had been touring elsewhere in Europe. It was difficult to judge how hungry our new arrivals would be after a tiring trip by plane, car or ferry. Would they enjoy a hearty pasta or a simple snack? This classic Mediterranean vegetarian dish was perfect to have on hand as it can be served in many ways: as a topping for bruschetta, as a sauce for pasta or as an accompaniment for grilled fish or meat.

Istrian Potatoes
Serves 4 to 6

Sniff this dish as it comes out of the oven and you'll think that you're in Northern Italy. Prosciutto, parsley, tomato, garlic, olive oil, Parmigiano Reggiano and cream blend together to create a tasty dish with flavors common to many parts of Italy and to the Istrian Peninsula.

4 large potatoes, peeled and cut into 1-inch cubes (about 2 pounds)
1/4 pound prosciutto, finely diced
2 Roma tomatoes, diced
4 cloves garlic, minced
1/4 cup parsley, chopped
Salt and freshly ground pepper to taste
2 tablespoons olive oil
1/2 cup milk
1/2 cup heavy cream
1/2 cup grated Parmigiano Reggiano cheese

Preheat the oven to 350 degrees and butter a 2-quart baking dish. In a large bowl, toss together the potatoes, prosciutto, tomatoes, garlic, parsley, salt, pepper and olive oil. Turn the mixture into a buttered baking dish. Combine the milk and the cream and pour over all. Cover with foil and bake for 30 minutes. Remove the foil and sprinkle the cheese over all. Continue to bake for an additional 30 to 45 minutes or until potatoes are cooked through and the top is golden.

Tomatoes growing in a front yard

Potatoes Braised with Spinach
Serves 4

This flavorful combination of a leafy green vegetable and potatoes is cooked together in a single pot and is ready to serve in less than 20 minutes. Traditionally made with mangold, a leafy green vegetable similar to spinach, it is popular throughout Dalmatia.

3 tablespoons extra-virgin olive oil

1 small onion, finely chopped (about 1/2 cup)

3 cloves garlic, minced

1 pound thin-skinned potatoes, peeled, halved lengthwise and thinly sliced

Salt and freshly ground pepper to taste

1/2 cup water

1/2 pound spinach

Additional extra-virgin olive oil (optional)

Pour the olive oil into a medium sauté pan and place over medium heat. Add the onion and the garlic and sauté until the onion is transparent, about 5 minutes. Stir in the potatoes, salt, pepper and add the water. Cover and simmer over low heat until the potatoes are just tender, about 10 minutes. Stir in the spinach and cook until the spinach is completely wilted. Taste and correct the seasoning. Drizzle with additional olive oil, if desired.

Cook's Notes:

• I like to use Yukon Gold or red-skinned potatoes.

• For a slightly different twist, try substituting red or green chard. Regardless of which greens you choose, be sure to use your very best olive oil.

POTATOES FIRST APPEARED in the Mediterranean in the late 16th century when they were imported to Spain from the New World. Initially used as fodder for pigs, they soon became a part of the Spanish menu and were often found in many stew-like dishes. It was not long before they found their way eastward and into Croatia. Today, potatoes are a Croatian staple and they are frequently used in stew-like dishes.

Potatoes Sautéed with Paprika
Serves 4

Paprika stirred into simple pan-fried potatoes provides both a flavor kick and a welcome blush. For a spicier dish, add hot paprika; and for a smoother flavor, select a mild variety, or try a combination of both. Just be sure to use a high-quality product. If possible, find a Croatian paprika or select a Hungarian variety.

4 medium new potatoes (about 1$^1/_3$ pounds)
2 tablespoons olive oil
2 teaspoons paprika (mild or hot or a combination)
Salt and freshly ground pepper to taste

Wash, scrub and thinly slice the potatoes. Warm the oil in a medium fry pan and stir in the paprika, salt and pepper. Immediately add the sliced potatoes and stir until all the potatoes are evenly coated with the paprika and oil combination. Cover the fry pan and cook over medium heat for 20–25 minutes, stirring occasionally, until the potatoes are tender.

THE ISLAND OF HVAR, the sunniest place in the Adriatic, proudly and justifiably boasts about its outstanding wine and beautiful lavender fields. The island's jewel, Hvar Town, presents an almost flawless, magical and mystical image of a 13th century Roman walled city, complete with a flag-flying castle perched high on top of the hill.

Hvar Town also offers the perfect place for a waterfront stroll. Head in one direction and you meander through a beautiful old park and suburban community of old villas. Head off in the other direction and end up at the Franciscan monastery and church. Today, these ancient buildings are being lovingly and beautifully restored. The old refectory has been furnished with traditional tables and benches that ring a room whose primary focus is the spectacular 17th century painting of the Last Supper by the Italian artist, Matteo Ignoli. Little imagination is required to visualize dozens of robed monks sitting down to a simple meal featuring satisfying and easy-to-grow potatoes.

Potatoes Simmered with Tomatoes
Serves 4

This dish is easy to prepare, flavorful and flexible. You can add more onions and use fewer potatoes or adjust the quantity of tomatoes to suit your taste. It can be made an hour or two in advance and simply reheated when it is time to serve.

1 large onion, thinly sliced (about $1/2$ pound)
2 tablespoons olive oil
4 medium potatoes (about 1 $1/2$ pounds), peeled, cut in half lengthwise and thinly sliced
3 cloves garlic, minced
2 large tomatoes, diced
Salt and freshly ground pepper to taste
2 tablespoons parsley, finely chopped

In a large fry pan, over medium heat, sauté the onion in the olive oil until it becomes very limp, about 7–10 minutes. Add the potatoes, garlic, tomatoes, salt and pepper and mix well. Cover the pan and simmer, stirring or shaking occasionally, until the potatoes are tender, about 20–25 minutes. Sprinkle with parsley and serve.

I LOVED MY EARLY MORNING walks through tiny Croatian villages, especially during the spring, summer and early fall growing seasons. In this part of the world, front yards are not spaces consumed with lush green lawns but instead they are brimming with colorful, aromatic and productive kitchen gardens. Each change in the season highlighted different crops: springtime onions, peas, lettuce and strawberries; summer tomatoes, peppers, beans and eggplants; and autumn squash, cabbage, Brussels sprouts and potatoes. These walks always provided inspiration for our fresh, local and seasonal menus.

Red Cabbage Sautéed with Apple
Serves 6 - 8

On a cool and breezy day in early autumn, this dish is the perfect accompaniment to grilled pork chops. The combination serves as a bittersweet reminder that the days of gathering around the barbecue may be numbered and that hearty and tasty cold weather dishes will soon emerge from the kitchen. Serve this warm slaw throughout the winter with roast pork, ham, chicken or beef.

$^1/_4$ **cup olive oil**

1 medium red cabbage, about 2 pounds, cored and thinly sliced

1 large red onion, peeled and thinly sliced

2 Granny Smith apples, peeled and finely chopped

$^1/_4$ **cup brown sugar**

2 tablespoons honey

$^1/_4$ **cup red wine vinegar**

$^1/_4$ **cup red wine**

Salt and freshly ground pepper to taste

$^1/_4$ **cup water**

Heat the oil in a large deep skillet over medium heat. Add the cabbage and the onion and stir-fry for 15 minutes or until the vegetables are wilted. Stir in the apples, sugar, honey, vinegar, wine, salt and pepper. Reduce the heat to low and add a scant $^1/_4$ cup of water. Simmer, covered, until tender (about 1 hour) stirring occasionally and adding more water if necessary. Serve warm or at room temperature.

Cook's notes:

• For a dressed-up flavor, reduce the red wine vinegar to 2 tablespoons and add 1 tablespoon of balsamic vinegar.

• Apple juice or cider can be substituted for the red wine.

Roasted Eggplant and Red Pepper Sauce (*Ajvar*)
Yield: about 4 cups

Almost as popular as ketchup in Croatia, this tasty sauce appears as an accompaniment for grilled meats and poultry. Commercially prepared varieties line the shelves in the grocery stores, some mild and some with a genuine spicy kick.

1 large eggplant
2 large red bell peppers
1/2 teaspoon chili flakes (or to taste)
1/2 cup olive oil
2–4 cloves garlic, minced
1 (14 1/2-ounce) can tomato sauce
Salt and freshly ground pepper to taste
1 tablespoon vinegar

Preheat the oven to 400 degrees. Wash and dry the eggplant and the bell peppers. Cut the eggplant in half lengthwise and place cut-side down on an oiled cookie sheet. Bake at 400 degrees until the eggplant is soft and pierces easily with a knife, about 45 minutes. Allow the eggplant to cool and scoop the pulp into the bowl of a food processor.

As the eggplant cools, cut the peppers in half, removing the core and seeds. Flatten the peppers with your hand. Cover a cookie sheet with aluminum foil and place the flattened peppers, skin side up, on the cookie sheet. Place under the broiler and broil until the peppers are charred on all sides, checking and moving the peppers every 5-10 minutes to char the skins evenly. Place the charred peppers in a bowl, cover with plastic wrap and allow to cool.

Peel the peppers and place them in the food processor bowl with the eggplant. Add the chili flakes, olive oil, garlic, tomato sauce, salt, pepper and vinegar and process until smooth.

Pour the sauce into a medium saucepan and simmer over low heat for 45 minutes, stirring frequently. The sauce should be thick, the consistency of ketchup. Cool and refrigerate for up to 1 week or freeze in small containers for future use.

THE HISTORY OF THE EGGPLANT reaches way back. It was first known in the Assam and Burma regions of Asia 4,000 years ago. From there the great Arab caravans carried it to northern Africa and eventually it was adopted by the Mediterranean peoples. They called it *Solanum insanum* as it was thought by physicians and botanists of the time to cause fevers and epileptic seizures in their patients. (The Italians kept the original name, transforming *Solanum insanum* into *melanzana*.)

As it spread, people grew to like this unique vegetable, originally considered to be an ornamental plant. It was the Anglo-Saxons who thought the small fruits reminded them of eggs. Hence the name, eggplant.

Zucchini with a Cinnamon Twist
Serves 4

Ground cinnamon brings new life to the simple zucchini. Quick, easy and enticingly aromatic, this side dish is destined to become a favorite.

2 tablespoons olive oil
2 cloves garlic, peeled and minced
1 pound small zucchini, thinly sliced
$1/2$ teaspoon salt
$1/4$ teaspoon freshly ground pepper
$1/2$ teaspoon sugar
2 tablespoons parsley, finely chopped
$1/2$ teaspoon ground cinnamon

In a large sauté pan, over medium-high heat, sauté the garlic for 30 seconds in the olive oil. Add the zucchini, salt, pepper and sugar. Stir-fry for 6 to 7 minutes or until the zucchini is tender and slightly golden. Remove from the heat; stir in the parsley, and sprinkle with cinnamon. Toss quickly and serve immediately.

THIS SIMPLE DISH is another reminder of Croatia's importance as a center of trade along the old spice route. Throughout the centuries, spice trading was conducted largely by sea routes with stops that included China, the East Indies, India, the Middle East and into the Mediterranean. Since Venice was a key Mediterranean destination, the Croatian harbors in the Adriatic offered safe refuge along the way. During this era cinnamon was said to have been more valuable than gold.

The Flavor of Italy ...
the Istrian Peninsula

Before we got to Croatia, Bill and I had spent more than a year cruising the Italian coast: exploring the tiny coastal villages, discovering the centuries-old wonders of Rome, and experiencing the various and nefarious sides of Naples. We had also traveled inland to investigate the small, historic hill towns and visit the larger cities of Milan and Florence. Throughout our Italian travels, we developed a self-indulgent habit—a midafternoon pause to enjoy a delicious, satisfying and energizing gelato. Finding this afternoon classic Italian pick-me-up was always easy. It seemed like every place we visited had at least one gelato shop.

Large or small, in the center of a busy square or tucked away on a side street, those emporiums almost always featured an intensely flavored and richly colored handmade product. And if the day happened to be blistering hot (or even just sunny and warm), I would succumb to temptation and order a cup or cone with not just one but two rich, cooling and refreshing flavors.

As a chocoholic, one scoop was always a deep, dark, rich, thick and smooth *cioccolato*. And the other choice was almost always a bright contrasting fruit flavor ... peach (often with small chunks of sweet, locally grown peaches), or deep red and slightly seeded raspberry, or my all time favorite *fruita de bosco* (fruit of the forest), a concentrated blend of tasty and colorful blackberries, blueberries and boysenberries. No matter what combination I selected, every lick would provide a refreshing, luscious burst of flavor. And if I were lucky enough to combine the chocolate with the fruit flavor into a single swish of the tongue, I would be reminded of yet another favorite sweet ... rich and creamy fruit-flavored chocolate truffles. Those wonderful little morsels, usually purchased one by one from an outstanding chocolatier, were treats we savored only on very special occasions.

Those memories of Italian gelato, created by small local producers using only the freshest and the best ingredients, provided me with my first hint of the "Italian connection" when we arrived in the region of Croatia known as Istria. In the tiny villages and larger towns in this region, I discovered multiple gelato stands on the summertime-busy waterfront quays and throughout the year, there was always a gelato shop tucked somewhere along the narrow, winding and twisting streets. But the outstanding gelato was just one of the many "Italian connections" we discovered throughout Istria. In fact, many first-time visitors to Istria often ask: "Are we really in Croatia or have we somehow crossed the border into Italy?" The question is justified. Many sights, sounds and smells in Istria seem to shout, "This is Italy."

❈ ❈ ❈

The region of Croatia known as Istria is a large triangular peninsula that juts into the northern Adriatic and points toward Italy. It is a borderland where Italian, Croatian and Slovene boundaries meet and where the cuisine of the region reflects a complex history spanning many centuries of domination and rule by various empires ... Venetian, Austro-Hungarian, Italian and Yugoslav.

Geographically separated from the continental mainland by the Dinaric Mountains, Istria seems destined to experience an ever-changing nationality. In the last century alone, residents born on this soil were, at one time or another, considered to be Austrian, Italian, Yugoslav or Croatian citizens. Today's borders are the result of a 1954 decision that designated most of Istria as a part of Croatia. One notable exception is a narrow strip of land that includes access to the sea and belongs to the small independent nation of Slovenia. Further confusing the issue is the always-emotional question of nearby Trieste. Now a part of Italy, many Istrians still consider Trieste to be a part of their territory and many Triestites consider Istria to be a part of Italy.

Along the coast, reminders of the Italian connection are constant; road and restaurant signs appear in both Croatian and Italian and conversations on the streets are overheard in highly animated Italian and relatively calm and guttural Croatian. And as I have already confessed, my own personal indicator of Italian custom is the availability of flavorful, handmade, smooth and rich gelato.

Near the Adriatic, the Mediterranean/Italian traditions of fresh seafood, creamy risottos, smooth olive oils and fine wines dominate the palate. But throughout the peninsula those flavors are commingled with the plentiful bounty of the fertile Central European valleys: velvety polenta, rich egg pastas, hearty game, thick sausages and mushrooms rich with the earthy flavor of the forest. The result is a diverse menu that may seem confusing, but it satisfies many palates.

Today there is no indication that either the Italian or the Continental influence is receding. In fact each July and August the Italian population in Istria swells as hordes of Italians, along with their German and Austrian neighbors, flock to the Adriatic seaboard for their annual seaside excursions. Lured by the promise of sunshine and the miles of spectacularly serrated coastline, sun worshippers line this rocky shore. They prostrate themselves on the pebbly beaches of secluded coves or, if they are seeking more comfort, they head to the smoothly cemented surfaces thoughtfully provided by the local towns, restaurants and hotels.

※ ※ ※

Bill and I were repeatedly lured to Istria by the enchanting towns and villages, the inviting green and fertile countryside, the rich history and, of course, the gelato. Our visits to Pula, located at the southern tip of the peninsula and the largest settlement on the peninsula, provided us with many wonderful discoveries: ancient Roman ruins, gracious Venetian residences and modern shops often housed in centuries-old architectural landmarks.

In my opinion, the Roman amphitheater is the most impressive sight in Pula. Remarkably well preserved, this extraordinary First century arena is one of the most magnificent structures of its kind in the world today. Built entirely of local limestone and standing over 100 feet high, the outer wall boasts two rows of 72 beautiful arches. If you enter the arena and close your eyes, you can almost hear the 20,000 spectators cheering on the gladiators—screaming for more blood and gore! Just don't expect to sit down ... the spectator seats were removed in the Middle Ages to be used as building materials for medieval construction. Recycling has been practiced in Pula for centuries.

In an area hidden below the coliseum and originally designed to house the equipment and the beasts for the gladiatorial events, we discovered a museum devoted to the history of Istrian wine and olive production. Filled with beautiful old amphora, ancient stone grinding wheels, giant wine presses and large troughs designed to funnel the oil and the grape juice into storage vats. This display clearly demonstrated the size, scale and importance of these products throughout the Roman era.

Along with the ancient equipment, copies of old maps and drawings were posted. As we studied the scale drawings of a large Roman villa, we began to comprehend another slice of Roman history ... the size and scale of this old villa were comparable to today's small town. We realized that huge numbers of diversely skilled and knowledgeable citizens were needed to maintain, feed and protect the holdings of the wealthy and land-rich Romans.

Pula was also a great place to provision the boat (aka: do the grocery shopping). Conveniently located near the marina was a beautifully restored old market building with an adjacent outdoor farmers' market that featured row upon row of fruit and vegetable stalls. I loved visiting the old market building. Inside there were at least 10 little cafés (each with a *barista* who had his or her own following), an outstanding fish market, a large meat and cheese market and a number of specialty food shops ... often with goods imported from Italy, Germany and/or Austria. Thanks to the diversity of the Istrian population, shoppers at this market were guaranteed a wide selection of products: oysters, tuna, fresh sauerkraut, *pršut* (air-cured ham), wild asparagus, truffles, *kobasice* (a thick, slightly spicy sausage), a seemingly endless variety of dried beans and giant bags of arborio rice and golden polenta.

No matter where we sailed in the Mediterranean, finding fresh fish was almost always a matter of timing and luck ... especially in regions where the availability of the catch was dependent upon the success of small, local, independent fishermen. One day in Pula, I had both timing and good fortune on my side. I arrived at the old market building just as a local fisherman appeared with a large trolley (think Home Depot contractor's trolley) at the fishmonger's booth. Extending over both ends of that trolley was one very large, recently-hauled-from-the-sea tuna. In less than an hour all that remained of that tuna was a silky sheen of spent blood on the trolley and the surrounding floor. Chefs, housewives, green grocers, bakers ... everyone who happened to be at the market descended upon this stall and anxiously stood in line and shouted their orders to the blood-spattered man and woman who were cutting, weighing and wrapping the delicacy. I was thankful and pleasantly impressed that the fishmonger heard and honored my request—spoken in very rugged Croatian—for a kilo of tuna. As I hurried back to the boat to refrigerate my "fresh catch," I was already making menu decisions ... dinner that night would have to be a fresh, melt-in-your-mouth sashimi and dinner the following night would be two lovely portions of slightly seared tuna served with just a drizzle of fruity olive oil, a squeeze of lemon and a sprinkle of Croatian sea salt.

❖ ❖ ❖

Just north of Pula, on the west coast of the peninsula, is the relaxed old fishing village of Rovinj. Whenever we sailed into her harbor, lined with colorfully painted homes and shops, we felt like we were entering a small Italian port. The multihued pink, coral, blue, yellow and turquoise buildings provided a light-spirited holiday atmosphere and offered a refreshing contrast to the monochromatic limestone-gray homes and buildings with brown shutters that are common throughout much of Croatia.

Originally an island, this egg-shaped limestone rock became a peninsula when it was connected to the mainland in the 18th century. Here, time seems to stand still. The centuries-old city plan has not changed ... narrow and twisting alleys wind their way skyward, snaking around an incomparable assortment of tightly wedded stone and stucco buildings. Strolling through Rovinj's neighborhoods is like strolling through an outdoor museum. Buildings and their additions have evolved over a period of more than 500 years and reflect the talents of many generations of architects, builders, stonemasons and woodworkers.

Late one morning, as we climbed the steep and cobbled streets, sniffed the onions and garlic sautéing for the midday meal, and listened to the phones ringing and the children laughing and shouting, we talked about the fact that these ancient buildings—with their tiny interior spaces—have been home to many, for many generations. As we walked, we lauded the decisions of the early citizens who met the challenges of tiny interior spaces by constructing chimneys and fireplaces as exterior extensions. Centuries later, those additions still provide function and architectural character as they cling ornamentally and precariously to the building sides.

When in Rovinj, it is almost mandatory to climb to the top of the hill for a visit to the Cathedral of Saint Euphemia. The large copper statue of Saint Euphemia perched atop the nearly 200-foot-high Baroque church tower is familiar to sailors arriving from sea ... she is their beacon of welcome. But this statue also provides an additional service to the area's citizens ... she was constructed on roller bearings, a feature that allows Saint Euphemia to serve her flock as a weather vane.

The stories and folklore that surround Saint Euphemia's life provided vivid and often diverse tales depending on the narrator. Each source had a slightly different twist but all shared a common theme. My favorite version explained that Euphemia was born in the year 290 A.D. At a very early age she became a Christian and because of her faith, the Roman emperor Diocletian tortured her mercilessly. Finally, in the year 304 A.D., after a series of gruesome forms of torture, she was thrown to the lions. Her body (my calculations indicate that she was a mere 14 years old) was then taken to Constantinople, where it remained for nearly 500 years. Then, one dark and stormy night in the year 800 A.D., Saint Euphemia's body, encased in its sarcophagus, appeared in a spectral boat off the shore of Rovinj. The sarcophagus washed ashore but the townspeople were unable to move it. Suddenly a young boy appeared with two spectral cows. Through the efforts of this boy and the phantom cows, Saint Euphemia was moved to the Christian church high upon the hill. To this day, her body remains in its sarcophagus within the cathedral.

❖ ❖ ❖

In was also in Rovinj that I realized that over the years I had personally established three very important "Commandments for Italian Food Lovers." These mandates had gradually evolved while cruising and traveling throughout Italy; wonderful weeks, months and years filled with careful, calorie-packed research. I realized that each commandment holds true in Istria. The first commandment is the result of numerous late afternoons and evenings spent consuming dozens of cone shaped vessels filled with at least two flavors of gelato. The second and third commandments required many afternoons and evenings devoted to devouring a huge number and a wide variety of pizzas, each suitably accompanied by generous quantities of *vino locale.*

Commandment #1: The best gelato is always scooped from a stainless steel tub. Any shop or kiosk displaying gelato in a plastic tub does not warrant a second glance. The plastic-packed product has undoubtedly been factory produced and just doesn't measure up to the handmade varieties.

Commandment #2: The best pizza comes from wood-fired ovens. This commandment requires no further explanation.

Commandment #3: In small, local restaurants, drink the *vino locale.* Often made by the restaurant owner or a member of his or her family, it is always good value and is almost always a suitable accompaniment to your meal.

❋ ❋ ❋

When in Istria, it was fun to rent a car and head inland to explore. There we found a landscape of rolling hills and moderate mountainsides; gently sloping pastures, generations-old farms, small forests and well-tended vineyards. Dotting the roadsides, the rustic hand-painted *vino* signs served as friendly invites to stop and sample some of the local wines, wines that have made the viticulture of this region recognized throughout the world. And after many tastings, Bill and I can confirm that the Merlots and Cabernet Sauvignons of Istria stand proud. However, it is the Istrian Teran, a dark ruby-colored red, and the Malvasia, a yellow/white dry wine, that enjoy the widest distribution of the wines from this region.

Although the inland population is somewhat sparse and the villages small and scarce, we always found a place to stop, to take pleasure in a late-morning cappuccino and to enjoy lunch in one of the storybook-like hilltop villages. While on the road we savored simple homemade pasta served with finely shaved truffles, creamy seafood risottos, and big and spicy *kobasice* served atop a bed of sauerkraut. This varied cuisine, available in even the smallest village, continued to remind us of the unsettled and often violent history of this area. However, with a sunshine-drenched and beautiful pastoral setting overlooking the rolling hills and vineyards, it was difficult for us to imagine anything other than joy and peace.

Our favorite time to head inland was fall, when local folks were harvesting the grapes and scavenging the wild mushrooms from their hiding places deep within the forests. At this time of the year, we would often notice old farm vehicles parked along the roadside. We quickly learned that if the trunks were closed, it was an indication that somewhere in the nearby woods someone was on the hunt for wild porcini (or perhaps even the highly treasured truffle). But, if the trunk was left open, this was the sign that the vehicle's owner was offering his small mushroom harvest for sale. For me, it was a major dilemma when there were several vehicles stopped along the road. It was impossible to decide which vendor might have the best porcinis at the best price. However, once we pulled over, my decision was made ... I could never resist purchasing at least a few of those incredibly delicious gifts of the land from the humble and hopeful farmer who stood before me.

One late autumn day our porcini stop introduced us to a charming father/son team. The son, who spoke excellent English, carefully explained that the wild mushroom season lasts for about 30 days each fall. Our late October timing was pushing us toward the limits of the season; fresh porcinis would not be available for much longer. We indulged and purchased close to a kilo of beautiful fresh porcinis—more than enough for several feasts.

Back in the car we debated and then we decided ... tonight it would be farm-fresh eggs scrambled with rich cream and fresh, wild mushrooms. The following night we would invite the Dutch couple moored next to us for dinner and serve a creamy, mushroom-rich Istrian pasta. Life was good. I loved being a tourist traveling with her own kitchen.

Inspecting the catch

Coliseum remains

Fresh porcini

Laundry

Vines

Capers

Pasta, polenta and rice are staples in the Croatian diet. Small amounts of rice or noodles may be added to a light broth to begin a meal, or hearty servings of pasta, rice or polenta may provide the base for a rich and flavorful sauce-enhanced entrée.

Some of the simplest and best pasta dishes have peasant origins ... delicious meals created with those most basic ingredients: flour, salt and water. Occasionally an egg is added to the dough. Additional ingredients depend on the season and/or the catch. And when ingredients are truly scarce, dishes like *Mljet Makaroni* are served.

As you experiment with these recipes, picture yourself working in a little farmhouse in a coastal Croatian village. Your surroundings are simple, your home is small and your kitchen tools are limited ... just a few pots and bowls and a couple of good knives. But your kitchen garden, brimming with seasonal produce, is just outside the door; the family wine kegs are full; there's lots of local olive oil and plenty of homemade cheese rounds stored away. Healthy, hearty meals will soon be on the table.

PASTA, POLENTA & RICE

Bowtie Pasta with Peas, Spring Onions & Lemon
Serves 4 to 6

Bursting with the flavors of springtime, this quick and simple dish is just the answer for a hectic weekday dinner.

4 tablespoons extra-virgin olive oil, divided
2–3 ounces pancetta, chopped fine
3 cloves garlic, minced
1 bunch green onions, thinly sliced
1 pound bowtie pasta
2 cups green peas, freshly shelled
2 lemons, zest only
¼ cup fresh parsley, finely chopped
Coarsely ground sea salt
Coarsely grated black pepper
Parmigiano Reggiano cheese, freshly grated

Heat 2 tablespoons of olive oil in a small sauté pan over medium heat. Add the pancetta and sauté until crisp and lightly browned, about 3–4 minutes. Stir in the garlic and sauté for 30 seconds. Stir in the green onions and set aside.

Meanwhile, bring a large pot of water to a boil and stir in the pasta. Cook until not quite al dente. Add the peas and continue to cook until the pasta is al dente. Drain the pasta and the peas and place in a large serving bowl. Add the pancetta/onion mixture, the lemon zest, parsley, salt, pepper and the remaining olive oil and toss together. Top with Parmigiano Reggiano cheese and serve.

Cook's Notes:

• Pancetta is a type of bacon common in Croatia and Italy. It is cured with spices and salt but is not smoked. It can be found in specialty food stores and delicatessens throughout the United States. If pancetta is not available, you can substitute bacon.

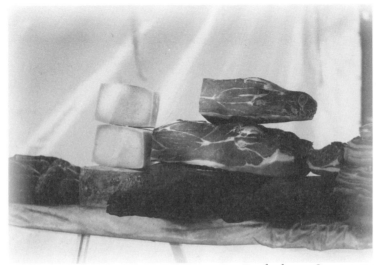

Fresh cheese & pancetta

THE START OF THE 21ST CENTURY signaled the beginning of major change in Croatia. The war was history, but its pains lingered. Communism was being replaced by capitalism … creating frustrations for some and opportunities for others. Generations within the same family struggled with different values and different expectations. Seniors clung to the old expectations and mourned the loss of their communist-sponsored economic safety net while the younger generations were ready to move forward to promote themselves and their nation as a part of the world economy. Yet social values and economic conditions continued to demand that these generations live together in the same household.

We observed and listened to many of these challenges. In fact, this recipe evolved from a springtime visit to the family garden of the warm and generous parents of a Croatian friend. Grinning with pride, they showed us their lovingly tended garden: a generous potato patch, stately columns of spring onions and tidy rows of green beans. Our mouth-watering enthusiasm was obvious when we discovered the pea patch—tender vines covered with bright green leaves, twisting tendrils and perfectly formed pods gently swollen with sweet and tender baby peas. By the time we were ready to return to the *Klatawa*, we were loaded down with a grocery bag filled with succulent, fresh peas—the perfect inspiration to create a casual communal evening meal for several nearby neighbors and ourselves.

Croatian-Style Spaghetti Bolognese
Serves 4 to 6

2 tablespoons olive oil

2 ounces pancetta, chopped fine

3/4 pound lean ground beef

1 large onion, chopped fine

2–4 cloves garlic, minced

1 stalk celery, chopped fine

1 carrot, grated

1 (28-ounce) can tomatoes, crushed

1 (6-ounce) can tomato paste

1/2 cup red wine

1 1/2 teaspoons dried oregano

2 teaspoons sugar

1 bay leaf

Salt and freshly ground pepper to taste

1 pound spaghetti

Parmigiano Reggiano, freshly grated

Heat the olive oil in a medium saucepan over medium-high heat. Add the pancetta and sauté until it is beginning to brown and the fat is released, about 3–4 minutes. Add the ground beef and stir to break apart. Continue to sauté and stir until the ground beef begins to brown, about 5 minutes. Reduce the heat to medium–low and stir in the onion, garlic, celery and carrot. Cover and allow to "sweat" until the vegetables begin to soften and the onion becomes transparent, about 10 minutes. Stir in the tomatoes, tomato paste, red wine, oregano, sugar, bay leaf, salt and pepper. Cook over low heat for about 1 hour, stirring occasionally.

When the Bolognese Sauce is nearly finished, cook the spaghetti in boiling water until al dente. Drain the pasta and transfer to individual serving plates or bowls. Remove the bay leaf, spoon on the sauce and serve with freshly grated Parmigiano Reggiano cheese.

Cook's Notes:
• Pancetta is a type of bacon common in Croatia and Italy. It is cured with spices and salt but is not smoked. It can often be found in specialty food stores and delis. If pancetta is not available you can substitute bacon.

As I sat at my tiny desk in the master stateroom on *Klatawa* one warm, sunny, late summer day, I debated the pros and cons of including this recipe. After all, some variation of Spaghetti Bolognese appears on so many family tables that it could be considered boring. On the other hand, it is a mainstay in many Croatian households and a regular on many restaurant menus.

My thoughts were suddenly interrupted by a distinctive hum emanating from the Scottish-flagged vessel in the adjacent slip. Our neighbor's guest and lifelong friend had begun his late morning serenade to the marina on his nearly 100-year-old bagpipe. On this particular day, he was playing a series of haunting, traditional melodies of his native land.

I stopped, listened, enjoyed and ruminated. Although Spaghetti Bolognese may not share a history of 20 centuries or more (the length of time for which the history of the bagpipe can be traced), it has been a tradition throughout the Mediterranean and in Croatia for many generations. Decision made: the lasting popularity of Spaghetti Bolognese more than justified its inclusion. 🎆

Istrian Pasta
Serves 4 to 6

This dish illustrates the great things that can happen when several food traditions are merged. In this recipe, butter, bacon and rich, heavy cream from the Alpine regions of Croatia and Slavonia are combined with the typically southern Italian ingredients of pasta, garlic, olive oil and a bit of tomato.

3 tablespoons butter

4 ounces sliced bacon, cut into $1/4$ inch strips

2–4 cloves garlic, peeled and chopped

1 medium onion, finely chopped

1 pound mushrooms, cleaned and sliced

$1^1/2$ cups heavy cream

1 large Roma tomato, washed and finely chopped

$1/3$ cup parsley, finely chopped

$1/2$ teaspoon salt

$1/2$ teaspoon freshly ground pepper

1 pound spaghetti

$1/2$ cup Parmigiano Reggiano, freshly grated

Over medium-high heat, melt the butter in a large, deep skillet. Add the chopped bacon and sauté until the bacon is crisp and lightly browned, about 4 minutes. Add the minced garlic and onion and stir until barely translucent, about 5–7 minutes. Toss in the mushrooms and continue stirring until the mushrooms are lightly browned and most of the juices have evaporated, about 5 minutes. Stir in the cream, tomato, parsley, salt and pepper. Cook and stir over moderately high heat until the sauce thickens, about 3–5 minutes.

As the sauce nears completion, cook the pasta until just al dente. Drain but reserve 1 cup of the cooking liquid. Add the pasta to the sauce and toss gently over moderate heat until well coated. Add pasta water in ¼ cup increments until a creamy sauce forms.

Transfer to a large serving bowl and top with freshly grated Parmigiano Reggiano cheese.

Cook's Notes:

• This recipe is best if an assortment of mushrooms such as cremini, shitake, chanterelles and porcini can be used. If only fresh white mushrooms are available in the market, certainly go ahead and make this dish. However, the flavor can be greatly enhanced by adding 1 ounce (or even less) of reconstituted dried porcini mushrooms.

• Dried porcini mushrooms are available at Italian markets, specialty food stores and some supermarkets. Reconstitute the dried mushrooms by covering them with boiling water and allowing them to soak for 15–20 minutes. Lift the mushrooms out of the water and squeeze out the excess liquid. This liquid contains a lot of flavor as well, so be sure to use it; but be careful not to pour out any sand or dirt that may remain in the bottom of the soaking vessel.

Mljet Makaroni (When There is No Seafood)
Serves 4

The original recipe calls for goat cheese preserved in olive oil, a standard ingredient in many rural Croatian homes. In order to adapt the recipe for use in American homes, I have substituted the readily available Parmigiano Reggiano. The dish remains wonderfully satisfying … thanks to the chewy texture of the pasta, the rich and aromatic garlic and the earthy flavor of extra-virgin olive oil.

3 cups of flour
1 scant cup of water
1^1/$_2$ teaspoons salt
1 cup Parmigiano Reggiano, coarsely grated
4–6 cloves of garlic
^{1}/$_2$ cup extra-virgin olive oil
Salt and freshly ground pepper to taste

Make a dough by mixing the flour, water and salt. On a smooth, floured surface lightly knead the dough until it is somewhat smooth. The dough should be stiff but not sticky. Shape the dough into 4 balls and let rest for 10 minutes. Working with 1 ball at a time, on a floured surface, roll out the ball to form a rope. Cut the rope into pieces, each about the size of a pecan. Rub and roll each piece between your hands, making a large pasta (*makaroni*.) Set the pastas aside. Each piece should be about ¼ inch in diameter and 2½–3 inches long. Continue until all the dough is used. Cook the *makaronis* in boiling water for 12–14 minutes and drain.

Heat the olive oil in a small saucepan. Add the garlic, salt and pepper and fry until the garlic becomes slightly reddish. Take a heatproof glass or ceramic bowl and fill the bottom with a thin layer of *makaroni*. Pour over some of the garlic and oil and grate some cheese on top. Repeat with *makaroni*, oil, garlic and cheese until all ingredients are used; finishing with the cheese. Serve.

MY FRIEND, JANY, GAVE me the original recipe for this dish. As she shared it, she explained that this was her mother's recipe for the meal she would serve when the man of the household returned from his daily fishing expedition without any fish. Originally prepared on her home island of Mljet, it is a typical island recipe, made from the simplest pantry ingredients.

Penne with Mushrooms and Gorgonzola
Serves 4 to 6

If you like blue cheese, this recipe is guaranteed to be an instant winner!

2 tablespoons butter
1 pound mushrooms, cleaned and sliced
3/4 cup white wine
4 ounces Gorgonzola cheese, crumbled
1/2 cup cream
1 pound penne pasta
1/4 cup parsley, finely chopped and divided
Salt and freshly ground pepper to taste

Melt the butter in a large sauté pan, over medium-high heat. Stir in the mushrooms and sauté until all the juices are released. Add the wine and simmer for 1 minute. Reduce the heat to low and add the Gorgonzola cheese. Stir until the cheese is melted. Add the cream and simmer until the sauce is slightly thickened.

Meanwhile, cook the penne in a large pot of boiling water until it is not quite al dente. Drain the pasta reserving 1 cup of the cooking liquid. Add 2 tablespoons of parsley, salt and pepper to the sauce. Toss in the penne and stir over low heat for 2–3 minutes to finish off the pasta and to combine the flavors, adding small amounts of pasta water if necessary. Garnish with remaining parsley and serve.

Cook's Notes:

• This is a very rich pasta. I like to serve smaller than normal portions on a bed of fresh baby spinach for a first course or as a meatless entree. Alternatively, top the pasta with a pan-seared chicken breast, for an elegant main course.

• For a different twist, eliminate the parsley garnish and top with roasted red seedless grapes. To roast the grapes, toss the grapes with olive oil and roast in a preheated 450-degree oven for 15–20 minutes or until grapes are browned but still firm.

WE FIRST TASTED this rich and creamy penne pasta at the restaurant Jurin Podrum in the town of Stari Grad (Old Town) on the Island of Hvar. Tucked away on a narrow, cobbled street, this small and intimate restaurant was a favorite stop.

Spaghetti Marinara with Fresh Herbs
Serves 4 to 6

Fresh herbs and seasonings are readily available in rural Croatia. Rosemary, marjoram and oregano grow wild along the roads, and you'll find flavor-enhancing capers tucked into the seemingly endless miles of rock walls. Moreover most kitchen gardens have a few favorite herbs planted in amongst the veggies. By mid summer herbs are in abundant supply throughout the land.

Fresh in flavor and low fat, this tasty and aromatic dish is incredibly easy to prepare. Simply adjust the quantities, and you have a dish that is suitable for a single diner or for a group of eight or more.

$1/4$ cup extra virgin olive oil

2–4 cloves garlic, minced

2 cups Roma tomatoes, chopped

2 tablespoons capers (chopped if large)

15 black olives (preferably Kalamata), pitted and chopped

Sea salt to taste

Freshly ground pepper to taste

$1/2$ cup parsley, chopped

$1/2$ cup basil, chopped

2 teaspoons each: rosemary, thyme and oregano, chopped

1 pound spaghetti

Parmigiano Reggiano, grated

Heat the olive oil in a large sauté pan over medium heat. Add the garlic and sauté for 2–3 minutes. Stir in the tomatoes, capers, olives, salt and pepper and simmer uncovered for about 5 minutes. Toss in the parsley, basil and mixed herbs.

Meanwhile, bring a large pot of salted water to a boil and cook pasta until al dente. Drain, reserving 1 cup pasta liquid. Toss the pasta into the pan with the sauce, stir over medium heat for 2–3 minutes until pasta is well coated, adding more pasta cooking liquid if needed. Serve with grated Parmigiano Reggiano cheese.

DROPPING AND SECURING AN ANCHOR in a secluded and quiet cove is easy compared to some of the challenges faced by sailors when they try to "Med moor" at a dock or quay. The system, designed to accommodate the largest number of boats in the smallest amount of space, provides endless challenges for the captain and crew of cruising sailboats as they attempt to complete this often-unpredictable exercise. The goal is straightforward: to maneuver the stern of the boat toward the quay and then secure the dock lines from the boat to the (hopefully present) shore-mounted cleats.

The challenges include but are not limited to the following: 1) many sailboats do not reverse in a straight line; 2) winds are always the strongest, least predictable and coming from the wrong direction during this maneuver; 3) throwing and successfully attaching a line ashore is impossible from a distance of more than 10 feet; 4) the mooring space available is always less than the beam of your boat; 5) despite our fantasies, liberal coatings of olive oil will not help the "squeeze".

Furthermore, before the stern can be tied to land, it may be necessary to drop the anchor off the bow in order to guarantee that the boat will not continuously and damagingly smash against the concrete dock or quay. Once this often frustrating and sometimes lengthy mooring exercise is successfully completed, the Captain always requires a cold beer and the First Mate needs to relax, read, sip a glass of wine and decide on a very simple dinner plan. Spaghetti Marinara with Fresh Herbs is a perfect choice. ▨

Med mooring

Spaghetti with Lemon and Caper Sauce
Serves 6 to 8

I think this simple dish is one of the best ways to enjoy Mediterranean capers. In fact, it shows off three key Mediterranean ingredients: excellent olive oil, fresh lemon and the intensely flavored capers. Serve as a first course or as a side for grilled or broiled seafood.

1 pound spaghetti

$1/4$ cup extra virgin olive oil

$1^1/_2$ tablespoon capers, drained

Zest of 1 lemon

Juice of 1 lemon

Sea salt, to taste

Freshly ground pepper to taste

In a small saucepan, over a medium-high heat, combine the olive oil, capers and lemon zest. Simmer for 3–5 minutes. Remove from the heat and stir in the lemon juice. Meanwhile, cook the pasta according to package directions. Drain, reserving 1 cup pasta water. Toss the pasta into the pan with the sauce, stir over medium heat for 2–3 minutes until the pasta is well coated, adding more pasta water if needed. Taste and adjust the seasonings.

Cook's Notes:
• If capers are large, chop them into the size of small capers.

MY QUEST TO FIND a caper plant, the bearer of that ubiquitous Mediterranean ingredient, began with our travels in France and continued through Italy, Greece, Turkey and finally Croatia. I could never identify this elusive plant in its native ground. I was told that it was a sprawling dense vine or shrub that clung tenaciously to rocky hillsides and to stone walls or buildings. I was also told that it grew "all over," even in the tiniest crack or crevice. It was not until one early summer afternoon when I was wandering the streets of Dubrovnik with my friend Jany, that she identified it for me. Laden with white and light purple flowers, the vine suddenly appeared to be everywhere. Jany further explained that what we enjoy in our recipes are the unopened buds, picked early in the morning, blanched and pickled.

Spaghetti with Seafood
Serves 4 to 6

1/4 cup olive oil

1 medium onion, chopped fine

3–4 cloves garlic, peeled and minced

1 (14 1/2-ounce) can tomatoes, diced

2 tablespoons tomato paste

1/2 cup dry white wine

1 teaspoon sugar

1/4 cup flat leaf parsley, chopped fine

Salt and freshly ground pepper to taste

1 pound mixed seafood, at least 3 different varieties:
   thinly sliced calamari, cubed boneless white fish fillets,
   minced clams, cleaned prawns, mussel meat, etc.

1 pound spaghetti

Chopped parsley for garnish

Parmigiano Reggiano (optional)

Heat the oil in a large sauté pan over medium heat. Add the onion and sauté gently for 5 minutes or until the onion becomes soft and translucent. Stir in the garlic and sauté for an additional 2–3 minutes. Add the tomatoes, tomato paste, wine, sugar, parsley, salt and pepper. Simmer uncovered for 10–15 minutes or until sauce is slightly thickened. Add the seafood and stir over medium–high heat for 3–4 minutes or until seafood is almost cooked.

Meanwhile, bring a large pot of salted water to a boil and cook the pasta until not quite al dente. Reserve 1 cup of pasta water. Drain the pasta and stir into the sauté pan. Toss and cook the pasta and the seafood over medium-high heat, adding the reserved pasta water as needed, until the sauce and pasta are well combined, about 2 minutes. Pour into a serving bowl, sprinkle with parsley and pass the cheese if desired.

IT'S NOT UNUSUAL TO FIND a small freezer tucked away in the corner of tiny food markets in rural Croatian villages. This freezer is often filled with a surprising variety of protein sources: a few chickens, some packages of sausage, a couple of pork chops, a plastic bag or two of octopus and some flat styrofoam packages of mixed seafood.

These 200 gram (about ½ pound) packages of frozen, mixed seafood usually include squid, octopus, artificial crab, mussels and baby shrimp … all cut or sized for rapid cooking. Perfect for seafood risotto or pasta, one package creates a flavorful meal for two. In the United States, a pre-mixed seafood combination is sometimes available at fresh fish counters or in the freezer compartment. If you need to create your own mix, keep in mind that the flavor of this dish will vary based on your selection of seafood. Be sure to use at least 3 different varieties and do try to include calamari. It is typically Croatian and it adds great flavor.

Basic Polenta
Serves 4

The texture and consistency of cooked cornmeal or polenta can vary significantly. It can be prepared to be stiff and firm, or more liquid can be added so that it remains soft and loose. When polenta is being topped with a flavorful sauce, the choice is yours.

In the United States, there is a wide choice of dried polenta or cornmeal products in the market place. I prefer to use a "quick cook" variety, as regular polenta will typically take about 35 or 40 minutes of attentive stirring to prepare. Whatever brand you choose, follow the package instructions and feel free to add seasonings and flavors of your choice (herbs, finely chopped veggies, cheese, etc.). Topped with your choice of sauces, polenta is a flavorful alternative to pasta, potatoes or rice.

> 4^{1}/$_{2}$ cups water or broth
> 1^{1}/$_{2}$ cups cornmeal (yellow or white)
> Salt to taste
> 2 tablespoons butter or olive oil
> 2 tablespoons grated cheese (optional)

Bring the water to a boil in a medium saucepan. Slowly, and in a steady stream, stir in the cornmeal with a wooden spoon. Lower the heat and cook, stirring constantly, for the length of time recommended on the package. Serve immediately or pour out on an oiled surface and allow it to set until firm. Refrigerate overnight. Cut with a taut string and grill or fry in olive oil or butter.

Cook's Notes:

- Cornmeal can "sputter and spit" so be sure to use a long-handled wooden spoon and stir cautiously to avoid burns.

- To help prevent lumps, mix the cornmeal with 1 cup of cool liquid before adding it to the hot liquid.

- For a special presentation, spray decorative molds or custard cups with a cooking oil and fill with hot polenta. Allow to cool and invert onto a serving plate. Note: molded polenta can be covered and re-heated in the microwave.

MAIZE, GROUND INTO CORNMEAL, was first introduced to northern Italy from the New World shortly after 1500. From there, it quickly spread throughout Europe, becoming a staple in many peasant homes. Polenta can be made with either finely or coarsely ground yellow or white cornmeal. ▨

Rich and Creamy Polenta
Serves 4 to 6

Polenta may have humble roots, but it can be dressed up to put on a sophisticated air and be right at home at the most elegant and discerning table. Throughout Croatia, as the number of well-traveled international tourists increases, finer restaurants are transforming this simple product into a specialty dish.

In Dubrovnik, I have been served tiny, shell-shaped bites of polenta as a garnish on a yummy, tomato-based frog leg stew, and several times we enjoyed tiny pieces of fried polenta that had been cut into rounds, diamonds and squares seasoned, fried in olive oil and served as an appetizer. But maybe best of all, is this delicious, creamy version which—I should warn you—can become addictive.

> 2 cups milk
> 3/4 cup butter
> 1 cup sour cream (or yogurt)
> 1/2 teaspoon salt
> 1 cup corn meal
> 1/2 cup cold water (or more as needed)
> 1 cup diced fresh Mozzarella or cottage cheese
> 2 tablespoons chopped parsley (optional)

In a thick-bottomed saucepan, combine the milk, butter, sour cream and salt. Over low heat, slowly bring the mixture to a boil, stirring often and carefully watching so that the mixture does not scorch.

Combine the cornmeal with the cold water and, stirring constantly, very slowly add the cornmeal to the milk mixture. Over low heat, stir with a long-handled wooden spoon until the mixture thickens. Add the cheese and continue to stir until the mixture begins to leave the side of the pan. Garnish with chopped parsley and serve hot.

Cook's notes:

• The entire cooking process will vary, taking between 10 and 25 minutes as different brands of polenta (cornmeal) vary in cooking times. The finished polenta should be soft and creamy but should retain some of its texture. Add more water or more cornmeal if necessary.

• Mixing the cornmeal with cold water before adding it to the hot liquid helps to prevent lumps.

Rizi I Bizi (Rice and Peas)
Serves 4 to 6

As is, this tasty yet simple risotto recipe reflects its humble beginnings. Dress it up with small shrimp, and it is ready for the most elegant dinner party.

> **3 tablespoons olive oil**
> **1 medium onion, chopped fine**
> **2 cups rice**
> **6 cups chicken stock**
> **Salt and freshly ground pepper to taste**
> **2 cups frozen peas, defrosted**

Heat the olive oil in a medium saucepan over medium heat. Add the onion and sauté until translucent, about 5 minutes. Add the rice and continue to stir for 2 minutes, until rice is well coated with oil and begins to become translucent.

Meanwhile, bring the chicken stock to a simmer. Reduce the heat to low to keep the stock hot. Stir in 1 cup of chicken stock and continue to stir until almost all the liquid is absorbed. Add more stock. Continue to stir and add stock in ½ cup increments until the rice is nearly al dente. Add green peas and continue to cook, stir and add stock until rice is al dente. Place on individual serving plates and serve.

Cook's Notes:

• Generally, I like my risotto to spread gently across the plate, leaving a small ring of sauce around the edge of the dish. However, if I'm using the risotto as an accompaniment on a plate that includes other foods, I prefer it to be a bit "tighter." I then add a bit less stock at the end. Taste and appearance are all a matter of personal preference.

• To dress up this dish and turn it into an elegant meal, substitute 1 cup of wine for 1 cup of the chicken stock. Along with the peas, add 1 pound of small, shelled, raw shrimp that have been cleaned and deveined. This addition will increase the cooking time by about 4 minutes.

• Variation: Some Croatian cooks prefer to cook the rice and peas separately and then toss them together in a quick stir-fry: Heat 3 tablespoons olive oil in a large sauté pan and stir in 1 small finely chopped onion. Sauté until the onion begins to turn translucent and then add 2½ cups cooked rice and 10 ounces of cooked and drained peas. Stir until well combined. Season with salt and pepper to taste and serve.

THE BEST OUTDOOR MARKET in Dubrovnik is located in the adjacent town of Gruž. Here there are 4 or 5 long rows of permanent fruit and vegetable stalls and a large, covered, open-air seafood market. Just a 15-minute bus ride from the marina, it was where I headed for fresh seafood and to stock up on fresh fruits and vegetables when we were "at home" in Dubrovnik. Although the bus was efficient, it was sometimes awkward getting all of my purchases back to the boat … especially if I was stocking up for an extended trip or a boatload of guests.

Those were the times when I turned to our friends, John and Judy, on the sailing vessel, *Lindisfarne*. A number of years ago, they became the proud owners of a "Russian taxi." Originally built for use in Russia, their shiny white, 4-passenger sedan, complete with the yellow rooftop taxi sign, somehow found its way to the UK. Because it was a left-hand-drive vehicle, it was eventually sold for use on the continent. Long story short, John and Judy became the owners; and we, their lucky friends, ran many errands and discovered lots of out of the way restaurants in the "Russian taxi"… always without the meter running!

After a trip to the market, we would often plan a communal dinner. These gatherings provided a time to chat about what was new or unusual at the market that day, and they also provided an opportunity to create a special meal with ultra-fresh fish and produce. *Rizi I Bizi* was a springtime favorite.

Seafood Risotto
Serves 4 to 6

Serve this Seafood Risotto with a seasonal salad and good crunchy bread.

2 tablespoons olive oil
1 medium onion, peeled and finely chopped
2–3 cloves garlic, peeled and finely chopped
1 cup dry white wine
4 cups chicken broth
2 cups short-grained rice (preferably Arborio)
Salt and freshly ground pepper to taste
3–4 Roma tomatoes, diced
$1/2$ cup parsley, minced
$1/3$ pound small shrimp, peeled
$1/3$ pound sea scallops
$1/3$ pound firm-fleshed fish, cut in small chunks
1 teaspoon fresh lemon zest
Parsley sprigs for garnish

Heat the olive oil in a heavy, medium-sized saucepan. Add the onion and sauté over medium heat for 5 minutes. Add the garlic and continue sautéing for 2–3 additional minutes. Meanwhile, in a separate pan, combine the white wine and chicken stock and bring to a simmer.

Stir the rice, salt and pepper into the onion/garlic mixture and then add about 1 cup of hot liquid. Stir to combine the ingredients and then stir frequently until nearly all the liquid is absorbed. Stir in an additional ½ cup of hot liquid. Continue to stir and add hot liquid in ½-cup increments until the rice is about three-quarters cooked and most of the liquid has been used (about 15 minutes).

Stir in the tomatoes, parsley and seafood. Stir constantly until rice is al dente and seafood is cooked, adding more liquid as needed. Add the lemon zest at the very end. Taste and adjust the seasonings. The risotto should be thick and creamy, with enough liquid to allow it to spread gently across the plate.

Cook's Notes:
• For a tasty and attractive change, serve on a bed of steamed fresh small peas in their pod. Their crisp texture and bright color help to create a beautiful and nutritionally balanced dish.

IT WAS NOT UNTIL the 15th century that rice made its initial journey from the Far East into Italy and Croatia. Since then, this inexpensive and easily stored product has become a staple in both nations. Creamy risottos, are a favorite preparation. Made with a short-grained rice, the unique texture and flavor is achieved by first toasting the rice in oil and then gradually adding hot liquid. Finally butter and/or olive oil and/or grated cheese are gently stirred in. The result is a moist, flavorful and creamy dish. Throughout the centuries, risotto has held the place of honor in many humble homes. Today, rich and creamy risottos are signature dishes in many Croatian restaurants.

Springtime Cruising ...
Sunsets and Seafood

It was the middle of May 2002 and at long last the wet and windy storm-packed days and nights of late winter and early spring were history. In Dubrovnik, the strong winds and incessant rain had been replaced by gentle breezes, clear sunshine and the blissful anticipation of summer. The hotels and restaurants were hustling to finish construction projects, arrange new furniture and print fresh multilingual menus. The tourist season was slowly cranking up and there was an optimism and anticipation that this tourist-dependent economy would see a marked increase in visitors, perhaps even reaching the longed-for records established prior to the war.

Likewise, *Klatawa* was ready to go. She was scrubbed and buffed. Her topsides were bright white and shining, with nary a trace of that relentless red mud, the telltale gift of southerly winds and rains delivered by winter clouds formed over the Sahara desert. And her mechanical systems had been tested and approved. The Captain was anxious to return to the seas and the First Mate was looking forward to investigating new villages, discovering quiet anchorages and reaping the bounty of Croatia's springtime markets.

For the last few weeks, Bill and I had been greeting and reuniting with sailing friends as they returned from winter trips to their homelands. We had gathered together for pre-dinner wine tastings and for late-morning cappuccinos, catching up with life events and local gossip. Now shouts of "safe sailing" and "bon voyage" could be heard across the docks as "the Dubrovnik winter fleet" completed its springtime chores and began to vacate winter berths. Some cruising boats would head east to Greece and Turkey while others would take a westerly course to Italy, France or Spain. For a few, it would be the year to leave the Mediterranean and head through the Straits of Gibraltar toward the Caribbean and the United States. And for at least one yachtie, the Red Sea beckoned, with possible stops in Egypt, Saudi Arabia and Eritrea. And then there were those of us who had simply chosen to spend another year sailing Croatia's captivating Adriatic coast.

As members of the international sailing community, we've been privileged to meet and form friendships with lots of folks from the UK. The more time we spend with our British friends, the more their habits and traditions rub off ... an afternoon cuppa, a succulent joint for dinner and an almost genetic fondness and respect for the sea. Throughout time, British livelihoods have depended upon the sea: fishing, trade and naval protection of their island nation. Not surprisingly, such dependency has given rise to multiple superstitions. One such superstition, adhered to by many cruising friends, demands that a ship never begin a sea voyage on Friday. Consequently, with bright sunshine but decidedly unfavorable winds, we cast off our lines on Thursday ... waiting until Saturday was more than *Klatawa's* Captain could endure.

Six bouncy and saltwater-soaked hours later, we arrived at Polace Harbor on the northeast coast of the island of Mljet. It is always a joy to reach this destination but it is especially satisfying to enter this beautiful, well-protected anchorage after slogging through turbulent, uncomfortable seas. Once within the sheltered sanctuary of the harbor and surrounded by lush, green Mediterranean woods of pine and holly oak, the wind still howls but the water remains relatively flat.

There is a magnificent sense of safety and security that settles over the Captain and crew when the anchor is lowered and successfully set—a feeling of comfort that has been shared by sailors throughout the centuries. Throughout history, the soothing green confines of the harbors on Mljet have welcomed many visitors. To the ancient Greeks, it was known as the home of Calypso, the nymph who held Odysseus prisoner for seven years and in Roman times the apostle Paul is said to have stopped for an extended stay as he traveled throughout the Mediterranean. Today, tourists from many nations arrive by ferry and personal yacht (throughout Europe, any sailboat is known as a yacht) to enjoy the pastoral beauty and to explore the architectural ruins.

Polace Harbor is one of our favorite Croatian anchorages and this day, while at sea with the waves crashing over *Klatawa's* bow and depositing another layer of sea salt on the boat and on us, I longingly awaited our arrival. I thought about strolling the narrow, dusty stone road that meanders along the shore and connects the seasonal shops, restaurants and cafes and I could almost smell the fresh espresso brewing and taste the baker's bread, warm and fresh from the oven. And I smiled to myself in anticipation of the friendly greeting from the elderly lady, dressed in widow's black, whose toothless smile frequently welcomes us to her special island—sometimes presenting us with a single rose or geranium plucked from her nearby garden.

This afternoon my patient anticipation was quickly rewarded. Within minutes of dropping the anchor, our dinghy was in the water and with the help of our small outboard engine, we were bouncing over the small, wind-whipped waves toward land. On the way, we chatted about making a dinner reservation at one of the waterfront restaurants and maybe even indulging in the local *piéce de résistance*, fresh lobster. A Mljet specialty, freshly caught lobster is patiently grilled over an open fire and blessed with frequent bastings of locally produced, garlic-infused olive oil. Applied with a heavy-duty sprig of rosemary, oil-basted, wood-fired Mljet lobster is known for its distinctive and delicious flavor.

As we strolled the shoreline, we realized that the early spring activity on Mljet mirrored the hustle and bustle that we had left behind in Dubrovnik. Local shopkeepers and restaurateurs were getting ready for what was sure to be a very busy tourist season. New waterfront dining docks were being constructed in front of existing restaurants and new homes (most with an extra apartment for paying guests) were springing up along the hillside. As we looked around at all the activity, we were grateful that much of this island is protected from rapid growth—thanks to its designation as a national park.

But in the designated growth areas, we couldn't help but wonder how all the new construction would fare. Were these new buildings built to last as long as the 5th century Roman palace, whose crumbling remains still cling picturesquely to the harbor's edge? Or would they age gracefully like my favorite Mljet ruins, located on a scenic islet in the middle of one of Mljet's two inland lakes, the 12th century Benedictine monastery and church of St. Mary? Hopefully, some of these new buildings will stand the test of time.

※ ※ ※

It is always difficult to leave the natural beauty of Polace Harbor. However one of the best features of the Dalmatian coast is the proximity of multiple, desirable sailing destinations. The next beautiful anchorage or comfortable marina is never far away. On this trip, our next stop was the island of Korcula. In less than three hours, we were comfortably "Med moored" at the marina in Korcula town.

Here the setting was completely different. From our berth we looked out over an enchanting town of 3,000 and asked ourselves: "Is this a Hollywood set or do ancient castles, magnificent churches and towering campaniles with this strength, beauty and character really exist?" (For the uninitiated, "Med mooring" is the standard method practiced throughout the Mediterranean for securing boats and yachts to land. The front end of the boat or bow is secured away from the shore by dropping an anchor or picking up an existing mooring line. The boat then backs in toward the quay and lines are secured to the shore from the back end or stern. In this way, boats are squeezed together side-by-side, allowing the maximum number to be secured to shore. It may sound straightforward and easy but it can be tricky and frustrating—even for the most experienced captain.)

With each stop in Korcula, I became more enamored and enthralled with the beautiful architectural details that help characterize this town. Throughout the centuries, the stonemasons and sculptors worked in magnificent harmony with the architects to create street after street of striking and unique facades. It takes but a short stroll to realize that each building claims at least one magnificent feature: a delicate stone carving, a special wood door or a beautifully arched stone window.

Korcula prides itself as the birthplace of Marco Polo and although there is much debate regarding the validity of this claim, the locals have designated an old building, complete with watchtower, as his birthplace. Tourists flock there to visit and consider the life of this famous explorer and travel writer. From the tower there is an inspiring view of the surrounding land and the sea where I could silently ask myself, "Was it this view of the water that inspired young Marco Polo to set out to explore the seas and head for China in 1271?"

Korcula's ancient walls, magnificent stone buildings and cobbled streets also provided the setting for summertime performances of the Moreska sword dance. For over 400 years, this traditional Mediterranean dance was performed throughout the region. Now Korcula is the last place where this time-honored story of the White King and the Black King vying for the love and attention of the beautiful princess is still reenacted. Men and young boys dressed in traditional costumes dance, swirl and strike opponents with flashing and clashing swords. Just watching the high-energy, emotion-packed presentation is exhausting.

※ ※ ※

The scenic mile-wide channel between the Peljesac Peninsula and the island of Korcula is almost always windy. Thermally induced winds funnel through the 10-mile-long channel, sometimes blowing from the northeast and sometimes from the southwest. Like most cruising sailors, Bill and I usually prefer to have the wind at our back and as we headed north this warm and sunny day late in May, we were in luck. A gentle 10-knot southwesterly breeze blew at our stern. We set the sails, sat back and relaxed and enjoyed a lunch of fresh, crisp-crusted bread, leftover pieces of thinly sliced lemon-garlic chicken, mild sheep's cheese, sliced cucumbers and green olives. It was a memorable afternoon sail, made more pleasing by the wholesome, succulent and sugary-sweet locally grown strawberries that we savored for dessert.

Scattered along a portion of the roughly scalloped Korcula coastline is a beautiful string of smaller islands and islets whose shores are dotted with the remains of small private chapels, monasteries and churches from centuries past. In various stages of decay and/or renovation they blend seamlessly into the white limestone terrain ... forcing the eye and the mind to focus carefully in order to separate the man-made formations from those designed by nature. Always identifiable, however, are the campaniles: The tall, elegant bell towers that were surely inspired by the stately grace of the nearby Mediterranean cypress trees.

This May, thanks to the late winter and early spring rains, we experienced an exceptionally verdant landscape on the Peljesac peninsula. Large areas of green pine and tender young scrub were brightly splattered with generous expanses of dazzling yellow broom. This luxuriant and colorful display provided a sharp contrast to the steep and rocky white limestone cliffs that define much of the peninsula. As we sailed quietly along, we identified a number of vineyards scattered along the south-facing coastal areas. Over the centuries, farmers scouted out and laid claim to areas where the geography was hospitable and where the aspect to the sun was ideal for growing vines. Those early farmers made wise decisions—today, many of Croatia's outstanding wines are produced in this region.

※ ※ ※

Spread out along the edge of a small, horseshoe-shaped bay at the west end of the Peljesac peninsula is the tiny end-of-the-road village of Loviste. Nestled in a sheltered bay with relatively shallow waters, a mud bottom (ideal for holding the anchor) and a picture-postcard setting, this bay provides the perfect small boat anchorage. Here at the tip of the peninsula, gentle hills roll down to embrace the sea. But several miles inland, beyond those hills, is a range of steep and jagged mainland mountains. When the sun plays off their harsh ruggedness, their presence provides a powerful contrast to the gentle seaside setting.

Our first visit to Loviste remains deliciously memorable, and is the reason for our frequent returns. On that quiet, sunny and warm late-autumn afternoon we anchored, hopped into the dinghy and motored toward what appeared to be the center of commerce along a quiet but reasonably developed waterfront. We tied the dinghy to a concrete wall and strolled slowly along an almost deserted waterfront, past a small market that proudly displayed a few fresh fruits and vegetables along with a generous supply of fresh bread, past a small hotel with a huge front veranda lined with inviting rocking chairs and past several homes sporting signs promoting rooms for travel-weary vacationers. Our trip around the village took just a few minutes but we were able to scope out several restaurants that appeared to be eager to serve the few tourists who venture this far off the traditional sightseeing trails.

Since it was late in the day, we decided to stop for a glass of the renowned and respected local product ... red wine. Attracted by the western outlook toward the open sea and the palm-frond-shaded patio that clung to the water's edge, we decided to stop at Restaurant Brasa. The western exposure was perfect for watching the setting sun and the fleet of very small fishing boats working the waters just beyond the entrance to the harbor.

By our second glass of very nice red, we decided to remain exactly where we were for dinner. With the deep burnt-orange of the fading sunset lingering over the smooth water, we beckoned our host and informed him of our desire. He appeared happy to have us as dinner guests so we were surprised when he suggested that we might want to postpone ordering our entrée. Our quizzical looks prompted him to explain that his son was out fishing with the small fleet that we had been observing and he was hoping that he would return soon with a few squid. To keep us happy and to stave off our hunger, our host recommended that we start our meal with the octopus salad.

Just as we were lapping up the last bits of the glorious, fresh-olive-oil-laced warm octopus and potato salad, the son returned from the sea. About 13 years old, he had been fishing alone in the family's small, well-maintained classic wooden boat, equipped with a small outboard motor. We sensed victory in the spirited way he handled the boat. And as he closed in on the dock, we quickly caught his energized smile of success. He swiftly tied the boat to the dock and proudly handed over four fresh squid to his dad. Within minutes, those squid were cleaned, brushed with olive oil, dusted with sea salt and grilled. Placed on our plates with a sprig of rosemary, drizzled with a bit more olive oil and served with a wedge of lemon, they were the tastiest, most tender squid—ever.

fishing nets hanging out to dry

Seafood

While cruising the Adriatic Coast of Croatia and adjacent islands, we were repeatedly lured ashore by the rich, belly-rumbling scent of wood-smoke infused with the aromas of red meat or fresh seafood cooking on a restaurant's open-fire grill. These often rustic, sometimes jerry-rigged grills, complete with brick and/or local stone chimneys, were at times located along the shore—outside and in the open and right in the pedestrian path. Other times, this hot spot of production was tucked away inside a tiny kitchen—well hidden from passersby and diners. Regardless of the grill's size, shape or location, experience taught us that the chefs working these grills were masters of their trade—knowing when to add more fuel to the fire, when to shift the coals and when to serve up the perfectly prepared entrée.

In those small, often seasonal restaurants, menus were rarely provided. Instead, we were likely to be greeted by our host who simply asked "meat or seafood?" If we responded "seafood," a platter of whole, variously-sized and shaped fresh fish was presented for our inspection. It was up to us to make our selection while we praised the restaurant owner for the fine array of fresh fish that he had made available. (We could, as a rule, assume that our host had also been the fisherman responsible for this catch.) Along this coast, the fish are relatively small and are usually served whole. Most of the varieties have names that we cannot pronounce, let alone remember.

The entrée question was then followed by two simple beverage questions: "Red or white?" for the wine and "Gas or no gas?" for the water. Although beer was almost always available, and spirits were occasionally offered, it was assumed that wine would be consumed with the meal. The wine was almost always a local bulk wine, frequently produced in the owner's own cellar.

In coastal regions, grilled seafood is considered the *piéce de résistance*. Preparations may vary slightly, but the universal approach is to simply grill the fish over glowing coals created from local hardwoods, drizzle with olive oil and serve. It doesn't get much better. 🮐

Seafood
SEAFOOD

Grilled Fish
Serves 4

In Croatia, "grilled fish" usually implies that an entire fish will be grilled and then presented to the diner(s) whole. Sometimes one fish will be large enough to serve two or more and sometimes two or more fish are required for a single serving. In America, it is often difficult to find fresh, whole fish. Never mind ... we have found that using fresh fillets provides a delicious alternative, and they are easier to eat!
Hint: Use a fish or vegetable grate (a porcelain or enamel-coated metal platter with lots of small holes designed to fit on the grill) when grilling fish fillets.

> **4 (6-ounce) fresh fish filets (halibut, salmon, sea bass, tuna)**
> **Sea salt**
> **Freshly ground pepper**
> **1 or 2 large rosemary stems (optional)**
> **Extra-virgin olive oil**
> **1 lemon, halved**

Preheat the barbecue and oil your seafood or vegetable grate. Wash the fish fillets and pat dry. Season lightly with salt and pepper. Using the rosemary stems, brush the fillets thoroughly with olive oil. Place the fillets on the preheated grill. While grilling, continue to use the rosemary sprigs to brush on olive oil. When the fish is seared and is beginning to cook through, about 3–5 minutes, carefully flip the fillets and cook until browned on the other side. The fish should break into firm flakes when pressed with a finger.

Remove the fish from the grill and squeeze fresh lemon juice over each piece and drizzle with extra-virgin olive oil. Sprinkle lightly with sea salt and serve accompanied by the garlic olive oil.

> ### ACCOMPANIMENT: GARLIC OLIVE OIL
> **1/2 cup extra-virgin olive oil**
> **1/4 cup garlic, chopped**
> **1/4 cup parsley, chopped**

Mix together olive oil, garlic and parsley. The sauce may be made several hours in advance and kept refrigerated for a week or longer. Serve with grilled fish.

Cook's Notes:

• If you prefer, the fish can be pan-seared.

• If large fresh rosemary sprigs are not available, gently rub each piece of fish with a few rosemary needles and use a basting brush to apply the olive oil.

• Do not put garlic on the fish while it is grilling as it could burn and ruin the flavor of the fish.

• If using fish that has been frozen, allow to marinate at room temperature for 30 minutes to an hour in a mixture of olive oil, garlic, rosemary, salt and pepper. Be sure that no pieces of garlic or rosemary cling to the fish when it is placed on the grill.

OLIVE OIL, used by the ancients for fuel as well as for medicinal, cosmetic and culinary purposes, is celebrated today for its nutritional virtues. It is known to be easily digested, act as an antioxident, help to assimilate vitamins A, D and K, lower bad cholesterol and raise good cholesterol.

Some of the best olive oil in the world is produced in Croatia, where there are trees that date back more than 17 centuries. Today, Croatian growers focus on traditional methods—handpicking the fruit and cold-pressing the harvest in order to preserve the distinctly Croatian flavors and qualities.

Grilled Squid

Be sure to use only the freshest and best ingredients for this quick and simple preparation. Savor the flavors of the Mediterranean Sea with the squid and the bounty of the Mediterranean land with the olive oil.

Fresh squid, cleaned
Extra-virgin olive oil
Minced garlic (optional)
Fresh lemon juice
Sea salt to taste
Freshly ground pepper

Depending on the size, allow 2–3 squid per person. Brush the cleaned squid with olive oil and grill for about 3 minutes per side. Sprinkle with minced garlic and freshly squeezed lemon juice. Drizzle with more olive oil and top with sea salt and freshly ground pepper and serve.

Cook's Notes:

• To clean squid, wash and pull the head away from the body. The innards should come away as well. Cut the edible tentacles from the head. Remove and discard the beak. Pull out the transparent backbone and remove any excess material from the body. Rinse under cold water and peel away the outside skin.

WE WILL ALWAYS REMEMBER the warm September evening when we dined at a small restaurant on the western tip of the Pelješac peninsula. Under an awning of twisted grape vines, we began our meal with an extraordinary octopus salad that was served warm and was made with diced new potatoes, fresh garlic, parsley and a fruity olive oil. Between the delicious octopus salad and the succulent squid, we knew we had found heaven. ▨

Stuffed Squid
Serves 4

Grilling squid is the quickest and easiest method to prepare this member of the cephalopod family, but I can also recommend preparing this inexpensive shellfish with a tasty stuffing. Sometimes the filling is as simple as the chopped tentacles, garlic, herbs and olive oil. Other fillings can be more complex. This recipe is adapted from several different versions that we enjoyed throughout our Adriatic travels.

1/4 cup olive oil, divided

4 cloves garlic, minced

1/2 cup green onion (mostly the white section), thinly sliced

1 1/2 pounds squid, cleaned and washed with tentacles removed and chopped fine

1 cup day-old bread crumbs

1/4 cup parsley, chopped

Salt and freshly ground pepper to taste

1 egg, beaten

1 cup diced tomatoes, canned or fresh

1 cup white wine

Chopped parsley for garnish

In a small sauté pan, sauté the garlic and onion over medium heat in 1 tablespoon of oil until transparent, about 5–7 minutes. Add the tentacles and stir for about 2 minutes. Add the breadcrumbs, parsley, salt and pepper and stir over medium heat for about 2 minutes. Allow to cool. Stir in the beaten egg and stuff the filling into the squid (see below). Secure the end with toothpicks.

Pour the remaining olive oil into a large sauté pan and heat the oil over medium-high heat. Add the squid. Top with the tomatoes and pour the wine over all. Cover and braise for about 5–10 minutes. Remove the cover, turn the squid and cook for an additional 5–10 minutes, just until the squid are tender. Remove the squid to a warm platter and tent with aluminum foil to keep warm. Over high heat, reduce the sauce until thickened and pour over the squid. Garnish with chopped parsley and serve.

Cook's Notes:

- To clean squid, wash and pull the head away from the body. The innards should come away as well. Cut the edible tentacles from the head. Remove and discard the beak. Pull out the transparent backbone and remove any excess material from the body. Rinse under cold water and peel away the outside skin.

- To stuff the squid, cut off the bottom end of a plastic water bottle and discard. Fill the remaining bottle with enough stuffing for 1 squid. Slip the bottle opening and neck into the squid and using the handle end of a wooden spoon, push the filling into the squid.

- Squid must be cooked either quickly at a high heat or simmered slowly on a low heat. Otherwise, the flesh will be tough.

Octopus Salad
Serves 4 to 6

Along the Adriatic coast, octopus salad appears on nearly every restaurant menu. Its simple, fresh flavor makes octopus one of the finest and most favored gifts from the sea. If octopus is not available, squid makes a tasty substitute. Just quickly sauté 1½ pounds of squid rings and tentacles in 2 tablespoons of olive oil until just tender, about 2–3 minutes, and proceed with recipe.

> **2 pounds octopus, cleaned**
> **2 wine corks**
> **2 bay leaves**
> **1/4 cup red wine vinegar**
> **1/2 cup extra-virgin olive oil**
> **2 cloves garlic, finely minced**
> **Salt and freshly ground pepper to taste**
> **2/3 cup green onions (mostly white part), thinly sliced**
> **1/4 cup parsley, chopped**

Place the octopus, wine corks and bay leaves in a large pot and cover with water. Bring to a boil and reduce heat. Simmer for 25–35 minutes or until just tender. Remove the octopus from the liquid and allow to cool.

If desired, remove the suction cups and skin by rubbing and rinsing away. Cut the tentacles into small pieces. Squeeze out the sharp core from the head and then cut the head into similar sized pieces. In a medium bowl, whisk together the vinegar, olive oil, garlic, salt and pepper. Add the octopus, onion, and parsley and toss together. Chill until ready to serve. Remove the octopus salad from the refrigerator a half hour before serving. The flavors are enhanced if served at a cool rather than a cold temperature.

Serve with thinly sliced baguettes or on a bed of lettuce leaves.

Variation #1 Octopus Salad with Diced Cucumber and Tomatoes
Add:

1/2 cup peeled and seeded cucumber, finely diced

1/2 cup tomato, finely diced

This combination adds a wonderful contrast of flavor and texture and will also help to increase the yield.

Variation #2 Octopus Salad with New Potatoes
Add:

1/2 pound steamed and peeled new potatoes, diced in 1/2 inch cubes.

This version is best served warm.

I LEARNED A LOT about octopus in the years we spent in the Mediterranean: how to catch it, how to cook it and how to enjoy it. Traditions and recipes may vary from region to region, but the custom of throwing a couple of corks into the cooking pot is practiced in every country we visited. There appears to be no scientific reason for the success of this technique, but it does provide wonderful results—an octopus that has been simmered with a few corks is sure to be more tender. In Croatia I learned another trick—cooking octopus does not require long hours of slow simmering; in fact, a more moist and tender product results from a shorter cooking time.

Dalmatian *Brudet*
Serves 4

In Croatia, a brudet usually refers to a one-pot dish. A seafood brudet is one that includes a combination of various kinds of seafood that is made distinctive by the measured use of vinegar. There are probably as many recipes for this dish as there are residents of the beautiful walled city of Dubrovnik.

This dish is not intended to resemble a soup but is meant to be eaten with a fork. Use a good crusty bread to sop up the luscious broth.

> 2 pounds mixed seafood (salmon, tuna, sea bass, halibut, snapper,
>   cod, sole, prawns, calamari, scallops, etc.)
> 3 tablespoons olive oil
> 1 large onion, finely chopped
> 5 cloves garlic, minced
> 1/4 cup parsley, chopped
> 1 teaspoon thyme
> Pinch of cayenne pepper
> 1 (28-ounce) can diced tomatoes
> 3 tablespoons red wine vinegar
> 1 cup red or white wine
> 1 1/2 teaspoons sugar
> Salt and freshly ground pepper to taste
> Chopped parsley for garnish

Remove all skin and bones from the seafood and cut into 1-inch chunks. If using prawns, remove head and shells. If using calamari, clean and cut the body into rings. Rinse all seafood and pat dry. Refrigerate until ready to use, keeping prawns, scallops and/or calamari separate.

In a large, wide sauté pan over medium heat, sauté the onion in the olive oil until the onion is very soft and translucent, about 15 minutes. Add the garlic and stir for an additional 2 minutes. Stir in the 1/4 cup parsley, thyme, cayenne pepper, tomatoes, red wine vinegar, wine, sugar, salt and pepper and simmer for another 20 minutes. Gently add the fish, stirring to coat each piece with the tomato sauce. Simmer gently, stirring occasionally, for 8–10 minutes or until fish is just beginning to appear cooked. Toss in prawns, scallops and/or calamari (if using) and continue to simmer until fish is tender and flaky and prawns, scallops and/or calamari are just cooked.

Spoon the brudet into wide bowls or deep-rimmed plates and sprinkle with fresh chopped parsley. Serve with polenta or crusty country bread.

Cook's Notes:

• For best flavor, use at least five varieties of seafood.

• This dish can be doubled, making it the perfect entrée for a dinner party. The tomato sauce can be made the day before and kept refrigerated. The seafood can be cleaned and cut up early in the day of the party, covered and refrigerated. When ready to serve, re-heat the sauce and cook the seafood. Just be sure to use a large, open and wide sauté pan—so the fish can cook quickly.

Marko's Poached Seafood
Serves 4

This is my interpretation of a delicious poached seafood dish that we have enjoyed several times at restaurant Kod Marko's on the Island of Sipan, where the owner/chef has one very firm credo: use only the freshest and the best ingredients.

4 medium new potatoes, peeled and sliced in ½-inch slices
1 medium onion, quartered and thinly sliced
1½ pounds firm fleshed seafood (halibut, sea bass, snapper), cut into large chunks
3–4 Roma tomatoes, sliced
8–10 sprigs fresh parsley
¼ cup extra-virgin olive oil
Sea salt
Freshly ground pepper
½ cup dry, white wine

In a 10-inch sauté pan equipped with a firm-fitting lid, layer the potatoes, onion, seafood, tomatoes and parsley. Drizzle with olive oil and sprinkle with salt and pepper. Pour in the wine and about 1 cup of water or just enough to have about ½ inch of liquid in the bottom. Cover and place over very high heat for 10–12 minutes. The fish should flake with a fork when the potatoes are tender. Bring the pan to the table and ladle the chunky soup and broth into large soup bowls. Serve with crusty bread to mop up the juices.

TUCKED ALONG THE WESTERN shore of the long, narrow and scenic bay known as Sipanski Luka on the Island of Sipan is a small, traditional, white limestone building complete with red tile roof, simple brown shutters and a small, inviting terrace. Built right at the edge of the sea, it appears to be the perfect picture-postcard Croatian home … especially during the summer, when a magnificent walled garden is filled with aromatic carnations of every possible hue and color.

However, the large *Kod Marko* sign on the retaining wall reveals the true identity of this attractive building. *Kod* is a Croatian word that, loosely translated, means "at our place" and Marko is the talented chef in residence. We have had many pleasurable visits to *Kod Marko* and have been consistently delighted with what Marko produces for our pleasure and enjoyment.

Salmon with Rosemary Port Sauce
Serves 4

Atlantic salmon is popular in Croatia and is often found on restaurant menus that feature Continental cuisine. This dish reflects the Continental influence and incorporates some of Croatia's best flavors.

4 (6-ounce) salmon fillets, preferably line-caught Pacific salmon
3 tablespoons flour
Salt and freshly ground pepper to taste
2 tablespoons olive oil
2 tablespoons butter, divided
2 teaspoons lemon peel, grated
½ cup port
5 sprigs of rosemary, divided
1 tablespoon balsamic vinegar

On a sheet of waxed paper, combine the flour, salt and pepper. Lightly dredge the salmon fillets in the flour and set aside.

In a 12-inch fry pan over medium high heat, stir together the olive oil and one tablespoon of butter. Add the salmon fillets and sauté, turning once, until they are just cooked, about 3–4 minutes per side. The fillets should be firm to the touch and flake easily with a fork.

Remove the salmon from the pan and place on a warm plate. Tent with foil to keep warm. Reduce the heat to medium and add the remaining tablespoon of butter, lemon peel, port and 1 sprig of rosemary to the pan. Whisk ingredients together to combine. Bring to a boil and add the balsamic vinegar. Continue to whisk until all the ingredients are well combined. Remove the sprig of rosemary and pour the sauce over the fillets. Garnish with additional sprigs of rosemary, if desired and serve.

Cook's notes:
- The kitchen rasp is one of my favorite kitchen gadgets. Originally a carpenter's tool, it has been refined for use in the kitchen. It is so easy to hold and to use … yielding lemon zest in a flash. It's also great for grating Parmesan cheese, nutmeg and fresh ginger.

THROUGHOUT THE CENTURIES, Croatians have had a rich connection to the sea. Many men went to sea to procure a simple catch to feed their families; many also fished commercially, providing seafood for those who otherwise had no access to that delicacy. Some worked to create the shipbuilding industry that still remains an important part of Croatia's manufacturing economy. Others went to sea as merchant seamen, engineers and captains, traveling the world and bringing back new perspectives, new ideas and new culinary experiences.

Seafood Skewers
Serves 4

Skewering is a wonderful way to use small quantities of a variety of fish. It is an ideal entrée to plan when shopping in the late afternoon just before a small fish market closes and the quantities of each variety of fish are likely to be limited. Although the garlic sauce is totally optional, we found this to be a special favorite amongst our garlic-loving cruising friends.

8 10-inch wooden skewers

1^1/$_2$–2 pounds firm fish fillets (halibut, sea bass, tuna, salmon, sea scallops, prawns)

24 bay leaves

Sea salt

^{3}/$_4$ cup extra-virgin olive oil

^{1}/$_4$ fresh lemon juice

8–10 cloves garlic, chopped

^{1}/$_4$ cup parsley, chopped

Soak the wooden skewers in warm water for 10 minutes. Cut the fish into 24 equal-size cubes (about 1–1½ inch square) and thread the cubes alternately with the bay leaves, onto the skewers. Salt the fish on all sides. Whisk together ^{1}/$_4$ cup olive oil and the lemon juice and brush over the skewered fish. Grill over hot coals until fish is cooked, rotating and brushing as necessary.

Meanwhile, combine the remaining olive oil, garlic and parsley. Pass the garlic olive oil with the fish skewers.

THE TERM MEDITERRANEAN DIET is frequently used to describe a nutritional model that reflects the traditional dietary patterns of some countries where diets focus on fruit, vegetables, bread, olive oil, seafood and red wine. It is low in saturated fat and high in monounsaturated fat and dietary fiber.

First publicized in 1945, but not gaining recognition until the 1990s, the diet is based on what seems to be a paradox. Mediterranean residents consume relatively high amounts of fat, but they have far lower rates of cardiovscular disease when compared to the population of other countries that consume similar levels of fat.

One of the main explanations for this may be the large amount of olive oil consumed by the Mediterranean people as compared to the large amount of animal fats typically found in the American diet. The olive oil lowers the cholesterol, blood sugar levels and blood pressure. Also, more red wine is consumed. The flavonoids and antioxident properties of red wine are said to have positive health-related attributes. In addition to these dietary factors, genetics, lifestyle and environment may also play a part.

Prawns (or Mussels) *Buzara*
Serves 4 (as a main course)

A buzara is a traditional Croatian dish made with mussels or prawns that have been cooked in a flavorful sauce of garlic, olive oil, parsley and breadcrumbs. The rules for creating a buzara are straightforward: a recipe may be prepared with or without tomatoes but it never includes onions. In order to create a more flavorful dish, the prawns are typically cooked in their shells. However, if you prefer a tidier meal, don't hesitate to remove the heads and shells before cooking.

> 2 pounds raw medium prawns
> 1/4 cup olive oil
> 4 cloves garlic, minced
> 2 tablespoons breadcrumbs
> 2 tomatoes, chopped (optional)
> 2 tablespoons parsley, chopped
> 2 tablespoons lemon juice
> 1 cup dry white wine
> Salt and freshly ground pepper to taste

Rinse the prawns under cold water and pat dry. In a large sauté pan, sauté the garlic in the olive oil over medium heat until softened, about 3-4 minutes. Add the breadcrumbs, tomato (if desired), parsley, lemon juice and wine. Season with salt and pepper and simmer for 5 minutes. Add the prawns and cook for about 4 minutes on high heat. Cover and simmer over reduced heat for 5-10 minutes, shaking the pan occasionally. Serve with crusty country bread.

Cook's Notes:
• A *buzara* can also be made with mussels. Allow 3/4–1 pound of mussels per person. Clean and remove the beards from all the mussels and discard any with broken shells before proceeding with the above recipe.

WE FIRST HEARD THE TERM *buzara* within an hour of our arrival in Croatia. Once all the customs formalities were cleared, our very hospitable customs agent shifted gears from being a process-oriented government official to a full-fledged chamber of commerce representative.

Using the charts on the wall in the Customs Office, he showed us some of his frequent anchorages, family villages and preferred restaurant locations. I of course, began to query him about his favorite foods and his family's gastronomic traditions. Topping his list of both family and personal favorites were "seafood *buzaras*"—flavorful dishes that were quick to prepare with a secret ingredient called breadcrumbs—the breadcrumbs pull together all the flavors. ▨

A Visit to the ...
Washing Machine

Dramatic, sheer-cliffed limestone mountains plunge into the azure-blue sea while random peaks erupt from glistening, crystal-clear waters to create a seemingly endless string of islands and bulging peninsulas. It is hard to envision a more magnificent coastline. Add an abundance of secluded beaches, numerous Roman ruins, medieval walled cities, succulent fresh seafood, tempting cakes and pastries, crusty breads, and some of the sweetest figs in the world and you have a perfect holiday destination. This is Dalmatia, a ribbon of land that stretches along the Adriatic coast for over 200 miles—from the medieval city of Zadar in the north to the large and beautiful Bay of Kotor (now a part of Montenegro) in the south.

But as the ribbon of land widens and reaches inland, a harsh contrast begins to emerge. The land becomes mostly arid and sparsely populated. A visit to this territory is both challenging and depressing. The poorly paved roads are pock-marked with deceptively deep potholes that severely slow the cautious drivers or provide a back-wrenching wake-up call to more aggressive ones. And there is little to say about the scenery. Dark and densely wooded mountains, vast rock-strewn valleys and barren windswept plateaus provide little inspiration for the sightseer.

Within this inland region, there are almost no picturesque towns or villages to lure the visitor ... no opportunities to stop and explore an ancient church, admire a colorful fresco or purchase a home-crafted souvenir. For the most part, there are just a few widely scattered walled settlements of 15 to 20 small, humble and dilapidated homes. The occasional sagging clothesline strung with bits of clothing or a rare gathering of children playing in a hard and dusty clay front yard provide the only hints that life exists behind the bleak and crumbling walls. There are few shops, no restaurants, no gas stations. Entrepreneurial activity is limited to an infrequent roadside stand offering a few jars of locally produced honey, a small round or two of cheese and a couple of brown sacks filled with potatoes. This too is Dalmatia. Clearly, Dalmatia encompasses two different worlds.

※ ※ ※

But there are reasons to head inland ... there are one or two havens of moderate prosperity in the midst of this bleak and inhospitable environment: there is an extraordinary national park and the town of Drniš and the region surrounding it produce some of the best air-cured hams in the world. Blessed with topographic conditions that maximize the natural curing and drying power of the strong and cold northeast wind known as the *bora*, combined with perfect moisture levels and temperatures, Drniš competes with Istria for the production of *pršut*, a Croatian national delicacy. And the Krka National Park is a nature-lover's dream.

Like many of the visitors who flock to Dalmatia for their sun-drenched seaside holidays, we discovered a unique place along the northern Dalmatian coast, where it is possible to travel by water to get a peek at the rugged inland geography. We entered the picturesque Krka River at the coastal town of Šibenik and enjoyed a short and fascinating eight-mile trip upstream to the historic town of Skradin and the entrance to the Krka National Park, notorious for the Krka waterfalls

This area is known as *karst* country, a region where the hills and mountains are composed of white, highly porous limestone. Throughout the ages, the Krka River carved a path through the rock and left behind a deep, rugged and dramatic canyon in some areas and a gently rolling verdant countryside in others. During our leisurely motor upstream, we observed the rapidly expanding commercial development along the banks of the river. Fish farms, oyster and mussel farms, restaurants and even a winery or two lined the river's edge.

Since private boats are prohibited to travel on the river beyond the town of Skradin, we moored *Klatawa* at the ACI Marina and began our visit to Krka National Park. Our experiences on this very special day were captured in my journal:

Some days are so interesting, fun and stimulating that you want to remember every single minute. Today was one of those days.

In the company of good friends Rob and Liz off the British sailing yacht Autumn Dream, *we began the day with a 20-minute taxi-boat ride up the Krka River to the entrance of the Krka National Park, where the well-touted Krka waterfalls are located. Unlike most of the spectacular and dramatic waterfalls around the world that are celebrated for their height, the Krka waterfalls are renown for the large number of falls that appear to bubble up out of limestone cliffs and course rapidly through thick tropical vegetation.*

Today, for the four of us, it was more than the waterfall activity that captured our attention. The consistently moist botanical environment of the park encourages the growth of a huge variety of plants, trees and animals. According to our guidebook, there are 18 different kinds of bats and 222 species of birds residing in this limited area. And, at this time of the year, the air is musky and earthy ... rich with the aroma of numerous fig trees loaded with ripe and overripe fruit.

Once we had explored the lower falls, we had to decide if we should take the four-hour river trip to the upper falls. Reviews from friends had been mixed, but we had the afternoon stretching ahead of us with no other plans. We decided to make the trip. In retrospect, we definitely made the right decision.

Our timing was perfect. A small, wooden tour boat was just about ready to depart from the dock. The four of us piled in and with 10 passengers on board, this little boat rode very low in the water. We proceeded up the river and quickly realized that our "captain" was an outstanding navigator and tour guide. Several times, he maneuvered us close to the tall, lush water grasses that defined the shoreline and positioned the boat right at the foot of a powerful water-

fall—dousing us with a welcome and wonderfully cooling spray. And at various points along our journey, he stopped the boat and had us reach overboard to feel the water. The water temperature in these select locations was cooler and the flow was different. These sites were "upswellings"—places in the riverbed where a smaller, cold underground stream emerged and then merged with the main river.

Our first land stop was the Franciscan monastery on the small island of Visovac. By now, it was late morning and the day was growing hotter and hotter and more and more humid. As we arrived at the small visitors' dock, we observed five friars gathered in the limited shade of the island's boathouse. Despite the heat, they each wore their signature full-length brown wool robes. I could not help wishing on their behalf that the church would provide them with lighter-weight "summer uniforms."

Nestled into a small forest of elegant cypress trees and dating back to the early 15th century—with expansion and restoration through the 18th century—this large, serene and well-maintained monastery boasted a unique combination of Byzantine and Mediterranean architecture. An exceedingly beautiful, peaceful and placid place, it invited the heart and soul to stop and linger. I paused to think about how wonderful it would be to spend three or four days in quiet "retreat." Although that may be possible, I did not have the opportunity to inquire.

Back on the boat, we continued to wend our way up the river to our second and last stop—the upper falls. The captain tied his vessel to the wooden dock and the four of us stepped up and out onto land. Following the official park signs, we immediately began our hike up the long set of stairs that would take us to the upper falls. We had just begun our climb when a very confident and professional-appearing woman halted and informed us in excellent English that the falls were not "falling." She introduced herself as Maria and told us that since it was late summer, the water levels were extremely low. Instead, she suggested that we visit her "restaurant" located in the nearby old mill building. We joked amongst ourselves that there was probably lots of activity at the falls but this was her way of attracting business. Never mind, on this hot and steamy day, a cold drink and a leisurely lunch under the brightly colored picnic umbrellas held a lot of appeal. As we wandered along the path toward the mill, Maria also mentioned that it might also be possible for us to take a pre-lunch dip in the "washing machine."

But first she suggested that we go inside the old, gray-stone mill building and decide on our lunch: Dalmatian pršut, homemade cheese and homemade village bread. A liter of white wine and some deliciously cold water completed our selection. (In fact, the menu was very limited. These were our only choices—except for a bottle or two of soft drink.)

Once our choices were made, we left the cool shade of the old mill building—intriguing with its dirt floor, tilting walls, sinking roof and extraordinary collection of antique kitchen implements, wine making equipment, farm tools and numerous antique three-legged stools—and headed out to the "washing machine."

Located at the edge of a rapid-moving cold-water stream, the "washing machine" was a large, open, and firmly anchored wooden tub. Our hostess told us that this "machine," resembling an over-sized wine cask, has been in use for centuries: to cleanse wool, make felt and to do the family laundry. Today, on a steamy-hot late August afternoon, we were ever so grateful to cleanse and cool ourselves.

Bill went first, and then one at a time, we took five-minute turns lowering our fully clothed bodies into the turbulent waters. We leaned back slightly, into the rushing waters, and luxuriated in the cool, powerful liquid flow. By the time we climbed out, we felt refreshed and indulged ... our body temperatures had dropped, our skin had been washed and it was as though we had each indulged in a personal, professional massage.

When we emerged from our dip, we found our lunch ready and waiting on a vine-shaded trestle table: a large round of cheese, a chunk of pršut, a round loaf of crusty and chewy home-made bread and a small bowl of fresh figs. We satisfied our thirst with a liter of golden "vino locale" and numerous jugs of refreshing cold water. It was a perfect lunch on what had become a perfect day.

Just as we were finishing our lunch, our hostess returned with a selection of digestifs—strong in flavor and, I am sure, high in alcohol. Liz and I sipped cautiously while Bill and Rob pleasurably downed theirs. In the welcoming shade of the old vines, the four of us sat around, struggling to keep our eyes open. After a glass (or two) of wine, a sip of grappa, hot and humid air and a vigorous dip in the washing machine, we were all ready for an afternoon siesta. Just in time, Maria, our energetic hostess reappeared and asked if we wished to buy a piece of pršut or cheese. Both Liz and I quickly said "da." It would be great to take some local pršut and cheese back to our boats.

Returning to the old mill building to make our selections, Maria explained that her mother had made the cheese and cured the ham and that her father had made both the wine and the grappa. She went on to tell us about her personal life. She had grown up in a tiny nearby village but she now lived with her husband and children in Split, Croatia's second largest city. Just today, she had returned for a weeklong visit to help her parents redevelop their tourist trade. This region was severely damaged during the war and the family was hoping to rebuild its small business.

We chatted about making and curing pršut, about the importance of dry winter winds for curing and the fact that the town of Drniš is blessed with the ideal climatic conditions. With the mention of Drniš, Maria excused herself and went into the mill house to retrieve a local map. She pointed out that we were now just a few miles from Drniš and consequently they were *also blessed with the ideal climatic conditions for making this delicacy.*

Once inside the old millhouse, Liz and I selected a nine-inch round of cheese to share and Maria cut and wrapped a kilo-sized piece of pršut. *Just as we were about to say farewell, Papa appeared with a tray filled with fresh glasses and a jug of dark liquid. With a jovial smile and halting English, he offered to serve us yet another* digestif. *This time, it was a sweet and intensely flavorful cherry brandy. (I can't help but wonder if the offer of another sip is a bit of a ploy ... as he offers up another toast to his guests, he also indulges in another small drink for himself).*

After fond farewells and repeated thank yous, we returned to the tiny tour boat and enjoyed a relaxed trip down river—returning to the lower falls and boarding a second boat for our return to the marina.

Krka Falls

Poultry and Meats

In the past, poultry and meat dishes were served only on festive occasions. On Christmas and/or New Years, *sarma* (stuffed cabbage) was likely to appear on the table and on Easter you might have been treated to both a smoked ham and a roast lamb. Wedding feasts were special celebrations where village tradition determined the menu ... a suckling pig roasted on a spit or pork, lamb or chicken roasted "under the bell" or *peka*.

The *peka* is a dome shaped lid made of metal or pottery and designed to cover a round roasting pan. Together, when placed in an open-fire fireplace and covered with burning embers, the pan and *peka* create an oven-like chamber. This cooking technique, dates back nearly 3,000 years, and remains a favorite for special occasions ... holidays, weddings or special events. Lucky travelers can sometimes find *peka* meals featured on *konoba* (small, often family-owned restaurants) menus.

Historically, waterfowl were raised along the riverbanks while chickens roamed the yard ... laying eggs while being fattened with table scraps. And it was a sure sign that a holiday was approaching when the lady of the house began a special feeding program for the ducks and geese. Weeks in advance the geese and ducks were force-fed with naturally grown corn. This special care and treatment produced a particularly fat liver (in French known as *foie gras*), coveted for its silky-smooth, rich and buttery flavor. The soft feathers of these water birds were also treasured ... as they were used in eiderdown coverlets, pillows and sometimes even sold in the lucrative feather market.

Although the tradition of keeping ducks and geese along the river is waning, there are still a few river-front families who continue to raise them. While in Dubrovnik, my regular morning walk would take me past one such family and their ever-changing family of black and white ducks. Although I never observed any force-feeding, I was always aware when a major holiday or celebration had recently occurred.

Today chicken dishes are no longer a luxury; instead they're served frequently because they are often quick and easy to prepare. However, the traditional Croatian seasonings continue to remain favorites ... the zest or juice of a brightly flavored lemon, a handful of dried fruit, a dash of paprika, bay leaves, rosemary and/or capers. With so many seasoning choices, it is no wonder that there are so many flavorsome recipes. ▨

Poultry & Meats
POULTRY & MEATS

POULTRY

MEAT

Chicken Breasts with Tarragon-Apricot Cream Sauce
Serves 4

This recipe incorporates many traditional Croatian flavors … lemon juice, dried fruit and locally grown herbs. It is simple enough to prepare for a hasty weeknight meal yet elegant enough to serve to your most discriminating guests.

1/2 cup dried apricots, chopped fine
1/3 cup boiling water
4 boneless, skinless chicken breasts
Salt and freshly ground pepper to taste
3 tablespoons olive oil
3 cloves garlic, minced
3 tablespoons fresh lemon juice
1 1/2 teaspoons honey
1/2 cup port
3/4 cup heavy cream
1 teaspoon tarragon

Pour the boiling water over the apricots. Set aside to allow the fruit to plump.

Gently pound the chicken breasts to a uniform thickness and salt and pepper them to taste. Heat the olive oil in a large sauté pan over high heat and quickly brown the chicken breasts on both sides, about 3 minutes per side. Remove the breasts from the pan and place on a plate. Reduce the heat to medium and stir in the garlic. Stir in the lemon juice, honey, port and cream. Scrape up any bits that remain in the pan.

Add the tarragon and the apricots, including any remaining soaking liquid. Simmer the sauce slowly to blend flavors and to allow the sauce to thicken. Return the chicken breasts to the pan and simmer slowly until the chicken breasts are cooked through, about 8–10 minutes. Remove the breasts from the pan and place on serving dishes. Top with the apricot cream sauce and serve with pasta, rice, noodles or parsleyed potatoes.

Cook's Notes:

• When pounding chicken breasts to create a uniform thickness, place the breasts between 2 pieces of plastic wrap. This reduces spattering and minimizes the risk of tearing the meat.

• Lightly score the skin side of a boneless, skinless chicken breast before pounding. This "relaxes" the flesh and reduces the amount of pounding required to produce a tender product.

• I have also made this dish with orange, pear and plum flavored liqueurs, in place of the port. They all yielded wonderful results. The flavors are subtle, slightly different and each is uniquely flavorful.

THE ORIGINAL RECIPE for this dish called for *Vegeta*, a Croatian mixed-herb seasoned salt that is found in virtually every Croatian kitchen. This special seasoning is said to have evolved from the peasant tradition of growing, picking and drying seasonings such as parsley, celery, cayenne pepper, onion, bay leaves and rosemary and blending them together with salt. Since it is a trademarked product that is difficult to find in America, I have eliminated its use; but I must admit that there are times when I miss its unique, complex flavor. ▨

Chicken *Brodetto*
Serves 4 to 6

Similar to the all-time Italian favorite, Chicken Cacciatore, this Croatian dish earns its signature flavor from the unique addition of rosemary and lemon.

1 chicken (2^1/2 to 3^1/2 pounds),
   cut into individual portions (leg, thigh, wing, half breast)
Salt and freshly ground pepper to taste
3 tablespoons olive oil
1 large onion, diced
3 cloves garlic, minced
^{1}/2 cup white or red wine
1 (28–ounce) can diced tomatoes
2 tablespoons chopped parsley
2 bay leaves
2 sprigs rosemary
^{1}/2 lemon, thinly sliced

Wash, pat dry and season the chicken with the salt and pepper. Heat the oil in a large skillet over high heat and brown the chicken on both sides, about 3–4 minutes per side. Remove the chicken from the pan, pour off excess fat and reduce the heat to medium. Stir in the onion and garlic and sauté until the onion begins to turn translucent, about 5–6 minutes.

Return the chicken to the pan and add the wine, tomatoes, parsley, bay leaves, rosemary and lemon slices. Simmer over medium low heat for 30–40 minutes or until chicken is cooked through and tender. Taste, correct seasonings and serve with polenta or spaghetti.

THE ELAFIT ISLANDS are a chain of islands just off the coast from Dubrovnik. The Island of Sipan is the largest in the group; and the deep bay known as Luka Sipanska on the Northwest side of the island, is one of our favorite anchorages. In a tiny village at the head of the bay, the ancient farmhouses scattered along the main island road make it the perfect place for a therapeutic walk anytime of the year.

In the fall of 2000, our son, Douglas, daughter-in-law, Leslie, and then two-year-old grandson, Dawson, joined us aboard *Klatawa* for several weeks. During their visit, Sipan was a frequent destination as it offered a great protected bay in which to anchor and take extended rides in the dinghy. Moreover the old buildings, beautiful land, pleasant farmers and shopkeepers provided our family with all the wonderful attributes that made our stay in Croatia so enjoyable.

On one of our early morning walks we were greeted by a grinning, toothless, elderly grandfather carrying a large bunch of grapes just plucked from his vines. He extended his bounty to Dawson and a friendship was quickly forged. I will always remember those deep-purple morsels as the sweetest, most succulent grapes I have ever popped into my mouth. And as we were bidding a fond farewell, this grandfather reached in his jacket pocket and presented Dawson with a warm, bright yellow lemon. Stirred into our chicken pot that night, it was a welcome addition to this memorable dish. 🀫

Chicken in Lavender and Dried Plum Sauce
Serves 4 to 6

This recipe originated on the sun-drenched island of Hvar, where brilliant patches of lavender and rosemary carpet the soothing green hillsides. It is particularly significant and memorable as it represents my first experience in cooking with lavender, an herb that we now grow commercially and use frequently on our ranch in Southern California.

For this dish, I like to cut a whole chicken into 10 pieces: legs, thighs, wings and 4 pieces of breast. By quartering the chicken breast, each piece resembles the size of a chicken thigh. Thus the cooking time for the white meat is reduced and all pieces are cooked in about the same amount of time. Maybe best of all, this method creates more opportunities to share the white meat.

1 chicken (2^1/$_2$ to 3^1/$_2$ pounds), cut into legs, thighs, wings, and 4 breast pieces
Salt and freshly ground pepper to taste
3 tablespoons olive oil
^{1}/$_2$ cup chopped onion
3 cloves garlic, minced
2 medium tomatoes, chopped
2 teaspoons dried culinary lavender
1 cup red wine
^{1}/$_4$ pound chopped dried plums (prunes)
2 tablespoons parsley, finely chopped

Wash and pat dry the chicken. Season with salt and pepper. Heat the oil in a large skillet over high heat and brown the chicken on both sides, about 3–4 minutes per side. Do not crowd the chicken pieces. If necessary, divide the chicken and brown in 2 batches.

Remove the chicken from the pan and pour off any excess oil. Reduce the heat to medium and add the chopped onion and minced garlic. Stir for 5–6 minutes or until onion begins to turn translucent. Stir in the tomatoes. Crush the lavender with a mortar and pestle and add to the tomato sauce. Return the chicken to the pan and pour the wine over all. Cover and simmer for 15 minutes.

Remove the cover and stir in the chopped dried plums. Continue to simmer uncovered until the chicken is cooked through and tender, about 15 minutes. Garnish with parsley and serve with pasta, rice or polenta.

Cook's Notes:
• Culinary lavender is available at some specialty food stores or online at www.newoakranch.com. Although many varieties of lavender are suitable for cooking, the variety known as Provence is the most popular.

IT WAS ALWAYS FUN to have our friends Karen and Lee join us aboard *Klatawa*. They shared Bill's passion for sailing and my passion for food. We sailed hard, explored every possible market and ate extremely well.

When they linked up with us in Croatia in June 2001, one of our first stops was the village of Stari Grad on the beautiful island of Hvar. Hvar is especially known for her lavender fields, so we could not resist the temptation to take a mid-day excursion inland to inspect and enjoy hundreds of rolling acres, all covered in a stunning, aromatic purple haze.

Once back in town, we wandered along the waterfront and bought a package of lavender from a grinning, sun-wrinkled, peasant lady who assured us that the lavender was "good to eat." She even suggested that we try it in our favorite chicken recipe, a suggestion that both Karen and I agreed to implement ASAP.

Our next activity was to wander the winding side streets (actually narrow stone-paved alleys) in search of the obscure and elusive "Green Door." The "Green Door" was a destination that was rapidly building a reputation within the cruising community as the best source for reasonably priced bulk wine on the island.

Eventually, we found a green door in a quiet, seemingly deserted residential neighborhood. Intuitively we were confident that we had identified *the* place. We pressed the well-worn doorbell rather aggressively and before long the shutters on the second floor were flung open and we heard a voice calling from above. Within moments, we were greeted and welcomed at ground level by a smiling young woman whose English was as limited as our Croatian. But wine tasting and buying and selling are universal skills and it did not take us long to decide on and negotiate a price for a couple of jugs of a smooth and hearty red wine.

Back aboard *Klatawa*, we created this tasty dish by incorporating some of our recently acquired ingredients. ▧

Chicken in Paprika-Sour Cream Sauce
Serves 4

This recipe crosses the lines of both Mediterranean and Continental cuisine. Distinctly Continental with the use of butter, paprika and sour cream, this dish also contains a hint of the Mediterranean from the olive oil. Serve over wide egg noodles to continue the Continental influence.

1 chicken (2^1/$_2$ to 3^1/$_2$ pounds),
  cut into individual portions (leg, thigh, wing, half breast)
Salt and freshly ground pepper to taste
2 tablespoons butter
1 tablespoon olive oil
1 large onion, finely chopped
1 large green pepper, finely chopped (or ½ red and ½ green)
1 tablespoon paprika (sweet, hot or a combination)
^{1}/$_2$ cup wine (white or red)
^{1}/$_4$ cup cold water
1 cup sour cream
1 tablespoon flour
^{1}/$_4$ cup parsley, chopped

Wash, pat dry and season the chicken with salt and pepper. Heat the butter and oil in a large skillet over high heat and brown the chicken on both sides, about 3–4 minutes per side. Remove the chicken from the skillet, reduce the heat to medium and add the onion and pepper. Sauté until the pepper is soft and the onion begins to turn translucent, about 4–5 minutes.

Return the chicken to the pan and sprinkle with paprika. Add the wine and cover, simmering over medium-low heat until the chicken is cooked through, about 35 minutes.

Once again, remove the chicken from the pan. Whisk together the water, sour cream and flour and stir into the pan, scraping down the sides and the bottom. Bring the sauce to a high simmer and add the chicken, turning to coat all pieces. Simmer for 5 minutes. Remove to serving plates, spoon sauce over and garnish with parsley and a dash of paprika.

FOR THE MOST PART, Croatian cuisine has always been regional with distinctive local variations occurring within the two major categories of Mediterranean and Continental cookery. The Mediterranean or coastal traditions centered on olives, citrus, fresh vegetables and seafood while the Continental diet featured cabbage, potatoes, sauerkraut, dairy and red meat. As transportation improved and Croatians relocated throughout the country, the flavors have become increasingly blended.

Chicken Primošten
Serves 4 to 6

This satisfying one-dish meal features the favorite Dalmatian flavors of smoked bacon, sherry and capers. Close your eyes, think sunshine, take pleasure in the aroma and savor the wonderful flavors. You now have a taste of Dalmatia.

1 chicken (2^1/$_2$ to 3^1/$_2$ pounds),
   cut into individual portions (leg, thigh, wing, half breast)
^{1}/$_4$ cup flour
^{1}/$_2$ teaspoon salt
^{1}/$_4$ teaspoon freshly ground pepper
3 tablespoons olive oil
3 slices bacon, diced
1 medium onion, chopped
2 cloves garlic, minced
1 (14^1/$_2$–ounce) can diced tomatoes
^{1}/$_4$ cup dry sherry
2 tablespoons capers
1 pound baby new potatoes, scrubbed and halved
10 ounces frozen peas
3 tablespoons parsley, minced

Wash the chicken and pat it dry. Combine the flour, salt and pepper and dredge the chicken pieces lightly in the flour. In a large sauté pan, heat the olive oil over high heat until very hot but not smoking. Working in batches, add the chicken and brown on both sides. Remove the chicken to a plate and drain any excess fat from pan.

Reduce the heat to medium and add the bacon. Sauté until nearly crisp. Add the chopped onion and minced garlic. Sauté over medium heat until the onion begins to turn translucent, about 3–4 minutes. Return the chicken to the pan and pour the tomatoes, sherry and capers over the chicken. Cover and simmer over low heat until the chicken is partially cooked, about 15 minutes. Add the potatoes and peas and continue to simmer until chicken is cooked and potatoes are fork tender, about 25 minutes. Taste and adjust seasonings. Stir in the minced parsley and serve.

Serve with a crusty bread to soak up the tasty juices.

THE CHICKEN PRIMOŠTEN RECIPE WAS NAMED after the charming coastal village of Primošten, which means "over the bridge." Historically, this cone-shaped settlement, crowned with a humble church, was an island close to the mainland. Centuries ago, the narrow passage was filled in and Primošten became more accessible. Today, it is an enchanting settlement that lures sun-seeking tourists. For those traveling by pleasure boat, there is a very picturesque harbor, and for those traveling by car, there are accessible beaches and endless opportunities to linger in a waterside café. 🔲

Chicken Ragusa (Baked Lemon-Garlic Chicken)
Serves 4 to 6

Marinating this chicken overnight has two major benefits: the flavors are more intense and there is less fuss on the day you plan to serve it ... thus making it a perfect dish for entertaining. Serve Chicken Ragusa with rice, a green salad and a crusty loaf of bread. Consider doubling the recipe; the leftovers make a tasty chicken salad!

1 chicken ($2^1/2$ to $3^1/2$ pounds),
   cut into individual portions (leg, thigh, wing, half breast)
$1/3$ cup lemon juice, freshly squeezed
$1/3$ cup dry white wine
4 cloves garlic, minced
2 teaspoons honey
1 teaspoon dried thyme
1 teaspoon salt
$1/2$ teaspoon freshly ground black pepper
3 tablespoons butter

Wash the chicken, pat it dry and place in a large zip-lock bag. Whisk together the lemon juice, white wine, garlic, honey, thyme, salt and pepper in a small bowl. Pour the marinade over the chicken, seal the bag and rotate several times to coat each piece of chicken. Refrigerate, turning occasionally, for at least 2 hours, preferably overnight.

Preheat the oven to 400 degrees. Remove the chicken from the marinade and place, skin side up, in a roasting pan. Discard the marinade. Cut the butter into thin slices and distribute over the chicken. Bake until the chicken is cooked through and tender, approximately 45 minutes.

Cook's Notes:

• This chicken also makes a tasty barbecue. Simply add $1/4$ cup of olive oil to the marinade and omit the butter.

• You might want to double bag the chicken ... just in case bag number one leaks.

• When cooking and serving chicken, I like to cut the chicken breast in half and then chop each half breast in half again. This provides four very nice pieces of white meat.

• Line the roasting pan with aluminum foil; it makes cleanup a breeze!

Dalmatian Coast Chicken
Serves 4

Traditionally, the chicken for this dish was first boiled or roasted. Then the sauce was poured over the cooked chicken. This version is quicker and the flavors seep into the chicken while cooking, creating what I think is a more flavorful dish. Served with fluffy white rice and a mixed green salad, dinner is on the table in just about an hour!

1 chicken (2$^{1}/_{2}$ to 3$^{1}/_{2}$ pounds),
  cut into individual portions (leg, thigh, wing, half breast)
Salt and freshly ground pepper to taste
$^{1}/_{4}$ cup olive oil
4 anchovies
1 medium onion, very finely chopped
1 tablespoon capers
$^{1}/_{4}$ teaspoon pepper
2 tablespoons minced parsley
$^{1}/_{2}$ cup white wine
1 cup chicken broth
2 tablespoons fresh lemon juice
1 tablespoon red wine vinegar

Wash the chicken pieces and pat them dry. Lightly season with salt and pepper. Heat the olive oil in a large sauté pan over high heat. Add the chicken pieces and brown on all sides, about 4–5 minutes per side. Remove the chicken from the pan and cover with foil to keep warm.

Reduce the heat to medium and add the anchovies to the pan. Using the back of a wooden spoon, mash and stir the anchovies until they fully disintegrate. Add the onion and stir until translucent, about 3–4 minutes. Stir in the capers, pepper, parsley, wine, chicken broth, lemon juice and wine vinegar. Scrape down the sides and bottom of the pan and simmer the sauce over medium heat for 10 minutes. Return the chicken to the pan and spoon the sauce over each piece. Cover and simmer for 10 minutes. Turn the chicken and increase heat to medium-high. Do not re-cover. Cook for an additional 10–15 minutes, until chicken is tender and most of the liquid has evaporated. Serve topped with the sauce.

Cook's Notes:

• No one will ever know that this dish contains anchovies—unless you tell them! The anchovies add a wonderful flavor and complexity to the dish, so do try to use them. If you do omit them, add a little extra salt. It will still be a terrific dish.

Hundreds of years ago, along the Mediterranean coast, there was no refrigeration nor was canning available for preserving food. Consequently fishermen turned to salting their catch for preservation. The freshly caught fish were spread in a single layer in a wooden box, salted, layered and salted. This process was repeated until the box was filled. Then a weight was placed on the top to press out the excess liquids. To this day, many Mediterranean recipes still call for salt-dried anchovies, and they're still readily available in the Mediterranean countries.

Mystery Chicken (Chicken in Fig and Tomato Sauce)
Serves 6

Throughout the Mediterranean and particularly in Croatia, figs (as well as other dried fruits) are often used to add a sweet and complex flavor (and vitamins) to a variety of meat and poultry dishes. Aboard Klatawa, *this dish became a favorite. I love to serve it and keep the key ingredient a secret until the last bit of sauce is blissfully consumed.*

> 6 chicken thighs with skin and bones intact
> 3 chicken breasts with skin and bones intact, each breast cut in half
> 1/4 cup flour
> 1 teaspoon salt
> 1/2 teaspoon freshly ground pepper
> 3 tablespoons olive oil
> 1 large onion, finely chopped (about 1 cup)
> 1 cup dry white wine
> 1 (28–ounce) can plum tomatoes, packed in juice
> 1 teaspoon thyme, finely chopped
> 1 tablespoon basil, finely chopped
> 1 teaspoon rosemary, finely chopped
> 3/4 cup dried figs, finely chopped or 1 1/4 cups chopped fresh figs

Wash the chicken and pat it dry. On a sheet of waxed paper or aluminum foil, combine the flour, salt and pepper. Lightly dredge the chicken pieces in the flour mixture and set aside.

In a large sauté pan, heat the olive oil over high heat until very hot but not smoking. Working in batches to avoid crowding, add the chicken pieces to the pan. Brown on both sides, about 3–4 minutes per side. Remove all the chicken from the pan and pour off the excess oil.

Reduce the heat to medium and add the onion. Stir over medium heat until the onion begins to turn transparent, about 4–5 minutes. Add the white wine and deglaze the pan by bringing the wine to a boil, stirring and scraping any bits from bottom and sides of the pan. Return the chicken to the pan.

Using your hand, squeeze each tomato into the pan, crushing and breaking it into small pieces. Pour the remaining tomato juice over the chicken and sprinkle with the herbs and the figs. Stirring frequently, simmer over low heat for 35–45 minutes, or until the chicken is tender. The sauce should be thick and small chunks of tomato and fig should cling to the chicken. Taste and adjust seasonings. Serve with pasta, potatoes, polenta or rice.

Cook's Notes:

• This is a perfect "make ahead" dish. The flavor actually improves when refrigerated overnight.

• For a more "finished" appearance, remove the cooked chicken to a serving platter. Cover with aluminum foil to keep warm. Carefully ladle the hot sauce into a food processor bowl and process by pulsing on and off several times or until the sauce reaches a coarse but smoother consistency. Reheat the sauce before pouring it over the chicken.

• Warning: Because of the high sugar content in the figs, care should be taken to avoid scorching the sauce. Use a moderately low heat and stir frequently to avoid sticking. If you choose to refrigerate and then reheat this dish, bring it to room temperature and then gently re-warm.

- In Croatia, dried figs are often strung alternately with bay leaves. The bay leaf is said to act as both a preservative and an insect repellent.

Sailing in the Mediterranean provided us with countless rewards, including the opportunity to taste, enjoy and develop a genuine fondness for figs. On many occasions, we stood in the hot Mediterranean sun and plucked soft, plump and sweetly fragrant figs directly from a tree and immediately savored their sugary, juicy and succulent flavor. And as we wandered through late summer and early fall markets, we were known to share a home made "fig-string": a portable snack made by alternating sweet, sun-dried figs and bay leaves. We almost always bought these market treats from a smiling peasant lady who had painstakingly harvested and dried the figs from her own trees.

Rich in fiber, iron, calcium and potassium, figs were probably one of the first fruits dried and stored by man. Native to areas from Turkey to northern India, figs spread throughout the Mediterranean, where they have enjoyed both symbolic and spiritual significance in ancient and modern cultures.

Roasted Chicken and Vegetables
Serves 4 to 6

In most Croatian homes, this dish is reserved for Sundays and special occasions.

1 roasting chicken (3 to 4 pounds)
Salt and freshly ground pepper to taste
$1/4$ cup olive oil
$1/2$ teaspoon salt
$1/4$ teaspoon pepper
2 teaspoons fresh rosemary, chopped
1 8-inch sprig of rosemary
$1^1/2$ pounds potatoes, peeled and cut into wedges
4 large carrots, peeled and cut in half
1 medium onion, cut into 8 wedges
1 small eggplant, cut into 2-inch chunks
2 medium zucchinis, trimmed and cut in thirds
12 cloves garlic, peeled
$1/3$ cup water

Preheat the oven to 400 degrees. Rinse the chicken, inside and out, and pat dry. Sprinkle the cavity with salt and pepper. In a small mixing bowl, combine the olive oil, salt, pepper and chopped rosemary. Rub the exterior of the chicken with the mixture (you'll have some left over) and place the chicken, breast side up, in a large roasting pan. Tuck a sprig of rosemary in the chicken cavity.

In a large mixing bowl, toss the remaining seasoned olive oil with the potatoes, carrots, onion, eggplant, zucchini and garlic. Add the vegetables to the roasting pan, scattering them around the chicken. Place the chicken in the oven and roast for 15 minutes. Reduce the temperature to 350 degrees and roast for an additional hour and a half or until the legs move freely in their sockets and the breast temperature reaches 170 degrees.

Remove the chicken from the oven and tent with foil. Allow to rest for at least 15 minutes. Meanwhile increase the oven temperature to 425 degrees. Toss and stir the vegetables in the pan and return the pan to the oven. Continue to roast until all the vegetables are fork tender and golden brown, about 20 minutes.

Transfer the chicken and vegetables to a serving plate and keep warm. Add the water to the roasting pan and scrape up all bits from pan. If desired, reduce the pan juices, and then pour them over the chicken and vegetables. Serve immediately.

SINCE ROASTED CHICKEN IS A SPECIAL-OCCASION dish, we were honored to have it served to us at the home of our Dubrovnik friends, Jany and Boris. I have long admired Jany as the founder and executive director of DESA, an organization established at the peak of the recent war.

During the war, DESA brought together many of the distressed women who were living in the very cramped confines of refugee hotels. Under Jany's leadership, these women, many of whom were accustomed to a rural, land-based lifestyle, learned new skills, renewed a passion for traditional crafts and provided mutual support to one another. Surrounded by military action and with husbands off fighting, the women found DESA afforded them a valuable focus while teaching them useful and beneficial new skills.

Today, DESA continues to provide job training and professional development for women in a nation that entered the 21st century as a proud and independent nation. ▩

Beef Steak with Paprika-Cream Sauce
Serves 4

Croatian paprika is an excellent product and is used as a common seasoning throughout the land. Its popularity serves as a reminder of the strong ties, spanning many centuries, that Croatia shares with Hungary.

This simple dish is an excellent way to appreciate and to enjoy a fine paprika. Shop for the best and select an imported brand, preferably Hungarian, as it is unlikely you will find a Croatian version in your local American market.

4 6-ounce pieces boneless beefsteak
Salt and freshly ground pepper to taste
2 tablespoons olive oil
8 2-inch sprigs of rosemary
4 cloves garlic, minced
$2^1/_2$ teaspoons paprika
$3/_4$ cup red wine
1 cup heavy cream
Additional rosemary for garnish, if desired

Salt and pepper the steaks. Add the olive oil to a large frying pan and, over high heat, brown the steaks on both sides, about 2 minutes per side. Remove the steaks from the pan and reduce the heat to medium. Add the remaining ingredients and deglaze the pan. Bring the sauce to a simmer and cook for 5 minutes. Add the steaks. Simmer, turning once, until the meat reaches the desired doneness, about 10 minutes for medium rare.

Place the steaks on warmed serving plates. Remove the rosemary and reduce the sauce, if necessary. You should have about $3/_4$ cup of thick sauce. Pour the sauce over the steaks and garnish with an additional sprig of rosemary, if desired.

Beef Tenderloin with Rosemary Red-Wine Sauce
Serves 4

Any boneless steak will work in this tasty dish, but beef tenderloin makes it an extra special meal. If you're looking for an alternative to the salad and bread routine, try serving this steak with polenta or garlic mashed potatoes. Add fresh green beans and sliced juicy, red tomatoes for a balanced and colorful meal.
Warning: One sprig of fresh rosemary packs a lot of flavor, so be cautious with the quantities.

4 beef tenderloin steaks, about 1 inch thick
Salt and freshly ground pepper to taste
4 tablespoons butter, divided
4 cloves garlic, minced (1 tablespoon)
1 cup red wine
2 8-inch sprigs of rosemary, broken in half
4 4-inch sprigs of rosemary (optional)

Rub salt and pepper on both sides of the steaks. In a large, heavy-bottomed pan set over high heat, melt 2 tablespoons of butter and sear the steaks until they are browned on the outside, about 2–3 minutes per side. Do not crowd the steaks. Remove the steaks from the pan and tent with aluminum foil to keep warm.

Reduce the heat to medium and quickly stir in the garlic. Add the red wine and deglaze the pan by scraping down the sides and the bottom of the pan. Stir in the rosemary sprigs and return the steaks to the pan. Simmer until done, about 4 minutes per side for medium-rare.

Remove the steaks from the pan and place on serving dishes. Add remaining butter and whisk over high heat until the sauce is reduced to about 1/2 cup. Remove and discard the rosemary. Taste the sauce and adjust the seasoning. Pour the sauce over the steaks and serve.

Garnish with additional sprigs of rosemary, if desired.

Cook's Note:
• About 1/2 cup of sauce should remain in the pan. If more sauce is desired, whisk in small amounts of additional wine and butter.

Croatian Cruiser's Favorite Goulash
Serves 4

Don't be put off by the sauerkraut in this recipe. The slow simmering required in this dish blends all the flavors and the result is a delicious, richly complex dish.

1¹/₂ pounds beef (preferably chuck or round)

2 tablespoons olive oil

1 large onion, peeled, halved and thinly sliced

2 cloves garlic, minced

1¹/₂ tablespoons excellent-quality paprika (mild, hot or a combination)

1 (15-ounce) can peeled tomatoes, crushed

1 teaspoon sugar

Salt and freshly ground pepper to taste

1 (15-ounce) can sauerkraut

1 cup sour cream

After trimming the meat of fat and sinew, cut it into ³/₄-inch cubes. In a medium pot, sauté the onion in olive oil over medium heat until it is limp and translucent, about 10 minutes. Stir in the garlic and sauté for an additional minute. Remove the pan from the heat and stir in the paprika. Mix thoroughly and return the pan to a medium heat. Add the beef cubes and continue to cook, stirring occasionally, until the beef has released most of its juices. Stir in the crushed tomatoes, sugar, salt and pepper. Cover and simmer over low heat for ¹/₂ hour.

Wash, drain and chop the sauerkraut into shorter strands. Stir the sauerkraut into the beef, cover and continue to simmer for an hour, adding water in small amounts if necessary. Blend in the sour cream and simmer for an additional ¹/₂ hour. Serve over wide noodles, polenta or rice.

Klatawa Casserole
Serves 4 to 6

Reflecting the common flavors of many Mediterranean nations, this recipe evolved as we traveled throughout the Mediterranean Sea. Although no one country has offered this exact combination of flavors, it is reminiscent of many dishes we have tasted and enjoyed: a Greek moussaka, a Turkish kebab (this word describes a tangy stew as well as meat cooked on a skewer), and both a Dalmatian stuffed eggplant and a popular Croatian meat and eggplant casserole.

Be sure to allow at least 2½ hours for the casserole to bake.

1 medium eggplant (about 1¹/₄ pounds)

1 (28-ounce) can of tomatoes, peeled and diced

8 large cloves of garlic, minced

1 teaspoon sugar

1 teaspoon thyme

1 teaspoon oregano

¹/₄ cup chopped parsley

Salt and freshly ground pepper to taste

2 medium potatoes, peeled and thinly sliced

1 pound beef (preferably round steak or chuck), cut in ³/₄-inch cubes

1 large onion, cut in half lengthwise and sliced thin

1 red or green bell pepper, cleaned and diced

2 tablespoons olive oil

Preheat the oven to 325 degrees. Peel the eggplant and cut in 1-inch cubes. Place the cubes in a colander, sprinkle generously with salt and toss. Let rest for 15–20 minutes, rinse, drain and pat dry. Meanwhile, in a medium bowl, combine the tomatoes and their juices with the garlic, sugar, thyme, oregano, parsley, salt and pepper.

Oil a 3-quart casserole. Spread half of the potatoes in the bottom of the casserole and then top with the meat. Spread the remaining potatoes and spoon ¹/₃ of the sauce over the potato layer. In a medium bowl, combine the onion, eggplant, bell pepper and olive oil. Add to the casserole and cover with the remaining tomato sauce.

Cover and bake in a 325-degree oven for 2¹/₂–3 hours. To assure that the sauce is thick and flavorful, it may be necessary to uncover the casserole and baste with the juices from time to time. Serve with a hearty country bread.

Cook's notes:

• Salting and draining the eggplant is an important step as it helps to remove the dark and bitter juices from the eggplant.

• I like to add a pinch or two of sugar to my tomato sauce; it helps to reduce the acidity and to enrich the tomato flavor.

• For a different flavor, substitute lamb for the beef.

TODAY, THE PEPPER is considered to be a quintessential Mediterranean vegetable. But its roots are South American. Most likely a native of Brazil, the pepper was discovered by Columbus in Haiti. He took the seeds back to Europe where they grew easily and their popularity spread quickly.

Pasticada (Dalmatian Pot Roast)
Serves 8

This is definitely a dish that requires extra effort, so you'll probably reserve it for special occasions. But the results are worthwhile. When planning, keep in mind that the roast needs to marinate overnight.

4 pounds rolled rump roast

1/2 pound thick-sliced bacon, cut in 1/2-inch pieces

4 cloves garlic, thinly sliced

1/2 carrot, thinly sliced

Salt and freshly ground pepper to taste

1/4 cup Dijon mustard

4 tablespoons olive oil

1 medium onion, chopped

2 carrots, peeled and chopped

1 stalk celery, chopped

1/2 cup chopped parsley

1 cup red wine

10 dried plums, chopped

10 dried figs, chopped

1 apple, peeled and chopped

3 Roma tomatoes, chopped

2 bay leaves

1 tablespoon chopped fresh rosemary

1 teaspoon dried thyme

With a sharp knife, make 1 1/2-inch-deep, evenly spaced slits on all sides of the roast. "Lard" the roast by inserting either bacon pieces, garlic slices or the thinly sliced carrot into each hole. Salt and pepper the beef and rub with mustard. Place on a plate, cover with plastic wrap and refrigerate overnight.

About 4 hours before serving, remove the roast from the refrigerator. Preheat the oven to 325 degrees. Heat the oil in a large casserole over high heat. Brown the meat on all sides and remove the meat from the pan. Reduce the heat to medium and add onion, carrots, celery and parsley. Stir until vegetables are tender and slightly golden, about 7–9 minutes.

Return the meat to the casserole and add the wine. Cover tightly and place in the oven for about 2 hours. Throughout this time, turn the roast occasionally and add more wine or water if needed.

Add the dried plums, figs, apple, tomatoes, bay leaves, rosemary and thyme. Cover and continue to braise until the meat is very tender and the fruits are softened, about 1 1/2 hours.

Remove the meat from the casserole, place on a warm platter and cover. If the sauce is not thick enough, reduce it to the desired consistency over medium-high heat, stirring frequently to prevent scorching. Slice the roast and spoon some of the sauce over the slices. Serve with the remaining sauce along with gnocchi, noodles, mashed potatoes or polenta.

• Even if you are not serving 8 people, make the entire recipe. *Pasticada* is terrific reheated and the beef makes an incredible sandwich.

I FIRST TASTED *PASTICADA* while celebrating my birthday at Restaurant Alka in one of my favorite Croatian villages, Trogir. The haunting memory of the wonderful combination of sweet and tangy flavors remained with me … so much so that we returned to Alka several times. Each time I begged for the recipe, but my requests were always denied. As a result, this recipe is my attempt to re-create this special dish. I hope you will enjoy it as much as we do. ▨

Sarma (Stuffed Cabbage Rolls)
Serves 8

Although the recipe might appear a bit daunting and complicated, it is really quite easy. Probably the most difficult part of this dish is boiling the cabbage and carefully removing the outer leaves. Mixing up the stuffing and making the cabbage rolls is a breeze.

1 large head cabbage
1 pound ground beef
$1/4$ pound bacon, finely chopped
1 cup rice
1 egg
1 large onion, finely chopped
2 cloves garlic, minced
$1/2$ teaspoon cinnamon
$1/2$ teaspoon nutmeg
$1/2$ teaspoon red chili flakes (optional)
Salt and freshly ground pepper to taste
Sauce:
2 cups tomato juice (or sauce)
1 cup beef broth (or water)
Salt and freshly ground pepper to taste
2 cloves garlic, minced
$1/4$ cup brown sugar

Using a very sharp paring knife, core the head of cabbage and carefully place it in a large pot of boiling water. Cover and simmer for 15 to 20 minutes—long enough to allow the outer leaves to soften. Carefully lift the cabbage from the boiling water and allow it to cool enough to handle. Remove the 16 outermost leaves and, with a small paring knife, trim and reduce the thick center vein in each leaf so that it is flexible enough to roll.

In a medium bowl, place the ground beef, bacon, rice, egg, onion, garlic, cinnamon, nutmeg, chili flakes, salt and pepper. Using your hands, mix until well blended. Place about $1/4$ cup stuffing on each cabbage leaf. Fold in the sides and roll loosely to make a neat packet. Dice the remaining cabbage and place in the bottom of the casserole. Add the cabbage rolls, being sure to place them seam side down. Mix together the tomato juice, beef broth, salt, pepper, garlic and brown sugar and pour sauce over all. Cover and bake at 325 degrees for 2 to $2^1/2$ hours.

Cook's Note:
• Even though this recipe serves eight, I recommend you make the whole batch. It is a great dish reheated and it freezes well.

ASK ANY CROATIAN, whether living at home or abroad, for their nomination for the most traditional Croatian recipe, and *sarma* would more than likely capture most of the votes. *Sarma* is served at nearly every wedding, holiday or family gathering throughout the country. For many Croatian families, *sarma* is an important part of the New Year's Day menu … possibly because it is rumored to cure hangovers!

In northern Croatia, sauerkraut is frequently made from a head of cabbage that has been left whole, not just the shredded variety we know in America. In this region, *sarma* is often made with a whole leaf of sauerkraut.

Succulent Beef and Pork Skewers
Serves 4

This sweet and savory combination of flavors will quickly become a summertime favorite.

1 small eggplant
$^3/_4$ pound 1-inch-thick boneless center loin pork chops
$^3/_4$ pound 1-inch-thick boneless sirloin steak
1 large apple
2 tablespoons olive oil
Marinade:
2 cloves garlic, peeled and minced
$^1/_3$ cup olive oil
Juice of 1 large lemon, divided
Salt and freshly ground pepper to taste
Special Equipment: 4 long metal or wooden skewers

Cut the eggplant into 12 1$^1/_2$-inch square pieces. Generously salt eggplant pieces and place in a colander for at least 15 minutes to allow excess bitter juices to be drawn. Rinse and pat dry.

Meanwhile, prepare the marinade. In a small bowl, whisk together the garlic, the $^1/_3$ cup of olive oil, juice of $^1/_2$ lemon, salt and pepper.

Trim the excess fat from pork chops and cut the pork chops into 12 even pieces. Toss with the marinade, remove from bowl and set aside.

Trim the excess fat from the sirloin steak and cut into 12 even pieces. Toss with the marinade, remove from bowl and set aside.

Peel, quarter and core the apple. Cut each quarter into thirds. Add the remaining lemon juice to the remaining marinade. Toss the apples with the marinade, remove from the bowl and set aside.

Rinse the eggplant and pat dry with a paper towel. Toss with the remaining marinade and set aside.

Using large metal skewers, alternate the beef, eggplant, pork and apples on the skewers. Place on a large platter, cover with plastic wrap and refrigerate until ready to grill.

Preheat your barbecue. Place the skewers on the barbecue and grill until the meat is cooked yet moist, about 12–15 minutes, rotating so all sides are evenly exposed to coals. Drizzle with additional olive oil and serve.

WE FIRST ENJOYED this tasty combination of flavors at the restaurant Adio Mare on the Island of Korcula as we gathered with our son, Doug, daughter-in-law, Leslie, 2-year-old grandson, Dawson and good British friends Rob and Liz from the sloop, *Autumn Dream*. Korcula town is a stunning example of a walled 13th century city with seemingly endless narrow alleys and ancient buildings. This was a perfect meal that followed our village tour and our visit to the nearby (alleged) birthplace of Marco Polo. ▨

Lemon-Mustard Roast Pork
Serves 4 to 6

In Croatia, a roast has always been considered a symbol for a festive occasion ... a tradition that continues to this day when the roast is the focus of many celebratory gatherings of family and friends. In this recipe, the 24-hour advance marinating time serves as a reminder that a special event is approaching. This is a delicious dish ... perfect for your next dinner party.

    1 2-pound boneless pork loin
    1¹/₂ tablespoons Dijon mustard
    1 teaspoon salt
    1 teaspoon freshly ground black pepper
    3 cloves garlic, minced
    1 lemon, thinly sliced
    2 tablespoons olive oil
    Lemon wedges for garnish (optional)

Combine the mustard, salt, pepper and garlic. Rub the marinade evenly over the pork and cover the roast with lemon slices. Wrap tightly in plastic wrap. Refrigerate at least overnight and preferably for 24 hours. Remove the lemon slices and drizzle the roast with olive oil. Roast at 400 degrees for about 1 hour or until the thermometer reaches 160 degrees. As the roast is cooking, baste frequently with the juices, adding a bit of water if necessary. Remove the roast from the oven and allow it to rest for 10 minutes. Carve and garnish with additional lemon wedges, if desired.

Pork Medallions with Lemon-Cream Sauce
Serves 4

For a special occasion, substitute veal scallops; or for a tasty weeknight meal, use boneless, skinless chicken breasts.

1 pork tenderloin, about 1 pound
3–4 tablespoons fresh lemon juice, divided
Salt and freshly ground pepper to taste
2–3 tablespoons flour
2 tablespoons olive oil
$1/4$ cup white wine
$3/4$ cup heavy cream
2 tablespoons fresh parsley, chopped

With a very sharp knife, slice the pork into $1/3$-inch slices. Place the slices between two sheets of plastic wrap and, using a meat pounder, pound to $1/4$ inch, being careful not to puncture the meat. Sprinkle each medallion lightly with lemon juice and let rest for 10 minutes.

On a sheet of waxed paper, combine the salt, pepper and flour and lightly dredge each slice of pork. Add the olive oil to a large sauté pan and quickly sear each medallion over high heat, being careful not to crowd the meat. Remove the medallions to a plate and tent with aluminum foil to keep warm. Reduce the heat to medium-high and add the wine along with 1 tablespoon of the remaining lemon juice. When almost evaporated, stir in the cream. Taste and adjust the seasonings, adding more lemon juice, salt or pepper as needed. Return the medallions to the pan and turn each medallion several times, allowing each to cook about 1 minute per side. Remove to a serving plate, reduce cream sauce if necessary and pour the sauce over the medallions. Garnish with parsley and serve.

SPLIT, THE SECOND LARGEST city in Croatia, is large, sprawling and industrial. But it is well worth a visit just to explore its multitude of historic sights—including Diocletian's Palace. Built as his retirement home between 295 and 305 A.D. by Emperor Diocletian (who had achieved fame for his persecution of the early Christians), the "palace" boasts 220 buildings. It is a small walled town within the old city of Split and includes lots of shops, services, several museums and the octagonal Cathedral of St. Domnius. Today, more than 3,000 people live within the palace walls.

Split also has a very large daily farmers' market comprised of many permanent stalls surrounded by shops and kiosks selling seasonal products as well as clothing and housewares. One morning as I was trying to complete my shopping, I was lured into a small butcher shop by a clean and tidy window display of seemingly top-quality meat. Once inside, I purchased a *po* kilo or a pound of veal and tried this recipe. It was the best veal we have ever had!

Times are changing, and today good veal is both politically incorrect and very expensive. Since returning to the States, I have switched to using pork tenderloins when preparing this dish.

Pork Tenderloin "Poked" with Dried Plums
Serves 6 to 8

I've learned so much by watching and listening to the peasant women of rural Croatia. Their traditions and habits demonstrate simple techniques for the sustainable stewardship of their treasured land along with seemingly endless ways to add wonderful new and complex flavors to basic dishes and simple cuts of meat. This recipe also provides additional benefits thanks to the vitamin-packed dried plums.

Serve with buttered egg noodles and a fresh green vegetable. Quick and easy, the flavors are tantalizingly smooth, and the dish is special enough to serve at a dinner party.

2 pork tenderloins, about 1 pound each

12 dried plums, pitted and cut in half

Salt and freshly ground pepper to taste

2 tablespoons olive oil

2 tablespoons butter

1/2 cup dry white wine

3 tablespoons port or sweet sherry

1 cup heavy cream

1/4 cup chopped parsley

Preheat the oven to 450 degrees. Randomly make 1-inch-deep slits in the pork with a sharp knife. Insert a prune half into each slit and pinch closed. Rub the outside of the pork tenderloin with the salt and pepper and let rest for 10 minutes.

Melt the butter in a small bowl in the microwave and combine it with the olive oil. Brush the pork with the butter and oil mixture and place in a pan that is both ovenproof and safe to use on the stovetop. Roast for 10 minutes, brush once again with the oil mixture and reduce the heat to 350 degrees. Roast for an additional 20–30 minutes or until a meat thermometer inserted in the middle of the pork tenderloin reaches 160 degrees. Remove from the oven and place on a warmed platter. Tent with foil to keep warm.

Add the wine to the pan and scrape down the sides, removing any bits. Add the port and cream and reduce over medium-high heat until the sauce is thick and yields about 3/4 cup.

Carve the meat into slices and arrange on a warm plate. Pour the sauce over the meat and garnish with chopped parsley.

Cook's Notes:

- Although pork tenderloins are rarely sold separately in Croatia, they are the ideal cut for this rich combination of Mediterranean farm fresh flavors.

- Piercing a roast and inserting bacon, vegetables or other seasonings is traditionally referred to as *larding*. Using the term *poked* is more direct.

- For a different twist, substitute dried figs or apricots for the dried plums.

HISTORICALLY, HONEY OR DRIED fruits such as raisins, figs, prunes, apricots or apples were the only sweeteners available to cooks in many lands. Used throughout the year, the dried fruits were a valued source of vitamins and minerals, especially in the cold winter months.

Walnut-Crusted Pork Chops with Fig Sauce
Serves 4

It was late October, and there they were, proudly spilling out of the packing box and sitting conveniently right next to the dried figs. The first walnuts of the season had just arrived at the Mediator grocery store in Dubrovnik. Suddenly inspired, I decided to try a simple walnut crust on the pork chops I had just purchased and then top them off with a dried fig sauce. The dish was simple to prepare, and the flavors were richly autumnal. One more hint: don't deny yourself the pleasure of using bone-in chops. The results are definitely worthwhile—the chops will be juicier and tastier.

4 large, bone-in loin pork chops (about 1½ inch thick)
Salt and freshly ground pepper to taste
2/3 cup walnuts, finely chopped
1/4 teaspoon nutmeg
1/4 teaspoon cinnamon
2 tablespoons butter
2 tablespoons olive oil
10 dried figs, finely chopped
1/2 cup white wine
1/2 cup chicken stock or water

Preheat the oven to 450 degrees. Lightly salt and pepper the chops. On a sheet of wax paper, combine the walnuts, nutmeg and cinnamon. Divide the walnuts into four parts and firmly press onto both sides of the chops. Over medium-high heat, melt the butter in large sauté pan. Add the olive oil and stir to combine. Brown the chops on both sides, about 3–4 minutes per side. Watch carefully … allowing the walnuts to toast but not burn.

Transfer the chops to an oven-safe dish and bake at 450 degrees for 10 minutes. Reduce the oven temperature to 350 degrees and continue to bake for an additional 15–20 minutes, until the internal temperature of the chops reaches 160 degrees.

Meanwhile, add the finely chopped figs to the browning pan and deglaze the pan with the wine and stock. Boil and reduce the liquids until a thick sauce is formed. Spoon the sauce over the chops and serve. Serve with noodles, rice or potatoes.

WALNUTS ARE A CROATIAN favorite … you'll find them in salads, breads, cakes and cookies. But they can surprise you by appearing in savory dishes as well: Ground into sauces for meat, poultry or fish or used as a coating for roasts or chops, they are a flavorful and nutritious addition to many dishes.

Veal Medallions with Mushroom-Cream Sauce
Serves 4

If you prefer not to use veal, pork medallions or boneless, skinless chicken breasts make a nice alternative.

1 tablespoon olive oil

2 tablespoons butter

12 ¹/₂–inch veal scallops (about 1¼ pounds)

1 medium onion, peeled and diced

¹/₃ pound fresh mushrooms, cleaned and thinly sliced

1 cup heavy cream

1 tablespoon finely chopped parsley

In a 12-inch sauté pan, combine the olive oil and butter and warm over medium-high heat until the butter melts and begins to bubble. Add the veal scallops and fry until they are cooked through, about 2–3 minutes per side. Remove the veal from the pan, place on a platter and tent with foil to keep warm. Stir in the onion and sauté for 5 minutes. Add the mushrooms and sauté until the mushrooms have released all of their juices and the onion is transparent, about 5–7 minutes. Stir in the cream and reduce until the sauce is very thick, stirring constantly. Return the veal pieces to the pan, heat through and turn to coat with sauce. Place three medallions on each plate and serve topped with mushroom cream sauce. Garnish with parsley and serve with rice.

WHEN WE ARRIVED in Dubrovnik in the summer of 2000, the Croatian tourism industry was just beginning to recover from the devastating effects of the recent war. As a result, there were relatively few services available to boaters stopping at the marina—a facility that had, at one time, been first class. There was a gas dock, a marginally stocked grocery store, and a small café with a limited-menu restaurant.

In just a few short years, the grocery store had grown exponentially and the on-site restaurant had been remodeled and expanded. A second restaurant opened nearby and it is there that we first enjoyed Veal Medallions with Mushroom-Cream Sauce.

From Market ...
to Market

Big markets, little markets, fancy markets, simple markets. I love them all. During our years of sailing in the Mediterranean, I spent hours wandering the stalls of weekly farmers' markets, strolling through dozens and dozens of *supermercatos* (Croatian translation: a shop with shelves that may hold 50,000 varieties of food and household products—or 50) and browsing the displays of numerous butchers, fishmongers and bakers. These markets supplied us with food for our table, helped me keep track of the culinary seasons and provided me with treasured connections to local residents. Best of all, in Croatia I got plenty of hints on how to cook like the locals. Friendly vendors were willing—through an often humorous combination of halting words and expressive hand and facial signals to provide useful and tasty suggestions for serving a springtime fruit or braising a winter vegetable.

And markets were my best "mind medicine." Throughout the years, there were times when I felt down or lonely—missing the routine of a land-based lifestyle and the closeness of family and friends. And there were the times when my "sailing nerves" took control. Regardless of the cause of my gloom, my preferred panacea was a trip to a market. It was my chance to relax and mingle with local housewives, select the best of the proudly displayed seasonal produce and fantasize about the meals I would prepare aboard *Klatawa*, in my small but functional galley. And if the weather appeared to be unsettled or the forecast was stormy and we were still heading out to sea, I tried to ignore my churning tummy and remind myself of the pleasures that awaited me at our next destination ... for Croatia is a land of coastal living and there was almost always some type of market nearby.

Thankfully, my fear of sailing was not an everyday occurrence. I loved those beautiful warm and sunny days when the gentle salt-air breeze propelled us along the dramatic Dalmatian coast on calm, azure-blue seas. And I would have hated to sacrifice those extraordinary days and nights when we were tucked away in a quiet anchorage surrounded only by nature's wondrous gifts. However, I know of no place in the world where the weather is always predictable. Despite the remarkable technology that has been designed to capture all of the available weather information, it is still possible to get caught. And we were caught: thunderstorms with gale force winds and turbulent seas, pelting hail storms that hammered the decks and sudden *boras* (fierce northeast winds) that caught us unaware both at sea and at anchor. Each was a memorable event. And each was an experience that we survived.

But even on the most glorious days, it did not take much to get my stomach churning. An unusual cloud formation, a sudden shift in the wind, a change in the temperature or the sighting of very large waves on the horizon and my imagination took control. For me, what I feared the most was the *possibility* of a storm, the *possibility* of running aground, the *possibility* of becoming dismasted. Unfortunately, I allowed myself to imagine the worst. As a result, I could work myself into a totally miserable state. Not a condition that made me feel proud and certainly not a condition that made me feel good.

So why did I pursue the cruising lifestyle? Simply put, I love to travel, to experience new cultures and to gain new perspectives. Travel allows me to explore the local markets and feast my eyes upon mysterious native delicacies and colorful mounds of fresh fruits and vegetables. For me, it is a joy to watch the locals as they go about their market activity—painstakingly selecting their tomatoes, haggling over price or praising (or sometimes belittling) a merchant. And I love the challenges presented by a new market: listening to and trying to learn (at least a few words of) a new language, trading in a new currency and observing the local customs. But most of all, I love the process of buying local products, taking them home and preparing a satisfying meal. Traveling by plane and train and living in hotels would not allow for these culinary desires to become a reality. Cruising and living aboard our sailboat did.

▨ ▨ ▨

Exploring the coast and traveling in inland Croatia, I discovered an enormous variety of markets and market styles—a reflection of the amazing differences in Croatian lifestyles. Urban residents, who lead typical 21st century lifestyles, are apt to shop at a genuine *supermercato*, very often a part of a regional or national chain. At these markets, it is one stop shopping—everything that the dual-career family of four needs to put a hastily prepared dinner on the table. But what a contrast that *supermercato* is to the tiny shop that serves the 30 or 40 full-time residents in one of the remote villages that we found so irresistible throughout the islands and scattered along the coast. During our cruising season, it was those little markets in distant and isolated settings that provided us with our food lifeline.

In most of these villages, the few year-round residents lived their simple lives off the land and the sea. Consequently, the "market" was likely to be one simple shop with limited hours and limited inventory. If the shop had a reliable source of electricity (and that was not always the case), they may have stocked a few packages of frozen goods: chicken, chops, sausages and an octopus or two were the most likely choices. Well-packaged and preserved meats and cheeses, long-life UHT milk (milk that has been sterilized at ultra-high-temperatures and packaged in sterile air-tight cartons), bottled water, beer, wine and a limited selection of household products completed the inventory. In these distant locations fresh bread was rarely delivered daily. Most likely, it appeared a couple of times a week, arriving either by road or by sea.

Adapting to a bread delivery schedule was usually easy when compared to the challenge of finding fresh produce. In a rural society where nearly every home had a kitchen garden, produce available for visitors to purchase was unpredictable. Basics like potatoes, carrots and onions may have been wonderfully fresh, still caked with a bit of soil from the local housewife's vegetable garden ... or they could have been so wrinkled and shriveled that they appeared to be remnants from a century past.

But I really got excited and my adrenalin began to flow when I approached a tiny street market ... the beckoning aroma of syrupy-sweet fresh figs recently plucked from the tree, an irresistible pile of carefully mounded fuzzy peaches or picture-perfect bunches of deep purple table grapes or tiny zucchinis with their bright, tender yellow blossoms still attached. These were ingredients for extraordinary meals: figs wrapped in *pršut*, crepes filled with peaches or a simple summer pasta enhanced with gently slivered zucchini blossoms. My imagination (and our menu) was limited only by the selection of ingredients available from the market or already stored in our galley. In these small villages, provisioning was all about being in the right place at the right time.

Being in the right place at the right time could also mean being anchored in a quiet bay or tied to the quay in a small town when the market boat arrived. In this water-dependent nation, market boats were common ... and they came in all shapes, sizes and descriptions. When we anchored in seemingly deserted coves, we looked forward to the boat-side visits from small, traditional, old wooden fishing boats powered by noisy but reliable outboard motors. These brightly painted vessels were typically captained by a slow-moving, sun-wrinkled gentleman who would call out a cheerful *dobar dan* (good afternoon) as he lifted up his limited articles of trade for our inspection: a few bunches of grapes, a handful of walnuts, a couple of eggs and an occasional loaf of bread. We always made a purchase.

Those humble entrepreneurs represented an astounding time-warped contrast in style and expectations when compared to the newer, custom-equipped powerboats that were genuine markets on the sea. Often complete with commercial refrigerators and freezers, these market boats could provide all of the ingredients for a gourmet meal as well as all of the household products necessary to clean up the mess.

The amazing wonder of these markets at sea struck me one very hot summer day. I had just finished my grocery shopping on one of them and I was strolling back to our boat while slowly licking a frozen, chocolate-covered ice cream confection. All of a sudden, it occurred to me that I was on a small, uninhabited and barren island surrounded by ancient Roman ruins, and I was enjoying this quintessential modern-day delicacy. That was a genuine "wow" moment.

Then there were times when a market boat did not look like a market boat. I remember the warm, windless summer afternoon when we were stern-tied to the tiny quay clearly marked "for *yahts*" on the small island of Rava. At about 3 p.m., the *Anamarija* arrived and docked nearby. Freshly painted a brilliant white, the *Anamarija* is a small, private ferry that makes twice-weekly passenger and goods delivery visits to this tiny community. We watched with interest as the buff and efficient captain, with the help of his customers, unloaded a new kitchen sink, a large mattress, a smaller mattress and numerous brown boxes containing unknown but necessary goods destined for the nearby homes.

Once the passengers and goods were off-loaded, I expected the dock activity to subside. Instead, I noticed a steady stream of women, each carrying empty sacks and baskets and dressed in traditional black or dark navy cotton housedresses, head down from their hillside homes to gather on the small quay. They had come prepared for the *Anamarija's* next business activity, one that would take place in the adjacent small, whitewashed ferry-office building. As soon as the *Anamarija's* captain opened the door to the building, the women at the head of the line made an orderly entrance and quickly emerged with bags and baskets filled with long loaves of bread.

Inspired and energized, I grabbed my market bags and called out to my friend Judy aboard the sailing vessel *Lindisfarne.* We headed over to the dock to take our place at the end of the line. Standing patiently, we soon realized that there was a system in place. The bread was being distributed based on a well-worn list of names. All of the bread had been pre-ordered. We began to fret. Would there be any bread left over? Would we each be allowed to buy even one loaf? When we finally reached the front of the line, the news was good: we could each buy one, but only one, loaf of bread.

Soon all of the bread orders were filled, and the supply was gone. Chatting nonstop, the neighborhood women set their bread-filled bags and boxes down against the ferry terminal wall or under the huge single shade tree growing in the middle of the quay. They were obviously standing by for something more to happen. Apparently, there was more shopping to be done. For that task there was another system in place. Another line was formed and the ferry captain, this time with the assistance of his enthusiastic first mate, once again became a shopkeeper. Groceries, cleaning supplies and beverages were dispensed from his very limited inventory.

As before, Judy and I took our place at the end of the line. By the time it was our turn, I knew that my purchases would be limited. I could tell that the inventory was sparse, as I had watched the captain frequently shake his head "no" when customers requested larger quantities of a particular product. But patience did pay off. I was able to buy six cans of beer, two bottles of wine and a liter of milk. True to their Croatian heritage and their profession as shopkeepers, the captain and his first mate willingly issued cheerful advice: Buy a bottle or two of the local white *Malvazija* wine. It was the best they had available.

▩ ▩ ▩

Marketing was far more predictable in larger towns and villages. Like most of my Croatian friends and my cruising peers, I preferred to head to the local farmers' market in the early morning when the produce was the freshest and the selection was the greatest. Before each outing, my heart would beat a little faster in anticipation of the goodies that I might discover. With years of experience shopping these small, local markets, I had developed a few techniques. First, I made a list of the basics that were needed on board, and with that list in hand I would walk the market stalls and scope out the options. What kind of produce was available? Which stall offered the freshest harvest? Whose prices seemed most fair? Once I had looked it over, I began to buy, choosing from the best of the seasonal selections.

But my approach was different when we were preparing for an extended time at anchor. Those shopping expeditions would determine the menus for the following days and even weeks. When I was doing this "serious provisioning," I would remind myself that what I was seeing was probably growing in a field just a few hours ago. With produce that fresh, it would be smart to buy in quantity. After all, it could be weeks before a similar selection might be available. I had learned: if something looks good, buy it. More than likely, there would not be another chance.

Once I had purchased the produce, it was time to head to the butcher. For someone raised in America where most meat is pre-packaged, or at least tantalizingly presented in a carefully managed butcher case, living in a world where each quarter kilo (about a half a pound) of meat was custom-cut presented challenges. For starters, I had never realized how much my perusal of the butcher counter had inspired our meals. Did a package of pork chops prompt a barbecue or would we prefer chicken thighs braised in a slowly simmered sauce? What looked good in the supermarket display often determined our evening meal.

Now, imagine this scenario: a sparkling clean, glass-enclosed, eight-foot butcher case filled with 10 to 15 hunks of meat, average size ... at least 30 pounds. Each chunk is different ... more fat or less fat, well marbled or without a hint of those tenderizing veins, pale pink or deep red. The differences were there, but what did they mean to my untrained eye? If I pointed and made a request, would I be ordering beef, veal, pork, horse, lamb or even goat? However, a closer examination of the display case could provide an important clue: the small, medium or even very large and very naked head from the prized animal was often there, right up front and center. Croatian butchers often proudly displayed the animal head to assist their customers in identifying the origins of the meat.

But those large chunks of flesh may not have been the only choices. Often, hanging directly behind the butcher case on giant hooks suspended from the ceiling, were three to six entire sides of animals. Approximate weight ... more than I could guess. How could I ever decide what I wanted? Would a few chops cut from that poor, skinless lamb make a tasty meal, or would I rather have a small roast from that quarter of a cow hanging beside? Or what about a pound of something from one of those carefully displayed 30-pound chunks? Fresh, custom-cut meat was definitely a culinary pleasure. Selecting that fresh, custom-cut meat was definitely a challenge.

In most cultures, it is fair to expect that a butcher is there to serve: to cut, grind, fillet and trim your order at your request. That makes it sound so simple, so easy. Oh, how I wished it were so. Often aloof and frequently arrogant, Croatian butchers would repeatedly plead ignorance to my requests. I would smile, I would point, I would stumble with my vocabulary, and I would write my request in Croatian. Despite these efforts, I was still frequently ignored or challenged. I did, however, learn not to take this attitude personally. More than one Croatian friend told me that the butcher frequently considered himself to reign supreme in the local community. After all, as the self-appointed ruler of the cutting block, it was he who determined who in town got the most tender and the most flavorful cut of meat.

After the stress of dealing with the butcher, I found shopping at the bakery to be easy and pleasurable. Rich, yeasty aromas filled the air and the bakers usually displayed their selections on open shelves and racks. With careful maneuvering through these busy and often crowded shops, I could usually see what was being offered. By the time it was my turn, I was ready to make a decision about the bread for the day. It was easy to say *malu bjeli kruh* (small white bread) or *veliku crni kruh* (large dark bread). Or, maybe I would simply point to my selection. Often the toughest decision was whether to buy a whole loaf or half loaf. Yes, in that waste-not society, they would actually cut a portion of bread for you.

During the summer, our bakery stops were critical. In the blazing hot summer months, it was just too hot to bake bread in the close confines of a small boat galley. In fact, there were times when our days and our destinations were actually charted by our need for bread. We did not live by bread alone, but it was an all-important ingredient in our well-balanced Mediterranean diet.

In Croatia, with the big markets, little markets and floating markets, the process of gathering groceries may have been challenging and unpredictable but it was always interesting, fun and rewarding.

Breads

Kruh, the Croatian word for bread, is an important staple in the Croatian diet. Nearly every village has its own baker or a fixed schedule for when fresh bread will be delivered to your home from a nearby bakery. And throughout the islands, bread is delivered by ferry with pre-established orders arriving regularly in the distant villages. All around the country, it is not unusual to see small, well-worn delivery trucks providing home delivery to regular customers. On my early morning walks, I would follow the bread deliveryman as he drove through a neighborhood, carefully hanging bulging plastic bags on front gates. Those recycled grocery bags were filled with the daily loaves ... some fat and round and some long and slender. Each family's standing order was well-known by the bread man.

Breads
BREADS

Cornmeal Bread
Makes 1 large or 2 small loaves

Distinctively golden, richly aromatic and absolutely mouth-watering when fresh from the oven, this corn bread is yummy when served with a hearty bowl of soup. It is also scrumptious when sliced thin, toasted and used as a foundation for your favorite bruschetta or hors d'oeuvres spread.

2 cups warm water, divided

2 teaspoons sugar

$1^1/_2$ packages dry yeast

1 cup cornmeal

3–3 $^1/_2$ cups flour

1 teaspoon salt

1 tablespoon gluten (optional)

1 tablespoon olive oil

In a small bowl, combine $^1/_2$ cup warm water (110–115 degrees), sugar and yeast. Allow the mixture to proof until it becomes bubbly, about 7–10 minutes. In a separate small bowl, combine the remaining 1½ cups of warm water with the cornmeal.

In a large mixing bowl, mix together 2 cups of the flour with the salt, gluten, olive oil, cornmeal and yeast mixtures. Stir, adding more flour as needed, until a stiff dough is formed.

Turn out onto a well-floured surface and knead until the dough is smooth and elastic, about 8–10 minutes. Place in a lightly oiled bowl and turn once to coat all surfaces. Cover and set in a warm, draft-free place until double in bulk, about 50 minutes. Punch down and turn out onto a lightly floured surface and knead several times. Cover and let rest for 10 minutes. Form into one or two loaves, place in pans, cover and let rise until double in bulk, about 45 minutes. Bake at 350 degrees until golden brown, about 35–40 minutes.

Cook's Notes:
• Use a heavy ceramic bowl and warm it with hot water before oiling and placing the dough in to rise. This will help speed up the rising process.

THROUGHOUT CROATIA, almost every restaurant meal includes a basket of freshly sliced bread. Most often, it is simply the local version of white bread. But every once in awhile, a special variety is served: dark wheat, seeded rye or a yeast-based cornbread. One summer evening, in the island town of Mali Losenj, we were served a basket filled with several varieties, including a distinctive cornbread. We enjoyed and appreciated this welcome change in the bread selection; but as special as the bread was, we felt exceptionally privileged when we realized that we had been seated in a prime ringside position to watch a performance by Vinko Coce.

Every country has its music idols and Vinko Coce ranks high on the list of Croatia's most popular performers. His CDs can be heard throughout the nation and his name is frequently mentioned as one of the top performers of traditional Croatian songs. It was almost as much fun to watch the audience, young and old, male and female, as they sang along with every word of his songs. Each time I make this bread, I remember that very special starlit night, the music and the fans. ▩

Croatian Easter Bread
Makes 4 loaves

If you're planning on using a mixer fitted with a dough hook or a food processor equipped with a bread blade, be aware that this recipe makes a large volume. Be sure that your equipment is large enough for the job.

2 packages dry yeast
1 teaspoon sugar
$1/4$ cup warm water
9 cups flour
1 cup sugar
1 teaspoon salt
2 teaspoons lemon zest (or orange zest or a combination of both)
$1^3/4$ cups milk
1 cup butter
4 egg yolks
2 eggs
1 egg, well beaten
1 tablespoon water
$1/4$ cup coarse sugar

Stir the yeast and sugar into the warm water (about 105–115 degrees) and set aside to proof for 7–10 minutes. Meanwhile, in a large mixing bowl, mix together 4 cups of flour, the sugar, salt and lemon zest. Combine the milk and butter and warm just enough to melt the butter. Allow the mixture to cool to 120 degrees.

Meanwhile, whisk together the egg yolks and the 2 eggs. Once the milk and butter have cooled, add the egg yolks and the eggs and stir the liquid into the flour mixture. Mix until blended, gradually adding more flour until a stiff dough forms. Turn the dough out onto a well-floured pastry board and knead until the dough is smooth and elastic.

Place the dough in a large, lightly oiled bowl and turn once to coat all surfaces. Cover with a clean towel and put in a warm place until the dough has doubled in bulk, about 2 to $2^1/2$ hours.

Meanwhile, butter 2 large cookie sheets. Divide the dough into 4 pieces and form each piece into a ball. Place 2 balls on each cookie sheet, cover and allow to rise until double in bulk, about 45 minutes to an hour. After the dough has risen, starting in the center of each ball, make three $1/2$-inch-deep equidistant cuts radiating from the center into the top of each round.

Whisk together the remaining egg with 1 tablespoon water. Brush the top of each round loaf with the egg wash and sprinkle with coarse sugar. Bake in 350-degree oven for 30 to 35 minutes.

EASTER IS A VERY special holiday in Croatia. The majority of Croatians are Roman Catholic, and as such they observe the prescribed sacrifices of Lent. Therefore, the joy of the risen Christ on Easter Sunday is cause for personal as well as religious celebrations. Families attend church, bringing their carefully decorated eggs and traditional bread in their Easter baskets to be presented for the customary blessing by the priest. After mass, they gather with family and friends to share the special foods of the day and of the season.

Croatian Nut Roll
Makes 2 loaves

Like many special-occasion breads and desserts, the preparation for this sweet bread is time-consuming, particularly if you do not have a stand mixer with a dough hook. If you are making this recipe without a mixer, be sure to allow extra time for hand kneading. Any way you make it, you'll be glad you did. The pleasure of the first bite and the praise from family and friends will make every ounce of effort worthwhile.

 1 package dry yeast
 $1/4$ cup warm water
 1 teaspoon sugar
 $4^1/2$ cups flour, divided
 1 cup warm milk
 $1/4$ cup butter, melted and cooled
 2 eggs, beaten
 $1/2$ cup sugar
 $1/2$ teaspoon vanilla
 $1/2$ teaspoon salt
 2 tablespoons butter, melted (optional)

In a small bowl, mix together the warm water (110–115 degrees), yeast and sugar. Allow the mixture to proof for 7–10 minutes or until the yeast is foamy. In an electric mixer fitted with a dough hook, add 2 cups of flour, the warm milk, butter, eggs, $1/2$ cup sugar, vanilla, salt and yeast mixture. Blend together on low speed. With the motor running, slowly add the remaining flour. The dough should just form a ball but remain somewhat soft and sticky. If the dough seems too moist, add a little more flour. Continue to knead with the dough hook for 5 to 6 minutes, until the ball is smooth and elastic. Place the dough in a lightly oiled bowl and turn once to coat all surfaces. Cover the bowl with a clean towel and place it in a warm spot. Let the dough rise until it has doubled in bulk, about $1^1/4$ hours. Punch down the dough and turn out onto a lightly-floured surface.

Let the dough rest for 10 minutes and then cut in half and form into 2 balls. Roll each ball into a rectangular sheet, 9 inches wide and 15 inches long. Spread each sheet with half of the filling (recipe on following page), being careful to keep the filling $1/2$ inch from the edge. Beginning with the narrow side, roll up the dough, jellyroll style. Once the dough is rolled up, pinch the edge of the dough to the roll. This pinched edge will become the bottom of the loaf. Gently stretch the side edges of the dough and bring them down to the bottom of the loaf, being careful to encase all of the filling. Pinch to seal those edges. Place, seam side down, in oiled loaf pans. Cover and let rise in a warm place until doubled in bulk, about 1 hour. Bake in a 350-degree oven for 35 to 40 minutes or until golden brown.

Remove the loaves from the oven and immediately remove the bread from the pan and place on wire rack. While still warm, brush the tops with melted butter (optional).

NUT FILLING:

2 cups ground walnuts

1 egg, beaten

¼ cup brown sugar

2 tablespoons honey

2 tablespoons milk

1 tablespoon butter, melted

1 teaspoon cinnamon

½ teaspoon vanilla

Mix together the walnuts, egg, brown sugar, honey, milk, butter, cinnamon and vanilla. If the mixture seems too thick to spread, add a little more milk.

Cook's Notes:

• For an alternate filling, substitute 1½ cups of raisins which have been plumped in a small amount of water for the nuts or use a combination of nuts and raisins.

AMERICANS OF CROATIAN DESCENT often mention this recipe as a homeland favorite. There are many stories about competitions between village cooks to determine who could make the best Nut Roll. It is hard to believe that there could ever be a "loser" in these friendly contests as this bread is always delicious ... fresh from the oven or toasted the next day.

Crusty Croatian Bread
Makes 1 loaf

On some days we found ourselves anchored in a picturesque cove with no nearby source of bread and there were other days when more bread than we had on hand was needed for an impromptu gathering. In those situations, I turned to this recipe. It makes a simple, no frills loaf of bread that is easy and relatively quick to make. Another bonus: it lasts for several days so don't hesitate to double the recipe.

1 package dry yeast
$1/2$ teaspoon sugar
$3/4$ cup warm water
2 tablespoons butter
$2–2^1/2$ cups flour
$1/2$ teaspoon salt

Dissolve the yeast and sugar in warm water (110–115 degrees) and set aside to allow to proof for 7–10 minutes, or until the yeast is foamy. Mix the flour with the salt and then, using your fingers, blend the butter into the flour mixture until the butter is well distributed and about the size of small peas. Combine the yeast mixture with 2 cups of flour and stir until a stiff dough is formed, adding more flour if needed. Turn out onto a lightly floured surface and knead until smooth and elastic, about 8–9 minutes. Oil a medium-sized bowl. Place the dough in the bowl and then turn it over to coat all sides. Cover the bowl with a clean towel and place it in a warm spot. Let rise until double in bulk, about 30 minutes.

Punch down the dough and form it into a long loaf. Place the loaf on a baking sheet and let rise until double in bulk, about 45 minutes to 1 hour. Bake at 400 degrees for 20 minutes. Reduce the heat to 350 degrees and bake for about 15 more minutes.

Cook's Notes:

• This entire process can be hastened by using a food processor fitted with a plastic bread blade or an upright mixer fitted with a dough hook. Either way, cut the butter into the flour and the salt. Add the water and knead until smooth and elastic, about 4–5 minutes. Proceed as above.
Hint: If you're using an upright mixer, place the mixer in a dry sink. This will contain the mixer and eliminate concerns about the mixer wandering off the countertop.

UP UNTIL THE TIME that Louis Pasteur identified yeast as a product made from living a microorganism, yeast was considered to be either a form of witchcraft or magic. Today it is used in baking as a leavening agent (a product that causes a foaming action) that converts fermentable sugars into carbon dioxide. In order for yeast to work, the conditions must be right: sufficient air, moisture and heat. As the carbon dioxide forms bubbles, the dough will rise. When the dough bakes, it "sets" and the pockets remain, giving the baked product a soft and spongy texture. ▨

Golden Butter Bread
Makes 3 loaves

If you've ever wished that your bread was served pre-buttered or that your toast popped out smelling like a freshly baked and buttery croissant, then this bread's for you! It boasts a smooth, buttery texture with a crisp and slightly flaky crust.

I like to add a tablespoon of gluten (available in most well-stocked supermarkets) to the flour when I stir in the salt. The gluten helps this exceptionally rich dough maintain its light, airy texture.

1 package dry yeast
$1/2$ cup warm water
1 teaspoon sugar
6–7 cups flour
$2^1/2$ teaspoons salt
1 tablespoon gluten (optional)
$2^1/2$ cups milk, warmed
$3/4$ cup butter, softened

In a small bowl, stir the yeast and sugar into the warm water (110–115 degrees) and set aside to proof for 7–10 minutes. In a large mixing bowl, mix together 4 cups of the flour with the salt and the (optional) gluten. Stir in the milk and the yeast. Stir in additional flour, as needed, to make a stiff dough. Turn the dough out onto a floured board and knead until smooth and elastic, about 10–12 minutes. Form the dough into a smooth ball and place in a large, lightly oiled bowl. Cover with a clean towel and place in a warm, draft-free location for 1 hour.

Turn the dough out onto a lightly floured surface and cut into thirds. Form each third into a round ball and let rest for 10 minutes. Using a rolling pin, roll each ball into a half-inch-thick rectangle, approximately 10 by 14 inches. Spread 1/3 of the softened butter evenly over the rectangle, keeping 1 inch free of butter on all sides. Beginning at the 10-inch side, roll the dough, jellyroll style. Pinch the long edge together and fold the ends under. Pinch the end edges together. Place each loaf seam side down in a buttered bread pan. Cover with a clean towel and place in a warm, draft-free location until double in bulk, about 2 hours. Bake at 350 degrees for 45 to 50 minutes.

Honey Wheat Bread
Makes 2 loaves

This bread tastes great straight from the oven and it makes a wonderful breakfast toast. It's also an outstanding base for raisin bread—just stir in some sweet, plump raisins as you finish your kneading. Another feature is that the dough can be prepared and refrigerated for up to 2 days in advance—just remove from the refrigerator and punch down and proceed with the loaf shaping when you're ready. You'll have fresh bread hot from the oven just when you want it!

2 cups milk
$1/4$ cup honey
$1/4$ cup butter
2 packages dry yeast
$1^1/2$ teaspoon salt
2 cups whole wheat flour
2 tablespoons gluten (optional)
$3^1/2$–4 cups unbleached flour

In a small saucepan, combine milk, honey and butter. Heat over medium heat, stirring occasionally, until the butter is melted and the ingredients are just warm, about 115 degrees. Stir in the yeast and allow to rest until bubbles begin to form, about 7–10 minutes.

In a large mixing bowl, combine the salt, whole-wheat flour, gluten (optional) and 2 cups of white flour. Stir in the warm liquids and mix, adding more flour as necessary, until a stiff dough is formed. Turn out onto a well-floured breadboard and knead, adding more flour if necessary, until a smooth and elastic dough is formed, about 8–10 minutes.

Shape the dough into a ball, cover with a clean towel and place in a lightly oiled bowl, turning it over to coat all sides. Cover and let rise in a warm place until double in bulk, about 45–60 minutes.

Punch down and turn out on a lightly floured surface and divide in half. Cover and let rest 10 minutes. Shape into 2 loaves and place in 2 oiled 8½ x 4½ x 2½ inch loaf pans. Cover and let rise in a warm place until double, about 30 minutes. Bake at 350 degrees for 35 to 40 minutes. Remove from the pans and cool on wire rack.

THROUGHOUT OUR SAILING ADVENTURE, we were blessed by several visits from my adventurous in-laws. As octogenarians, they had spent time with us in Italy, Greece and Turkey. In the fall of 2000, they arrived to spend a couple of weeks aboard *Klatawa* in Croatia.

Always willing to try new dishes, they were immediately impressed by the variety of breads that we had available in the market at Dubrovnik. They especially enjoyed this slightly sweet wheat bread and it soon became a favorite creation from our galley.

No Need to Knead Sweet Bread
Makes 2 loaves

From start to finish, this tasty bread takes about 3¹/₂ hours to prepare ... but the active time involved is less than 30 minutes. Best of all, there is no reason why the process cannot be interrupted. It's an ideal bread to begin a day ahead and then refrigerate overnight. Early the next morning, remove the loaves from the refrigerator, bring to room temperature, and soon the aroma of freshly baked bread will lure everyone to the breakfast table.

1 package dry yeast
1 teaspoon sugar
¹/₄ cup warm water
¹/₂ cup butter
1 cup milk
2 eggs
¹/₂ cup sugar
1 teaspoon salt
1 teaspoon vanilla
4–4¹/₂ cups flour

Dissolve the yeast and sugar in warm water and allow to proof for 7–10 minutes, until the yeast is foamy. In a small saucepan, melt the butter over low heat. Stir in the milk and heat until warm, about 115–120 degrees. Pour the mixture into a large mixing bowl.

Meanwhile, lightly beat the eggs and set aside 1 tablespoon of the beaten egg for later use. Add the eggs to the lukewarm milk mixture and stir in the sugar, salt and vanilla. Gradually add the flour, 1 cup at a time, until a stiff batter is formed, beating well after each addition.

Cover and let rise in a warm place until light and double in bulk, about 1 hour. Beat down and let rise once again until double in bulk, about 45 minutes. Spoon into 2 well-greased loaf pans. Cover and let rise in a warm place until light and doubled in bulk, about ³/₄ of an hour. Stir the remaining egg with 1 tablespoon of water and brush the tops of the loaves. Bake in a 350-degree oven for 25–30 minutes.

Cook's Notes:
• These loaves will be slightly smaller than loaves made using other bread recipes.
• For a different flavor, omit the vanilla and add 1¹/₂ teaspoons lemon and/or orange zest.
  Or try adding ³/₄ cup chopped dried apricot, raisins, dried cherries or cranberries.
• This finely textured sweet bread makes excellent toast.

Pogacha (Croatian Flat Bread)
Makes 2 flat loaves

Croatians call it pogacha *and Italians call it* foccacia. *Either way, it's a yummy, relatively quick flat-bread—just 3 hours from start to finish with less than 30 minutes active time. If you happen to have a food processor or mixer with a bread hook, it goes even faster. On the other hand, good old-fashioned kneading gives you a bit of exercise and you might even manage to get rid of a frustration or two!*

1³/₄ cups warm water
1 package dry yeast
2 tablespoons sugar
4¹/₂–5 cups of flour, divided; plus more for dusting
1 tablespoon gluten (optional)
¹/₂ teaspoon salt
3 tablespoons olive oil
Cornmeal

In a small bowl, mix the warm water with the yeast and the sugar and set aside to allow to proof for about 7–10 minutes.

In a large bowl, combine 3 cups of the flour with the (optional) gluten and the salt. Stir in the olive oil and the yeast mixture and mix vigorously with a wooden spoon until smooth. Gradually add the remaining flour, stirring until the dough becomes very stiff.

Scrape the dough onto a lightly floured work surface. Dust hands with flour and knead until dough is smooth and elastic, about 8 minutes. Add more flour as necessary to prevent sticking.

Shape the dough into a smooth ball and place in a lightly oiled large bowl, turning once to coat all surfaces. Cover with a clean towel and let stand in a warm, draft-free location until doubled in bulk, about 1 hour.

Preheat the oven to 375 degrees. Punch down the dough and divide in two pieces. Shape each piece into balls. Cover and let rest for 15 minutes.

Stretch each ball into a 9-inch round, about 1 inch thick. Place each round on a large cookie sheet that has been sprinkled with cornmeal, adding one of the toppings listed below if desired.

Bake at 375 degrees until golden brown, about 35 minutes. Serve hot.

Optional Toppings:
Basic salt topping: Brush each round with an egg wash that has been made by whisking together 1 egg and 1 tablespoon of water. Sprinkle with coarse sea salt.
Rosemary/onion topping: Toss together 1 very thinly sliced small onion, 2 teaspoons chopped, fresh rosemary and 1 tablespoon olive oil. Spread over the *pogacha* and sprinkle with coarse sea salt.
Garlic topping: Thinly slice 2-4 cloves of garlic. Brush *pogacha* with olive oil and evenly distribute the garlic.

Cook's Notes:
• *Pogacha* can be baked, cooled and then wrapped tightly in foil for up to 2 days. Reheat in a 350-degree oven for 20 minutes. You may also freeze this bread for up to 3 weeks. Bring to room temperature and then reheat in a 350-degree oven for 20 minutes.

ALMOST NOTHING ATTRACTS ATTENTION like the aroma of yeast bread baking in the oven. Walk down a dock with a hot loaf or two and you will have folks flocking after you like a starving gaggle of geese. Freshly baked bread is a sure way to make new friends in any port (or neighborhood). ▩

Potato Bread
Makes 2 loaves

Since the amount of water used to cover and cook the potatoes determines the amount of flour required in this recipe, be sure that the water just covers the potatoes. Also, the nature of this dough tends to be very sticky—another factor that makes figuring out how much flour to add even trickier. Try to get a balance between slightly sticky and slightly manageable. It may take more flour than you think. If in doubt, go ahead and add it, this recipe is just about foolproof.

3 medium baking potatoes (about 1 pound), peeled and cut in 1 inch cubes
2 tablespoons butter
$1/3$ cup warm milk
1 package dry yeast
1 teaspoon sugar
4–5 cups flour
1 tablespoon gluten (optional)
$1^1/2$ teaspoon salt
1 egg, slightly beaten

Place the potatoes in a medium saucepan and barely cover with water. Bring to a boil and simmer until the potatoes are tender when pierced with a fork, about 15–20 minutes. Remove from the heat and add the butter. Mash the potatoes in their liquid and allow to cool.

Meanwhile, in a small bowl, mix the warm milk (115 degrees) with the yeast and the sugar and allow to stand until foamy, about 7–10 minutes.

In a large bowl, combine 2 cups of the flour with the (optional) gluten and the salt. Stir in the potato mixture, the yeast mixture and the egg. Using a wooden spoon, mix vigorously until smooth. Gradually add the remaining flour, stirring until the dough becomes very stiff.

Scrape the dough onto a lightly floured work surface. Dust hands with flour and knead until the dough is smooth and elastic, about 8 minutes, adding more flour as necessary to prevent sticking.

Shape the dough into a smooth ball and place in a lightly oiled large bowl, turning once to coat all surfaces. Cover with a clean towel and let stand in a warm, draft-free location until double in bulk, about 1 hour.

Preheat the oven to 350 degrees. Punch down the dough and divide into two pieces. Shape into two loaves and place in greased loaf pans. Cover and allow to rise until double in bulk, about 30–40 minutes.

Bake at 350 degrees until golden brown, about 45–50 minutes. Remove immediately from pans and allow to cool.

POTATOES, THOSE HUMBLE TUBERS, have been a staple in peasant homes throughout the world for centuries. Today they provide sustenance and pleasure everywhere on earth, as they are cultivated in virtually every climate. Grown throughout Croatia, it is easy to ignore the rows of potatoes that are planted in nearly every kitchen garden ... for there are no bright and shiny globes of fruit clinging to their vines to sparkle in the summer sun. There are simply rows of green leaves reaching up to the sun in order to feed the tender tubers growing below.

From our friend Pepi on the island of Iz, we learned of the importance of potatoes in the Croatian peasant diet; and we learned of the traditional awareness of the dangers of consuming potatoes tinged with green. These potatoes, full of toxic alkaloids (the result of too much exposure to light) are potentially lethal. He shared his village's warning that even pigs who are fed green potatoes have been known to die.

Healthy, untainted potatoes are used in many traditional Croatian dishes: tasty *brudets*, tender gnocchi and delicious breads. In this bread recipe, the peasant mantra of no waste is respected. The cooking water, rich in vitamins B and C and potassium, is used as the liquid for this satisfying bread. ▓

A Day With Pepi ...
Pottery and Pageantry

It was late July and it was hot. Hellishly hot.. The thermometer in the cockpit threatened to reach 110 degrees and the large white canvas awning (in sailing jargon, a bimini), designed to shield us from the sun's brazen force, didn't begin to protect us from the day's penetrating heat. To make matters worse, there was not a whisper of wind. In fact, the only hint of a breeze was the scarcely perceptible flow generated by *Klatawa's* sluggish, motor driven passage through the mirror-like waters of the Kornati Islands. We felt lazy. We had little motivation. We didn't know what we wanted to do or where we wanted to go.

On the bright side, our ever-reliable refrigerator continued to produce a seemingly endless supply of chilled water and thirst-quenching juices. But cool drinks provided little relief as the heat grew more intense with each passing hour. So by late morning, when we were ready to consider something more substantial than a liquid diet, I enthusiastically volunteered to dive headfirst into the depths of the refreshingly cold, top-loading refrigerator.

All too soon my mission into the cooling cavity was accomplished. I resurfaced with a few tiny vine-ripened tomatoes, a super-sweet seedless cucumber, a small plastic container of day-old left-over pasta primavera, a well-hidden chicken leg, a small chunk of Cambozola cheese and some leftover grilled red peppers that had been soaking in a garlicky balsamic vinaigrette. I found all these little treasures buried and tucked between a 10-pack carton of eggs, a paper bag full of mixed purple and white eggplants, a recycled grocery bag brimming with fresh green beans and the multiple liter-size containers of fruit juices and milk.

Spread out on a colorful Italian platter, it was the perfect lunch to pick at as we carefully checked our charts and to wend our way through the nearly 150 islands, islets and reefs that make the Kornati Islands the largest archipelago in the Adriatic. Sculpted out of light gray, almost-white limestone, these islands are rugged, barren and pretty much uninhabited. And in the bright summer sun, they appeared almost surreal—rocky lands, crosshatched with mile upon mile of three-foot-high stone walls, that emerge from what may be the bluest water in the world. In this shriveling heat, we felt stunted, insignificant and humbled by our surroundings.

According to our guidebooks, the Kornatis did not always look this way. Just a few hundred years ago they were a series of sparsely populated, lush green lands that provided ideal conditions for resident shepherds to graze their growing flocks of sheep. It was during that period that the seemingly endless miles of sculpturally handsome old stone walls that we admire today were built by the shepherds' hard-working wives. Those women painstakingly cleared the fields rock by rock and built the walls that defined each family's grazing lands.

Life was good for a couple of centuries but then things began to change. For several decades, the shepherds watched with distress as their green pastures became increasingly barren. Finally, motivated by the mistaken notion that clearing the land would encourage new growth, the shepherds burned off the vegetation. Sadly, the plant life failed to return. However, the stone walls remained, providing an everlasting tribute to the backbreaking efforts of those early female inhabitants. Now, as a new century begins, there seems to be a bit more green scrub appearing in the rocky crevices. There is hope that some vegetation might be returning.

※ ※ ※

This was not our first visit to the Kornatis. We had sailed through these islands several times and our images and impressions changed with each visit, each season, each day and each hour. We were always fascinated and entertained by the changing angles of the sun on the limestone hills and cliffs. Shadows emerge, shift slowly and then disappear. Sharp, rocky angles soften into gentle curves. And this day, as we looked out upon these islands and islets, surrounded by the clear and brilliant blue sky and the deep crystal clean azure blue Adriatic Sea, it was easy to understand the inspiration behind George Bernard Shaw's memorable words: "On the last day of the Creation, God desired to crown His work, and thus created the Kornati Islands out of tears, stars and the breath of the sea."

But our thoughts remained inescapably focused on the heat and the possibility of relief from it. We thought about a cool swim and we thought about the pleasures provided by green shade trees. Suddenly, our cell phone rang. It was our good friends Darryl and Jean aboard *Sheba Moon* calling to invite us to the annual *Iske Feste* (Iz Festival) on the nearby island of Iz. They promised shade trees and they guaranteed new experiences at the traditional Croatian festival. We readily agreed and made plans to rendezvous at the Veli Iz marina, just 20 miles away.

※ ※ ※

Leaving the stark and barren Kornati Islands, our approach to Iz provided a tantalizing and refreshing contrast. From a distance, the island appeared lush and green and we anxiously anticipated our arrival at the oasis. As we got closer, we were able to identify large olive groves, small farms and wide expanses of native woodlands. Iz looked shady, cool, inviting and revitalizing.

But the day was still very hot. Upon entering the small (despite the name *veli*, meaning big) enclosed harbor, the stifling calm and heavy air that engulfed the horseshoe-shaped space suddenly overwhelmed us. We questioned our decision to tie up in town and thereby sacrifice the cool and refreshing swim that anchoring in a nearby cove could provide. Our timing, however, required a now-or-never decision. Just two spaces remained for this popular festival weekend—space for us and space for *Sheba Moon*. We decided to stay.

Once our boat was successfully squeezed in between two other vessels already stern-tied to the dock, I headed off for an exploratory hike on this island that is home to 300 full-time residents. The temperature this afternoon remained well above the 100-degree mark, and my intended brisk walk became a sluggish stroll. I wandered aimlessly for over an hour along the waterfront and up through the dusty, narrow and meandering roads of the small village. It seemed that these freshly whitewashed homes with their red tile roofs were built a few feet farther apart than those on the mainland and on most of the neighboring islands. Consequently, the front-yard kitchen gardens were slightly larger, boasting a few more well-tended grapevines, an extra row or two of juicy multi-hued tomatoes, mangold (a spinach-like vegetable), red and green peppers and glossy white and purple eggplants.

Toward the end of my walk, I found myself back at the water's edge, wandering along a well-worn stone trail that headed toward a cluster of houses. At the foot of one narrow pathway that led up to the front entrance of one of these homes was a weathered driftwood sign that read *"Iska Keramika."* It was just the sign I had hoped to discover. According to my guidebook, Iz is the only island in Dalmatia that has a history of pottery making. As an avid ceramics admirer, I was eager to learn more about this traditional craft. I returned to the boat, shared my enthusiasm and quickly convinced Bill, Jean and Darryl to join me for a visit.

❈ ❈ ❈

The front door to the potter's studio stood wide open. As we stepped across the threshold, the earthy aroma of damp clay surrounded us and a soft, deep male voice beckoned us with a friendly *"dobar dan."* From deeper within the refreshingly cool, dark and cluttered space came another voice calling out *"dobar dan."* This one was bright, cheerful and feminine. As our eyes slowly adjusted to the low light, we returned this standard Croatian greeting and introduced ourselves. Then the short, slim and strong man dressed in clay-spattered shorts and T-shirt and seated at the manually operated potter's wheel introduced himself and his wife: Predrag Petrovic—*Pepi,* for short—and Jadranka Bukic-Petrovic *his* "store manager."

A sense of welcome pervaded the centuries-old space that served as Pepi's studio and pottery shop, now cluttered with jetsam and flotsam from the sea and pieces of ancient pottery. We immediately sensed this couple's respect for their culture, their craft and for their nation's past. Thankfully, both Pepi and Jadranka spoke excellent English and we were soon exchanging stories. We chatted about our sailing experiences, our families, our hometowns, and we learned more about Pepi's craft, about the island of Iz, about Croatia and about Pepi and Jadranka's families.

Pepi spoke patiently about the history of pottery in Dalmatia and his personal interest and involvement with this ancient craft. He explained that both clay and sand are required to make pottery and that clay suitable for making pottery is rarely found in Dalmatia. Although there may be pockets of clay on other islands, no one in Dalmatia has ever made pots any where except on Iz. Furthermore, there is no sand on the island so local *vrsta* (calcite stone) must be ground manually. It did not take us long to realize that making Dalmatian pottery is hard and demanding work—but the results are functional and long lasting. Pots from Iz have been used throughout the Adriatic for centuries and Pepi, a schoolteacher by profession, was dedicated to studying and preserving the traditional methods and designs.

At one time, there were more than 50 potters on the island. But at the time of our visit, only two remained—both faithfully creating the traditional rustic dishes that have been used for cooking and baking for centuries. Pots from Iz come in many different shapes, each created for a specific purpose: to store cheese in oil, to cook a *brudet* (a meat, fish or vegetable stew-like dish), to fry potatoes, or to cover bread or meat as it bakes or roasts. As Pepi described each vessel, Jadranka retrieved an example from the shelves that lined the walls of their studio. Many of these utilitarian pots require as many as three pieces: a small base in which to build a wood fire, a vessel for holding and cooking the food, and a lid. Because so many men from Iz were fishermen, many pieces were originally designed to be used at sea.

Throughout our conversation in this tiny, low-ceilinged, stone-walled studio, Pepi remained seated on his short, wooden potter's stool, chatting softly while calmly and steadily turning the wheel. In less than 30 minutes, he finished a pot—complete with an arched handle and a decorative pattern precisely etched into the soft clay with his wooden stylus. Finally, Pepi pulled a thin, taut thread across the base of the bowl, and skillfully removed the object from the wheel. As he set the finished piece aside and began working the clay for his next piece, he talked about the firing process.

According to the ancient traditions on Iz, there are three important steps required to create terra cotta. First, the clay pots are gently air-dried indoors (sometimes for days or even weeks). Next they are set out for at least a few days in the blazing hot summer sun and finally they are fired in a traditional wood-fueled open-pit fire. To help prevent the vessels from shattering in the intense heat of this last phase (temperatures reach between 800 and 900 degrees Celsius), the heat is increased gradually. It is this extreme heat that triggers the chemical change that transforms the clay into terra cotta. Our visit to Iz was perfectly timed. Late today they would fire a batch of pots.

▨ ▨ ▨

Armed with our cameras, we headed to the designated field. Soon, two young men and a woman, all dressed in standard blue work coveralls, appeared. They were pushing wheelbarrows padded with well-worn and dusty blue quilted blankets and filled with large *pekas* (dome-shaped lids that are used for baking bread and roasting meat) and bowls of varying sizes. They carefully spread the pots out one by one in the full sunlight and then headed off for another batch. Likewise, this second load was gently placed in the full sun. The day's powerful summer sun would slowly preheat the pots. The artisans suggested that we find some shade and return in several hours to watch the firing process.

By the time we returned, 50 to 75 pots had been meticulously arranged on a barren 10-by-20-foot patch of land that had been preheated by a ground fire. These pots of various sizes and shapes had been carefully stacked against one another—in a style reminiscent of a house of cards. Jean, Darryl, Bill and I kept checking the wind. As sailors, we were sensitive to the late afternoon breeze and hoped that the wind would remain calm enough for the project to continue. The potters did not seem to share our concern; they were confidently armed with buckets and watering cans.

After a brief strategy huddle, the "firing team" began to toss clumps of hay and straw on top of the pots. Once all the pieces were evenly covered, the fuel was ignited. Slowly, more and more handfuls of fuel were added. This gentle fire had to be kept alive for 20 to 30 minutes.

Once the clay was preheated, it was time for the serious firing to begin. Bunches of dried olive branches were piled upon the pots and the flames began to mount. The fast-burning fire was constantly hand-fed by what was now a four-member team. Our friend Pepi had appeared and was working front and center. The team watched closely as the wind, made stronger by the intense heat, started several runaway fires. Quickly, with buckets and sprinkling cans, the errant fires were extinguished. This extremely hot fire burned for about 10 minutes and then burned itself out.

As the last flames flickered, three team members reached for long cypress and acacia branches to brush away the ash that had accumulated in mounds on the rows of pottery. A nearby observer told us that these ashes must be cleared—otherwise they would form an unwanted layer of insulation over the pots. This firing process, using hot-burning olive wood, was repeated a second and a third time. After the third firing, success was declared. The clay pots had been transformed into terra cotta.

❈ ❈ ❈

In addition to continuing the ancient tradition of pottery, Iz has long been a cultural center celebrating music and theater throughout the centuries. As the new century began, local residents were focusing their efforts on rebuilding some of these traditions and the *Iske Feste* was part of that endeavor. Three days of games, music, poetry and dance were all part of the activities, which culminated with the age-old ceremony of "Crowning the New King."

As tradition demanded, the featured event began well past sundown. There was no moon and the sea was hauntingly calm. The entire village and hundreds of visitors had gathered along the shore in silent anticipation. Suddenly, like noiseless ghosts, the old king and his court were sighted in the harbor, arriving aboard several very old wooden sailing/fishing boats. In anticipation of this fairytale-like event, all the lights along the shore had been extinguished. The only visible light was cast by the time-honored oil lanterns hung on each of the vessels. The light from these lanterns spread a surreal and noble mood on both participants and observers.

The king's court included a large entourage of men and women all dressed in traditional costumes. These islanders are people with simple traditions. The men were dressed in rough-textured black pants, black vests and loose white blouses with long, ballooning sleeves. Their bright six-inch-wide red fabric belts wrapped their waists and matched the small red round hats atop their heads. Likewise, the women's clothing was simple: long, dark skirts and black vests over long-sleeved white blouses. Only a few of the vests boasted embroidery, and only a few women wore colorful necklaces. However, every female head was covered with a bright white *babushka*.

As the procession moved slowly off the boats and away from the quay, heading toward the ceremonial stage in the town square, the men and women began chanting ancient songs and verses. Finally, the old king stepped onto land. He was the last to leave the boat and he followed his increasingly boisterous court toward the town square. Even the king reflected his humble heritage. Beneath a somewhat elaborate and definitely well-used cloak, he was dressed just like the other men. It was, however, his colorful crown (could it possibly have been a fifth-grade craft project?) and his six-foot scepter topped with a bright yellow rubber ball that set him apart.

As a final gesture to royalty, a young male member of the king's court, dressed in a seafaring costume of cropped blue pants, a blue and white horizontally striped shirt and a red pirate-tied *babushka*, rotated three sheepskins across the ground. His job was to assure that the king's feet remained clean and comfortable. We guessed that this was the local version of rolling out the red carpet.

Once the key players were on stage, the official ceremony began. Given our Croatian-challenged ears, it was difficult to understand exactly what was happening. But thanks to a nearby English-speaking acquaintance, we were laughingly informed that the new king would be selected by the time-honored method of "whoever gets the longest stick wins." Tonight there would be a definite Mediterranean twist: The new king would be selected by drawing the longest *spaghet*.

Throughout the ceremony, we wondered which parts of this ritual were based on historical fact and which parts were the result of modern-day fun and fiction. One thing for certain, politicians throughout the world and throughout history have been and continue to be notoriously long-winded. There was little question that the entire ceremony could have been significantly abbreviated had the old king and the new king not spent so much time paying endless compliments to one another and to their loyal supporters. We also strongly suspected that the "magic potion" in the large-handled wooden vessel radically loosened the royal tongues as it passed freely and frequently between the old and the new kings.

❧ ❧ ❧

Early the next morning, we returned to the pottery studio to say farewell to Pepi and Jadranka. As we sat outside in the pleasantly shaded yard, surrounded by bits and pieces of old fishing boats and paraphernalia used at sea, we sipped a coffee-flavored liqueur and enjoy a selection of home-made cakes and cookies. We chatted comfortably and thanked our host and hostess for opening their studio, their home and their hearts to us. In just a few days, we had begun to forge a friendship; we had developed a sense of their personal history, their joys of family and friends and the sorrows imposed by the recent war. And we had learned of their dream to establish a pottery school, a place where pottery students from around the world could come to break away from the frenzies of urban life and to learn the local traditions and the ancient ways of making pottery.

Dessert

In the coastal regions of Croatia, dessert is not routinely served in homes or restaurants. As a matter of fact, there are those who will say that residents of this region do not favor sweets. The reason is climatic. Before refrigeration, rich foods did not keep during the long hot summers. Even today, there are rural areas where refrigeration is not available. Consequently, it is likely that as guests in homes and restaurants, you will be offered a local *grappa* as a *digestif* instead.

That is not to say that Croatians do not have a sweet tooth. Leavened sweet breads, cakes, cookies and pastries are served whenever friends and family gather and they are a tradition on festive occasions: special breads at Easter, fritters (raised doughnuts) at Christmas and crisp fried *hrustule* at Carnival time.

And there is no question about the Austro-Hungarian influence. The most traditional Croatian dessert is a torte ... a cake that comes in all sizes, shapes and flavors. Most involve several layers and require lengthy beating of egg whites and yolks ... customs that evolved long before the KitchenAid. Today's busy cooks are lucky—they can turn to store-bought pre-baked torte shells, filling them with whipped cream, custards and/or fresh fruits.

Fruits and nuts—the bounty of the Mediterranean climate—often end a meal. But if pears, grapes, strawberries, apricots, figs, oranges, cherries, lemons, dates and plums are not available fresh, you'll find them dried ... ready to nibble or use in a favorite recipe.

Desserts
DESSERTS

Apple Cake
Serves 12 to 14

The recipe for this cake came from Croatia, but the butter and sugar coating that creates the wonderful crust came from Klatawa. It has become a favorite—we've even been known to have a slice or two at breakfast.

4 eggs
2$^1/_4$ cup sugar, divided
1 tablespoon baking powder
2 teaspoons vanilla
1 cup vegetable oil
$^1/_4$ cup orange juice
1 teaspoon grated orange rind
3 cups flour
2 teaspoons cinnamon
3 large Granny Smith apples, peeled and diced

Preheat the oven to 350 degrees. Carefully butter a nonstick Bundt pan and heavily dust with sugar, being sure that all surfaces are well coated. In a large mixing bowl, using a wooden spoon, combine the eggs, 2 cups of sugar, baking powder, vanilla, oil, orange juice, orange rind and flour. In a smaller bowl, combine the remaining ¼ cup of sugar and the cinnamon and toss with the apples. Combine the batter with the apples and pour into the prepared Bundt pan. Bake at 350 degrees for 65 to 75 minutes or until a toothpick inserted in the center of the cake comes out clean. If desired, serve with Ginger Lemon Cream.

GINGER-LEMON CREAM
1 cup whipping cream, chilled
2 teaspoons grated fresh ginger
1 teaspoon grated lemon rind
1$^1/_2$ tablespoons honey
Whip the cream until soft peaks begin to form.
Add the remaining ingredients and whip until stiff peaks form.

Cook's Notes:

- This recipe makes a large, dense cake. You can split the batter between 2 prepared Bundt pans and reduce baking time by 15 to 20 minutes. The extra cake makes a wonderful hostess gift or freezes well for up to 1 month.

- It is easy to dress up this cake for guests. Just add a dollop of whipped cream, a scoop of ice cream or a slathering of Ginger-Lemon Cream.

- Add ¾ cup of raisins to the batter for a tasty and healthy alternative.

Chocolate Cherry Cake
Makes one 8-inch-square cake

This moist and simple cake can easily be transformed into a glamorous dessert. Just cut the cake into serving-size portions, place each piece on a serving plate and top with sweetened whip cream. Grate semi-sweet chocolate over the top and serve.

> 5 ounces semisweet chocolate
> 6 ounces butter
> 1 cup powdered sugar
> 1/4 teaspoon salt
> 4 eggs
> 3/4 cup sifted flour
> 1 1/2 cups pitted, canned and drained cherries

Preheat the oven to 350 degrees. Generously butter and lightly flour an 8-inch-square baking pan. Break up the chocolate and melt in a small, heavy saucepan over low heat, stirring constantly. Allow to cool.

Cream the butter and sugar together until light and fluffy. Add the salt. Separate the eggs and add the yolks, one at a time, to the butter and sugar mixture, beating well after each addition. Add the cooled, melted chocolate. Beat the egg whites until light and fluffy. Fold in 1/4 of the egg whites into the batter and stir lightly until well incorporated. Fold in half of the remaining egg whites. Fold in half of the flour. Repeat with the remaining egg whites and flour.

Spread the batter in the pan and sprinkle the cherries over the batter. The cherries will sink into the batter as the cake bakes. Bake 40 to 45 minutes or until a toothpick inserted in the center comes out clean. Note: this cake is best if made at least 6 hours in advance.

Cook's Notes:
• To melt the chocolate in the microwave, place the broken chocolate in a glass cup or bowl. Microwave on high power for 30 seconds. Stir. Repeat the 30-second cycle of heating and stirring until the chocolate is smooth.

EVEN THE MOST PROTECTED anchorage can provide challenges when the weather changes. Aboard *Klatawa*, the captain paid close attention to all available weather indicators: weather forecasts (when available), the barometer, the sky and that good old-fashioned sixth sense, intuition. So it was not surprising that when all indicators predicted a *sirocco* (gusty, humid winds from the south that often bring rain mixed with red Sahara mud) extra precautions were taken. Bill added another line to reinforce our bond to the mooring buoy to which we were tied.

As expected, the winds increased and their direction shifted ... not just once but several times, turning us around and around. The next day, when it was time for us to leave, we had a problem. The lines were twisted and the wind was blowing steadily at 20 knots, creating a lot of tension on those twisted lines. To make a long story short, Bill, with his wonderful logic and infinite patience, managed to undo the mess and we were on our way. The entire exercise created a little tension that could best be relieved by something sweet and something chocolate. I headed below to bake a Chocolate Cherry Cake.

Cream Cheese and Strawberry Torte
Serves 6

Readily available throughout Croatia are long-life sponge-cake torte shells. And, it is no secret why they are popular—they can be quickly filled with fruit, pudding or whatever happens to be on hand for an almost-instant yet elegant and tasty dessert. Such dessert shells are difficult to find in the United States so I often substitute a single-layer yellow cake mix or sliced, previously frozen pound cake.

1 9-inch single layer yellow cake

8 ounces cream cheese, softened

2 tablespoons heavy cream

2 tablespoons grated lemon zest

1/2 cup sugar, divided

1 quart strawberries

1 cup whipping cream

Cut the cake in half horizontally and place the bottom half on a cake plate. Using an electric mixer, whip the cream cheese until smooth and fluffy. Add the cream and lemon zest and gradually add the sugar, reserving 2 tablespoons for later use. Gently spread the cheese filling over the bottom layer.

Slice about 1 cup of the strawberries and arrange over the cream filling. Place the second layer of cake on top of the strawberries. Whip the cream until it becomes thick. Add the remaining 2 tablespoons of sugar and whip until soft peaks form. Spread the whipped cream over the top layer of the cake. Cut the remaining strawberries in half and arrange decoratively on top.

Luscious Loaf Cake
Yield 1 loaf

For a larger, more sophisticated presentation, double this recipe and bake in a Bundt pan. Dust with powdered sugar just before serving.

3/4 **cup butter**
1 3/4 **cup powdered sugar**
1 **teaspoon vanilla**
3 **eggs**
2 **cups flour**
1 **teaspoon baking powder**
Pinch of salt
1 **teaspoon lemon peel**
1 **cup raisins (or chopped walnuts, dried chopped apricots, dried cherries, etc.)**

Preheat the oven to 325 degrees. Butter and generously flour a 5 x 9-inch loaf pan. In a large mixing bowl, cream together the butter and the sugar. Stir in the vanilla and add the eggs, one at a time, beating well after each addition. In a separate bowl, stir together the flour, baking powder, salt, lemon peel and dried fruit then add to the egg mixture. Mix until all ingredients are well combined. Spoon the batter into the loaf pan and bake for 50 to 60 minutes or until a toothpick inserted in center comes out clean.

Cook's Notes:
• My favorite dried-fruit combination is ½ cup each dried and finely chopped apricots and dried cherries.

MANY OF THE EXPATRIATES that were a part of our international cruising community were retired or semi-retired. Although we came from all walks of life, we rarely talked "shop." But there were a few remarkable exceptions. One was our British dentist friend, Denis. Denis was semi-retired from his surgery in the UK, but he had set up a full dental office aboard his ketch, *Electra II*. Patients were always welcomed and professionally treated as he cruised throughout the Mediterranean.

In the summer of 2001, we were glad that Denis was nearby in his favorite Croatian anchorage off the village of Venisce. Our friend and guest, Lee, had broken a tooth and although it was not painful, it was annoying and uncomfortable. As we sailed into the anchorage, it was only moments before Denis was in his dinghy and rowing over to greet us. Soon he was aboard, introductions were made, a jug of wine was shared and an invite to dinner was extended. We settled into a friendly evening, sharing sailing tales and life stories. Before heading back to *Electra II*, Denis had set a time for the following morning to perform some "wet finger dentistry" on Lee's damaged tooth.

The next day, while Lee was being treated, Lee's wife, Karen, and I made this loaf cake as a thank you for Denis. ▓

Quick and Yummy Crustless Cheesecake
Serves 8

There was no food processor in Klatawa's, galley so I simply stirred together all the ingredients for this simple cheesecake. The results were not as smooth as this version but both styles are yummy.

> 1 pound cottage cheese
> 8 ounces cream cheese, softened
> 1/3 cup flour
> 4 eggs
> 1/4 cup butter, softened
> 1/4 teaspoon salt
> 1/2 cup cream
> 3/4 cup sugar
> 1 teaspoon lemon rind, grated

Preheat the oven to 350 degrees. Very generously butter a 6-cup ceramic tart pan or casserole dish and set aside.

Place all of the ingredients, in the order listed, in the bowl of a food processor. Pulse the mixture until the cottage cheese is smooth and all the ingredients are well blended, scraping down the sides of the bowl once or twice. Pour the mixture into the prepared baking pan and smooth the surface. Bake at 350 degrees for 50 minutes or until the center is just set. Remove from the oven and allow to cool slightly before cutting into pieces and serving.

Cook's Notes:
• For a special dessert, serve with sliced, sweetened strawberries.

CROATIANS LOVE CHEESE and a selection of cheese is often considered to be a wonderful way to begin or end a fine meal. However, if the cheese happens to be soft, mild and slightly sweetened, you'll often find it used as a filling for pastries, cakes, pancakes and pies. This quick and easy dessert provides a sweet cheese treat without the time-consuming pastry that traditionally encases a cheescake.

Sour Cherry (or Plum) Cake
Yield: one 9-inch-square cake

The sweet and crunchy optional topping for this cake is not traditional. However, sweet-toothed Americans seem to have a preference for this satisfying version. Try it either way and make your own decision. You can also serve this cake for brunch or with a cup of coffee for a mid-morning snack.

3/4 cup butter, softened

1 cup sugar

3 eggs

1 1/2 cups flour

2 teaspoons baking powder

1 teaspoon lemon rind, grated

1 teaspoon orange rind, grated

1/3 cup walnuts, finely chopped

3 cups cherries, drained if they are canned (or ripe plums)

Optional topping:

1/4 cup butter

1/4 cup sugar

1/4 cup brown sugar

1/3 cup flour

1/3 cup walnuts, finely chopped

Preheat the oven to 350 degrees. Lightly butter a 9 x 9-inch-square baking pan. Cream together the butter and sugar until light and fluffy. Beat in the eggs, one at a time. In a separate bowl, stir together the flour, baking powder, lemon rind, orange rind and chopped walnuts. Stir the flour mixture into the butter and egg mixture.

Spread a thin layer of batter over the bottom of the pan. Top with half the cherries. Spread the remaining batter and top with the remaining cherries. Blend together the topping ingredients and sprinkle over the top. Bake at 350 degrees for 45–50 minutes or until a toothpick inserted in the center comes out clean.

Cook's Notes:
• For a tasty alternative, substitute ripe plums for the cherries.
• If you are using fresh fruit, taste for tartness. If the fruit is exceptionally tart, you may want to mix a small amount of sugar into the fruit before adding it to the pan.

IN THE LATE FALL OF 2002 we were interviewed and filmed for a Croatian National Television program. The producers were curious about our live-aboard lifestyle during the sailing off-season. In order to provide several perspectives, we gathered together the few remaining cruising couples still living in the Dubrovnik ACI marina and invited the television crew aboard. As the program hostess asked her questions and the cameraman filmed, this cake was baking in the oven. We concluded the shoot with a slice of Sour Cherry Cake. ▩

Biscotine

Similar to Italian biscotti, Croatian Biscotine *tends to be more tender and easier to munch. And like their Italian counterparts, they are delicious when dipped into a piping-hot cup of coffee. This particular recipe features two favorite Dalmatian flavors: walnuts and cherries.*

1/2 cup butter
1/2 cup sugar
3 eggs
2 teaspoons orange peel, grated
Juice from 1 orange (about ¼ cup)
1 teaspoon vanilla
3 cups flour
1 tablespoon baking powder
1/2 cup walnuts, chopped
1/2 cup dried cherries

Preheat the oven to 350 degrees. Beat together the butter and sugar until light and creamy. Add the eggs, one at a time, beating well after each addition. Stir in the orange peel, orange juice and vanilla. Add the flour, baking powder, walnuts and cherries and stir until well mixed.

Turn the dough out onto a lightly floured pastry board and divide in half. Gently gather one half of the dough and roll into a log, about 12 inches long. Place the log on one side of a cookie sheet. Repeat with the second half and place parallel to the first log. Gently press to slightly flatten the logs. Bake at 350 degrees for about 35 minutes or until the logs are golden and they are beginning to crack. Remove from the oven and allow to cool for 20 minutes. Reduce the oven temperature to 275 degrees.

Using a bread knife, slice the logs diagonally into ¾-inch slices and place flat side down on a cookie sheet. Return to the oven and bake at 275 degrees, turning once midway through the baking, for 35 minutes or until the biscotine are dry and crisp. Store in a well-sealed container for 3 days or freeze for up to 2 months.

Croatian Christmas Cookies

These cookies are perfect for the holiday season as they retain the contrasting textures of the shortbread and the meringue for up to several weeks. Just keep covered and store in a cool, dark place. Cut into bars just before serving.

$1/2$ pound butter, softened

$1/2$ cup sugar

2 egg yolks

$1/2$ teaspoon salt

$2^1/4$ cup flour

4 egg whites

1 cup sugar

2 teaspoons lemon rind, finely grated

$3/4$ cup walnuts, finely chopped

$1^1/4$ cups currant jelly

$1/2$ cup walnuts, coarsely chopped

Preheat the oven to 300 degrees. Cream together the butter and sugar until light and fluffy. Beat in the egg yolks and salt and then gradually stir in the flour. Pat the dough into a thin layer in the bottom of a well-buttered cookie sheet. Bake at 300 degrees for 20 minutes.

Beat the egg whites until foamy. Gradually add the sugar and continue to beat until stiff. Add the lemon rind and fold in the finely chopped walnuts.

Spread the jelly over the warm dough and top with the meringue. Sprinkle with the coarsely chopped walnuts. Increase the oven temperature to 325 degrees and bake for 35 minutes. Remove from the oven and allow to cool for 10 minutes. Cut into squares.

SEATTLE, OUR FORMER HOMETOWN, has a large Croatian population that has gathered together for years to maintain and enjoy the rich traditions of their homeland. In 1976, the Yugoslav Women's Club compiled a cookbook and my friend, Mary K, was kind enough to lend me her copy of *Culinary Classics*. This recipe is adapted from that out-of-print publication.

Hrustule (Fried Cookies)

Light, crisp and crunchy, these cookies—traditionally served at Carnival—make the perfect accompaniment to a fresh fruit dessert. Just a word of warning—if they're not served immediately, sprinkle with more powdered sugar just before serving to refresh their appearance.

3 tablespoons butter (softened)

3 eggs, beaten

3 tablespoons sugar

1 teaspoon vanilla

1 ¹/₂ teaspoon grated lemon rind

1 tablespoon brandy or 1 tablespoon orange juice

2 cups flour (approximate)

Sifted powdered sugar

Oil for frying

In a medium mixing bowl, stir together the butter, eggs, sugar, vanilla, lemon rind and brandy until well blended. Add sufficient flour to create a firm dough and turn out onto a well-floured board. Knead until very smooth. Cover and chill for 1 hour.

Divide the dough into quarters and return 3 quarters to the refrigerator. Working with one quarter of the dough at a time, roll the dough out on a floured board until thin. Using a fluted pastry wheel or a pizza cutter, cut the dough into thin strips (about 1/3 inch by 6 inches). Tie each strip into a loose knot and drop into hot oil. Fry until golden. Remove from the oil and drain immediately on a brown paper bag or on paper towels. When cool, dust with powdered sugar and store in an airtight container.

THROUGHOUT THE TIME we were cruising and living aboard *Klatawa*, Bill and I returned to the States for the holiday season. During those visits, we liked to visit elementary school classrooms and talk about our travels ... providing insight for the students into the culture of the countries we had visited. We quickly learned that nothing kept the attention of restless puplis like the promise of food.

I first made this traditional Croatian sweet to take to a combined class of fifth and sixth graders in Easton, Washington. The kids begged for the recipe and their enthusiasm guaranteed that this recipe would be a part of this book. ▓

Fresh Figs with Port and Citrus
Serves 4

12 fresh figs
1 cup port
1/4 cup sugar
1 tablespoon honey (plus additional for drizzling)
1 stick cinnamon
1/4 cup fresh orange juice
1 lemon, zest only
Additional honey for drizzling

Preheat the oven to 400 degrees. Wash and dry the figs. Remove the stem and beginning at top, create 6 petals by cutting 7/8s of the way through each fig. Gently spread the petals and place in a buttered baking dish.

Meanwhile, combine the port, sugar, honey, cinnamon, orange juice and lemon zest in a small saucepan and bring to a boil. Boil for 5 minutes and then pour over the figs. Bake at 400 degrees for 10 minutes. Baste the figs with the pan juices and bake for an additional 5–10 minutes. Remove from oven and drizzle lightly with honey.

Optional: Serve with whipped cream enhanced with honey and lemon zest.

IT DOESN'T GET MUCH BETTER: a clear warm summer day sailing downwind through the azure-blue waters of the Adriatic Sea toward the oldest settlement in Dalmatia. The island of Vis (settled by the Greeks in 397 BC) is the most westerly of all the Dalmatian Islands and was, for many years, off limits to visitors. It was the primary base for the naval forces and the seat of command of Marshall Tito during World War II. Reopened to visitors in 1989, it is now a favored holiday destination for many Croatians.

On our initial visit, we explored our anchoring options. We ultimately decided on the pleasant bay at Komiza rather than the crowded harbor at Vis. For several hours, we swam, read and relaxed ... until the day began to cool. Then we hopped in the dinghy to go ashore. The town was a pleasant surprise. Most buildings featured wonderful architectural details and there was an astonishing sense of positive energy. As a special surprise, we discovered a fishing museum, complete with ancient spears, hooks, lines and the reconstructed remains of an old fishing *gaetja*—the traditional Mediterranean fishing boat. The entire museum was dedicated to the fishermen on Vis.

Back on the boat, we treated ourselves to this special preparation of perfectly ripened, local, sweet and juicy figs. It was a tasty way to end a memorable day. ▨

Poached Pears
Serves 6

Elegantly simple and richly flavored, poached pears are a favorite autumn dessert throughout the Mediterranean. Add a dollop of sweetened, whipped cream just before serving this make-ahead dessert and you'll have the perfect ending for a special dinner.

> 1 bottle decent red wine
> 1 cup sugar
> ¼ cup honey
> 2 cinnamon sticks
> 3 4-inch-long strips orange peel
> 6 firm pears

Combine the wine, sugar, honey, cinnamon sticks and orange peel in a pan large enough and deep enough to keep the pears submerged. Bring the liquids to a boil and reduce to a simmer. Meanwhile, peel the pears and place in a bowl of cold water. Drain the pears and place in the wine pot, making sure that all the pears are submerged. Simmer slowly, rotating the pears as needed, until pears are easily pierced with a sharp knife, about 50 minutes. Remove the pears from the syrup and set aside.

Increase the heat to medium-high and slowly boil the syrup until it resembles the syrup found in canned fruits. Strain the syrup and return to the pot along with the pears. Cover until ready to serve. To serve, place the pears in individual dessert dishes and drizzle generously with syrup.

Cook's Notes:

• Like the fine peasant women I have met and enjoyed throughout our travels, I too hate to waste good food ... especially something as sweet and tasty as the leftover syrup from this dish. I combine the remaining syrup with dried or canned fruit and serve as a warm sauce over ice cream or pound cake. My favorite is a combination of ½ cup finely diced dried apricots, 1 cup of syrup and 1 cup canned, drained cherries, simmered for 20 minutes in a small saucepan.

UNTIL SUGAR WAS PRODUCED, honey—the sweet and sticky fluid created by honey bees from the nectar of flowers—was the only sweetener available. (Sugar was introduced early in the 16th century but the first sugar factory—located in Silesia in central Europe—did not go into production until 1801.) The aroma, flavor and color of this natural sweetener varied according to the flower source ... citrus, lavender, acacia and sage were and still are popular varieties.

From time immemorial, honey has been considered the food of the gods. Through ancient lore and cave drawings the value of honey has been documented. European convents and monasteries were known for their beekeeping skills, drawings in prehistoric caves in Spain show people hanging from ropes trying to reach honeycombs lodged in rock holes, records from ancient Egypt attest to the importance of beekeeping and stories abound in Slavic, Germanic and British lore about the intoxicating properties of honey-made mead. Today, honey remains a favorite sweetener in both sweet and savory dishes. ▩

Basic Dessert Crepes
Makes 10 crepes

This recipe uses a minimum of ingredients to create tasty and easy-to-handle crepes that will last up to 4 days in the refrigerator or up to 1 month in the freezer.

1¹/₄ cup all-purpose flour
4 eggs
1 cup milk
2 tablespoons water
¹/₄ cup sugar
¹/₄ teaspoon salt

In a medium bowl, whisk together the flour, eggs, milk, water, sugar and salt. The batter should resemble heavy cream. If the batter is too thick, add a little more milk. If the batter is too thin, add a little more flour. For easy pouring, transfer the batter to a glass measuring cup. Allow the batter to rest for at least 10–15 minutes before proceeding.

Preheat a 10-inch nonstick omelet or crepe pan over medium heat. The pan is ready for use when a few drops of water, sprinkled on the surface begin to "dance." Using a paper towel, wipe a small amount of butter over the hot surface of the pan.

Pour a scant ¼ cup of batter into the bottom of the pan. Quickly tilt the pan to spread the batter evenly across the bottom. Allow the crepe to cook over medium heat until the bottom turns golden, about 2 minutes. Then, working carefully and quickly, release the edges of the crepe from the bottom of the pan by lifting the outside edges of the crepe with a heatproof rubber spatula. Very carefully, with the fingers of both hands, grasp the edges of the crepe furthest from you and quickly lift and flip the crepe. Cook on the other side until just golden, about 30 seconds. Slide out and stack each crepe on a plate as it is finished.

Repeat until all the batter is used, spreading more butter on the pan after each fourth or fifth crepe.

Cook's Notes:

• To make crepes for use in savory recipes, omit the sugar.

• Pre-made, purchased crepes can be substituted in all of these recipes.

Variation #1 Sinfully Simple Dessert Crepes
Serves 4

8 crepes
²/₃ cup strawberry jam or orange marmalade
¹/₄ cup butter (¹/₂ stick)
¹/₄ cup sugar

Divide and spread the jam or marmalade evenly between the 8 crepes and fold into quarters, forming a triangle with each crepe. Over medium heat, melt the butter in a large fry pan and add the folded crepes. Lightly brown on both sides, about 2 minutes per side. Place 2 crepes on each serving dish, sprinkle with the sugar and serve.

Cook's Notes:

- These crepes can be made in advance, filled with jam and folded. Refrigerate until ready to proceed with the recipe.

- A small scoop of ice cream or a dollop of sweetened whipped cream will make this simple dish extra special.

- Feel free to experiment with fillings. You might want to try a dessert fruit topping, a favorite canned pie filling or the Croatian favorite, Nutella. Be as indulgent as your conscience will allow!

Variation #2 Cheese-Filled Pancakes
Serves 4

1^1/$_2$ cups ricotta cheese
2 eggs
^{1}/$_2$ cup sugar
1 teaspoon vanilla
1 teaspoon lemon zest
8 crepes
^{3}/$_4$ cup sour cream
^{1}/$_4$ cup granulated sugar

Preheat the oven to 375 degrees. In a medium bowl, whisk together the ricotta cheese, eggs, ½ cup sugar, vanilla and lemon zest. Divide and spread the filling over the crepes and fold into quarters. Place the pancakes in a single layer in a buttered baking dish and top each one with a dab of sour cream. Bake at 375 degrees for 15 minutes. Sprinkle with granulated sugar and serve.

Variation #3 Crepes with Apple & Figs
Serves 4

2 apples, peeled, cored and coarsely chopped
^{1}/$_2$ cup dried figs, rehydrated and coarsely chopped
4 tablespoons butter, divided
Zest of 1 lemon
2 tablespoons fresh lemon juice
2 tablespoons honey
8 crepes
2 tablespoons butter
Sauce:
2 tablespoons butter
^{1}/$_2$ cup orange juice
2 tablespoons fresh lemon juice
2 tablespoons honey

Melt 2 tablespoons of butter in a 12-inch skillet over medium heat. Add the apples and the figs and stir about 5 minutes, or until the apples begin to soften. Add the lemon zest, lemon juice and the honey. Stir for an additional 2–3 minutes. Remove from heat and set aside.

Place equal amounts of the apple-fig filling in the middle of each crepe. Fold the crepes into envelopes; making sure that the entire filling is enclosed. Using the same pan, melt the 2 tablespoons of butter over medium heat and place the crepes, seam side down, in the pan. Sauté until golden, about 2 minutes. Carefully flip the crepes over and sauté the top side until golden, about 2 minutes. Place 2 crepes, seam side down, on individual serving plates.

Sauce: To the same pan, add the butter, orange juice, lemon juice and honey. Simmer over high heat for 1–2 minutes, stirring constantly. The syrup should be thick and bubbly. Drizzle the syrup over the crepes and serve immediately.

Cook's Notes:

- To rehydrate the figs, cover them with boiling water and allow to rest for 15 minutes.
- If you prefer, you can substitute dried apricots or raisins for the figs.
- Make ahead hint: Crepes can be made and assembled in advance. Place the filled crepes in a buttered, ovenproof dish. Drizzle with the syrup, cover and refrigerate. When ready to use, bring to room temperature. Dot each crepe with a small piece of butter and sprinkle lightly with sugar. Reheat in a 350-degree oven for 20 minutes and serve.
- To make the envelopes, fold the side of crepe closest to you over the filling and then fold over both the left and right sides. Complete the enclosure by folding over remaining 4th side.

THROUGHOUT CROATIA, pancakes (the variety we know as crepes) are a popular dessert. With recipes that are quicker and more straightforward than their French counterpart, it is easy to understand why they frequently appear on home tables and restaurant menus.

On warm summer nights while strolling along a busy town quay, who could resist the sweet aroma of a fresh pancake direct from the street vendor's cart? My mouth always watered as I watched my pancake come off the griddle ... would I request a generous slathering of hazelnut-chocolate rich Nutella or a thick fruit marmalade? Either way, it was sure to be delicious.

Rožata or Crème Caramel
Serves 8

A variation of this dessert is found in many parts of the world. Made primarily with whole eggs and cream, it is firm and wholesome, rich and creamy. The proportions of milk to cream are flexible. If you desire a richer custard, increase the cream and reduce the milk. If you wish to reduce the calories from fat, increase the milk and decrease the cream.

> 1³/₄ cup sugar, divided
> 1¹/₂ cups milk
> 1¹/₂ cups cream
> 2 2-inch-strips of lemon peel
> 5 eggs
> 2 egg yolks
> 1 teaspoon vanilla

Preheat the oven to 350 degrees. Butter 8 individual ramekins or custard cups. In a small saucepan over medium heat, stir ¾ cup of sugar until clear, smooth and golden brown. Working cautiously, divide the caramel syrup evenly among the ramekins or custard cups, tipping the dishes to ensure even distribution of the syrup over the bottom.

In a medium saucepan, combine the milk, cream, the remaining 1 cup of sugar and the lemon peel. Bring just to a boil and remove from the heat. Allow to cool for 10 minutes and strain.

In a medium mixing bowl, whisk the eggs until just beginning to froth. Whisking constantly, slowly add the hot milk mixture to the eggs and divide the custard among the ramekins or custard cups. Place the ramekins or custard cups in a water bath (see below) and bake until the custard is firmly set and a sharp knife inserted in the center comes out clean, about 40 to 50 minutes. Remove the individual dishes from the water bath and allow the *rožatas* to cool.

To serve, run a sharp knife along the outside edge of the custard and tip upside down onto individual dessert plates.

Cook's Notes:
- A water bath, also known as a *bain marie*, is used to keep the outside edges of a custard tender and light in color. To prepare a water bath, simply place the ramekins or custard cups in a large pan and pour enough boiling water into the pan to come halfway up the side of the dishes. Place in the oven and bake according to directions.

IN THE PAST, several drops of rose oil were used to flavor this very popular dessert. Today, however, this very precious and expensive oil is rarely used.

Recipes for *rožata* do vary. Hence the tradition of friendly competition that encourages many cooks along the Dalmatian coast to lay claim to the "original" *rožata* recipe. I have enjoyed many versions ... and they all taste good. ▩

Acknowledgements

Over the past seven years many talented and dedicated individuals from Croatia, the United States and around the world helped me build this book. To each of you I say a most sincere *thank you*. You provided, tested and tasted the recipes, snapped photos, shared adventures, coached my writing, critiqued and edited my words and encouraged this venture.

At the risk of omitting some very special family members and friends, I would like to say thank you to Toni Allegra, Don Anderson, Doug Andrianson, Kit Bakke, Judy Balas, Jo Ball, Jane Dobrovolny, LaNette Donoghue, Leslie, Doug and Dawson Evenden, Hope Frazier, Jean Fuller and Darryl Wideman, Joan Greathouse, Ian and Pippa Greenwood, Jany Hansel, Karen and Lee Hedge, Liz and Rob Jessop, MaryAnn Jankowski, Mary Karabaich, JoAnn and Don Moore, Diane Morgan, John and Judy Miller, Carole and Barry Patmore, Denis and Zina Pepper, John and Lois Post, Yvette Powell, Tracey Ryder, Dorothy Russo, Olga Singer, Chuck Shores, Audrey Stubner, Linda Swofford, Cricket Twichell, Marina Vitasovic, Kristin and Cameron Webster, Nita Whaley and RJ Wullich.

And to those who simply never gave up in asking, "How's the book?" I want to say a special *thank you* … your friendship, interest and gentle prodding kept this project going.

Bibliography

Bilus, Ivanka, Bozic, Rode and Brkan. *Desserts in Croatia*. Zagreb: Alfa Publishing, 1997.

Bilus, Ivanka, Brkan, Coric and Rode. *Croatia at Table*. Zagreb: Alfa Publishing, 1997.

Bilus, Ivanka, Rode and Brkan. *Cooking Around the World with Vegeta*. Zagreb: Alfa Publishing, 1999.

Bozin, Anna. *The Art of Croatian Cooking*. NSW: Jennifer Zanger Editing, 1997.

Center for Research and Improvement of Diet. *Croatian Cuisine the Modern Way*. Zagreb: Golden Marketing, 1995.

Goldstein, Ivo. *Croatia, a History*. Toronto: McGill-Queen's University Press, 1999.

Pavicic, Liliana and Gordana Pirker-Mosher. *The Best of Croatian Cooking*. New York: Hippocrene Books, 2000.

Plotkin, Fred. *La Terra Fortunata*. New York: Broadway Books, 2001.

Ronald Community Club, Ronald, Washington. *Favorite Hometown Recipe*. Waseca, MN: Walter's Cookbooks, c. 1990.

Valcich, Dennis. *Croatian Cookbook: A Walk Through Croatia*. Bonnyrigg, NSW, Australia: Valcich Publishing, 1994.

Wright, Clifford. *A Mediterranean Feast*. New York: William Morrow and Company, 1999.

Yugoslav Women's Club. *Our Traditional and Favorite Recipes*. Seattle, WA, 1976.

Index

Dubrovnik

Pepi's Pottery

The Peka

Coastal

Living

Soup's on ...

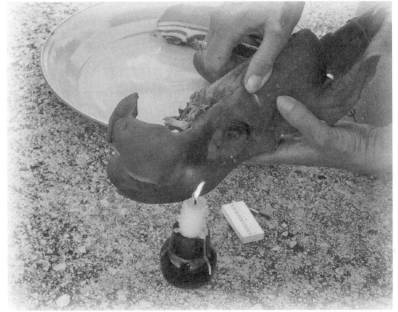

Singeing the pig's ear

The Story of this Book

I did not realize it at the time, but I began to write this book the day we arrived in Dubrovnik. Bill and I had just crossed the Adriatic Sea from Brindisi, Italy, on our sailboat, *Klatawa,* and had completed the required formalities when the friendly customs agent began talking about his family, their favorite foods, fishing spots and restaurants. His passion for time-honored recipes, respect for the land and commitment to family and tradition provided me with my first "taste of Croatia." He had immediately whetted my appetite to learn more.

Nor did I realize at the time that our Mediterranean sailing adventure would eventually lead us to Southern California, where we would become farmers growing Mediterranean-inspired crops: lavender, olives (for oil), a sweet and special tangerine called the "Ojai Pixie", and walnuts. Today, our landscape and our crops provide daily reminders of our Croatian experience … we are constantly challenged to learn new ways to organically nourish our crops, to preserve the land, to conserve our resources and to connect with our customers. Our thoughts often return to our memories of Croatian farmers and their patient care of soil, water and crops.

Nor did I realize at the time that the simple land-based peasant culture would provide us with a model for our changing American food focus—a focus that celebrates ingredients that are locally grown, organic, sustainable and seasonal and demands recipes that are nutritious, economical, straightforward and satisfying. (A reminder to all cooks: flavors in fresh ingredients can vary enormously … sometimes one clove of garlic can pack a powerful punch while other times two or more cloves may be required to achieve the same results. Tasting is a critical step when cooking with fresh ingredients.)

Bill and Karen Evenden

Croatia is a land of good cooks who consistently manage to work culinary magic with limited ingredients and tight budgets. In that land, I learned that the tastiest food is made from scratch with ingredients that are seasonal and locally grown … from the field to the fork.

A Taste of Croatia is both a travel memoir and an easy-to-use cookbook. Most of the recipes have been savored by generations of Croatians and all of the recipes have been adapted for use in American kitchens. Throughout the book, I've indulged in sharing some of our favorite memories and experiences via a series of short essays and brief anecdotes that grew out of our more than three years of sailing the Adriatic coast. I hope this combination of stories, facts and recipes will provide each reader with *A Taste of Croatia.*

Karen Evenden
Ojai, California
November 2007
www.tasteofcroatia.com